ISC
CONCEPTS
OF
ECONOMICS

In accordance with the latest syllabus prescribed by the Council for the Indian School Certificate Examinations, New Delhi.

ISC
CONCEPTS OF
ECONOMICS

Class XI

By :

Crystal David John
Ph.D. (Econ.)
Associate Professor and Former Head
Department of Economics
Stella Maris College (Autonomous), Chennai
Former Head
Department of Economics
Isabella Thorburn College, Lucknow

Jayalakshmi Sathyabharath
M.Phil. (Econ.)
Assistant Professor
Department of Economics
Stella Maris College (Autonomous), Chennai

Sushil Kr. Gupta
M.Com., M.A. (Econ.), B.Ed., PGDMM
Senior Teacher in Accounts & Economics
Dr. Graham's Homes, Kalimpong

OSWAL PUBLISHERS
1/12 Sahitya Kunj, M. G. Road, Agra-282 002

No part of this book can be reproduced in any form or by any means without the prior written permission of the publisher.

Edition : 2020

ISBN : 978-93-87660-83-0

OSWAL PUBLISHERS

Head office : 1/12, Sahitya Kunj, M.G. Road, Agra-282 002
Phone : (0562) 2527771 - 4, +91 75340 77222
E-mail : contact@oswalpublishers.com
Website : www.oswalpublishers.com

Preface

We feel immense pleasure in introducing the latest edition of 'ISC concepts of Economics' for class XI. The content has been composed keeping in mind a beginners' need to explore this critical subject. This edition strictly adheres to the latest syllabus prescribed by the Council for the Indian School Certificate Examinations. This book comprehensively explains the areas of microeconomics and macroeconomics.

Having a strong foundation for this subject is crucial as economics stands imperative in the current national and international dynamics, being applied in the arenas of business, engineering, planning, marketing, social sciences and various other fields, thus, making it a critical component of the curriculum. Explanations in this book are thought-provoking and also encourage a student to dive deeper into the subject. The language used is simple and lucid. All endeavours have been made to make this book student-friendly by simplifying the graphs, tables, and illustrations. A systematic summary at the end of each chapter for easy understanding and quick revision. Model papers given at the end of the book will enable the students to become familiar with the pattern of question papers for the board examination.

Constructive suggestions are acknowledged and would be incorporated in future edition.

– Publisher

SYLLABUS

*There will be **two** papers in the subject.*
Paper I - Theory: 3 hours .... 80 marks
Paper II - Project Work .... 20 marks

PAPER – I (THEORY) – 80 Marks

Part I (20 marks) will consist of **compulsory** short answer questions testing knowledge, application and skills relating to elementary/fundamental aspects of the entire syllabus.

Part II (60 marks) will consist of **eight** questions out of which candidates will be required to answer **five** questions, each carrying 12 marks.

Note: The syllabus is intended to reflect a study of the theory of Economics with specific reference to the Indian Economy. Therefore, examples and specific references to the Indian Economy must be made wherever relevant.

1. **Understanding Economics**

   (i) Definition of Economics: Adam Smith, Alfred Marshall, Lionel Robbins, Samuelson.

   Basic understanding of economics and economic phenomena to be explained especially in the context of the concept of scarcity and allocation of resources. Students may be introduced to the main points on which the various definitions of economics could be analyzed. Features of definitions and two-three criticisms.

   (ii) Micro and Macro Economics – Meaning and difference. Basic concepts: utility, price, value, wealth, welfare, money, market, capital, investment, income, production, consumption, saving, Business cycle, Aggregate demand and Aggregate supply.

   Meaning and difference between Micro and Macro Economics. A conceptual understanding of the terms: Human wants – classification; Factor of Production; utility – types and features, total utility, marginal utility and diminishing marginal utility; price – definition and general rise and fall in price; value – real vs nominal value; wealth – explanation of the term, classification (personal and social); welfare – economic welfare, social welfare and relation between wealth and welfare; money – barter economy vs money economy; market – meaning and size; capital – meaning; investment – meaning, investment as a process of capital formation; income – meaning, factor incomes; production – meaning; consumption – meaning; saving – meaning; individual saving and aggregate savings.

   The above terms to be explained with the help of relevant examples.

   (iii) Basic problems of an economy: what to produce; how to produce, for whom to produce; efficient use of resources.

   The basic problem of scarcity and choice must be emphasized. As this problem is universal in character, i.e. faced by all economies, irrespective of the economic system they follow, it must be explained using the concept of Production Possibility Curve. The three problems - what to produce, how to produce and for whom to produce - must be highlighted. The role of technology and a shift in the Production Possibility Curve (assumptions and features) must be explained.

   (iv) Types of economies: developed and developing; Economic system: capitalism, socialism and mixed economy; mechanism used to solve the basic problems faced by each economy.

   Characteristics of developed and developing economies; Development experience of India: a comparison with neighbouring country (China) in terms of growth, population and sectoral development (introducing regional and global economic grouping such as SAARC, European Union, ASEAN, G-8, G-20 - basic knowledge); different types of economic systems; definition, features, merits and demerits of capitalism, socialism and mixed economic system; mechanisms used to solve the basic problems under each economic system to be explained with the help of examples. The role of government along with the price mechanism to be emphasized. Price mechanism as a tool to solve economic problem.

2. **Indian Economic Development**

   (i) Introduction.

   Indian economy Post liberalization. Main features, problems and policies of agriculture, industry and foreign trade.

(ii) Parameters of Development.

Parameters of development: per capita income (definition and limitations); meaning and construction of Human Development Index. India and HDI as per the UNDP report.

(iii) Planning and economic development in India.

Planning and economic development in India : a brief explanations major objectives of all the five year plans. NITI Aayog : Objectives and role.

(iv) Structural Changes in the Indian Economy after liberalization.

Need, meaning, significance and features of liberalization, globalization and privatization of Indian Economy; disinvestment: meaning.

(v) Current challenges facing Indian Economy.

Poverty – absolute and relative, vicious circle of poverty, main programmes for poverty alleviation: A critical assessment of PAPs (Poverty Alleviation Programmes); Rural development. Rural creadit (need, purpose and sources); Agricultural manceting, defects and government measures to improve agricultural marketing; role of cooperatives, agricultural diversification; alternate farming/organic forming; meaning and importance.

Human Capital formation: How people become resource; role of human capital in economic development; Growth of education sector in India; Education – formal and informal (Meaning only); Unemployment-types of unemployment, causes for unemployment, Policy measures (after 2000).

(vi) Economic growth and development.

Economic Growth and Development – Meaning and difference.

(vii) Sustainable Development.

Effect of Economic Development on Resources and Environment.

Understanding the concept of Sustainable development; Need for sustainable development for improving the quality of life - looking at the deteriorating quality of air, water, food over time, developing an appreciation to sustain at least what exists for the generations to come.

Global warming – meaning and effects.

3. **Statistics**

(i) Statistics: definition, scope and limitations of statistics.

Statistics: definition, scope and limitations of statistics. Special emphasis to be laid on importance of statistics in economics.

(ii) Collection, organisation and presentation of data.

Collection of data - Sources of data: primary, secondary. Methods of collecting data: Some important sources of collecting secondary data; ways of collecting primary data; organization of data: meaning and types of variables, frequency; presentation of data: tabular and diagrammatic presentation (bar diagram, pie, line, histogram, polygon and ogive curve).

(iii) Measures of Central Value: average defined; type of averages: arithmetic mean; simple and weighted; median and mode; ungrouped and grouped data; numericals, relationship between mean, median and mode.

Measures of Central Value: average defined; type of averages: arithmetic mean; simple and weighted; median and mode; ungrouped and grouped data. Numericals only on mean, median and mode for both ungrouped and grouped data. Relationship between mean, median and mode – the nature of the frequency distribution – symmetrical, positively skewed and negatively skewed.

(iv) Measures of dispersion: definition, methods of studying variation - range; standard deviation; quartile deviation; the mean or average deviation; coefficient of variation.

Numericals on measures of dispersion required.

(v) Correlation: introduction, scatter diagram; Karl Pearson's coefficient of correlation; Spearman's coefficient of correlation.

Meaning and significance of correlation to be explained along with types and degrees. Scatter diagram, Karl Pearson's method (two variables, ungrouped data); Spearman's Rank Correlation to be explained with the help of numericals.

(vi) Index numbers: simple and weighted - meaning, types and purpose. Problems involved in constructing a Price Index Number.

What does an Index number show, measure or indicate (like a Price Index Number). Difference between simple and weighted – Price weighted or quantity weighted. Laspayre's, Paasche and Fisher's methods of index numbers (to be explained with the help of numericals). Wholesale Price Index, Consumer Price Index and Index of Industrial Production should be explained. Uses of Index Numbers. Problems involved in constructing Price Index Number – the choice of the base year, the number of commodities to be included (coverage), choice of prices and the method to be used.

(vii) Some Mathematical Tools used in Economics.

Equation of a straight line and slope of a straight line.

PAPER – II – PROJECT WORK – 20 Marks

Candidates will be expected to have completed **two** projects from any topic covered in Theory. Mark allocation for **each** Project [10 marks]:

Overall format	1 mark
Content	4 marks
Findings	2 marks
Viva-voce based on the Project	3 marks

A list of suggested Projects is given below:

1. Study consumer awareness amongst households through designing a questionnaire and collection of primary data.
2. Prepare a report on productivity awareness among enterprises through use of statistical data from statistical tables published in Newspapers / RBI Bulletin / Budget / Census report / Economic survey, etc.
3. Make a study of two cooperative institutions (example milk cooperatives, etc.) with a view to compare the organizational and financial structure of the organizations, production capacity and output, marketing strategies, sales, market share, etc.
4. Study in detail the South Asian Association for Regional Cooperation (SAARC) and its impact on Indian economy.
5. Prepare a report on the various poverty alleviation and employment generation programmes started in India, with special focus on MNREGA.
6. Compare the status of women of your State with that at the National level for the last ten years, on the basis of educational level, employment, etc.
7. Prepare a report on the forest cover in India, highlighting the following aspects:
   (a) Five States/Union Territories having higher and lower forest cover and compare the extent of forest coverage.
   (b) Causes for decrease in forest cover in the Country.
   (c) Measures adopted by the Central/State Governments to increase the forest cover.

Contents

1. Definition of Economics.. 13–20

    1.1   Introduction

    1.2   Wealth-oriented Definition-Adam Smith

    1.3   Welfare-oriented Definition-Alfred Marshall

    1.4   Scarcity-oriented Definition-Lionel Charles Robbins

    1.5   Growth-oriented Definition-Paul Anthony Samuelson

2. Micro and Macro Economics : Concepts.. 21-52

    2.1   Introduction

    2.2   Microeconomics: Meaning and Features

    2.3   Macroeconomics : Meaning and Features

    2.4   Differences between Micro and Macro Economics

    2.5   Human wants – classification

    2.6   Utility Analysis : The Marginal Concepts

    2.7   Utility : Meaning

    2.8   Price : Meaning and Concepts

    2.9   Value

    2.10   Wealth

    2.11   Welfare

    2.12   Money : Meaning

    2.13   Market

    2.14   Capital

    2.15   Investment

    2.16   Income

    2.17   Production

    2.18   Consumption

    2.19   Saving

    2.20   Aggregate Demand and Aggregate Supply

    2.21   Business Cycles or Trade Cycles

3. Basic Problems of an Economy 53–61
    3.1   Introduction

    3.2   Basic Problems of an Economy

    3.3   Opportunity Cost

    3.4   Rational Choice

    3.5   The Production Possibility Curve or the Product Transformation Curve

4. Types of Economies 62–84
    4.1   Economy : Introduction and Meaning

    4.2   Types of Economies

    4.3   Solution to the Basic Economic Problems

    4.4   The Development of India and China

    4.5   Regional and Global Economic Groups

5. Introduction to Indian Economic Development 85–98
    5.1   Indian Economy—Post liberalisation

    5.2   Indian Economy—Positive/Negative Impact

    5.3   Agricultural Sector in India—Problems and Steps taken by the Government

    5.4   Industrial Sector in India—Problems and Policies

    5.5   Foreign Trade : Problems and Policies

6. Parameters of Development 99–105
    6.1   Introduction

    6.2   Per Capita Income

    6.3   Quality of Life Index (QLI)

    6.4   Physical Quality of Life Index (PQLI)

    6.5   Human Development Index (HDI)

7. Planning and Economic Development in India 106–117
    7.1   Concept of Planning

    7.2   Objectives of Planning

    7.3   An Overview of the Five-Year Plans in India

    7.4   Achievements of Economic Planning in India

    7.5   Shortcomings of Economic Planning in India

    7.6   NITI Aayog

8. Structural Changes in the Indian Economy After Liberalisation.................118–125

    8.1   Introduction—Economic Reforms

    8.2   Need for Economic Reforms

    8.3   Meaning and Features of the New Economic Reforms

    8.4   Disinvestment : Meaning

9. Current Challenges Facing Indian Economy..126–145

    9.1   Introduction

    9.2   Poverty

    9.3   Rural Development

    9.4   Human Resources

    9.5   Education Sector in India

    9.6   Unemployment

10. Economic Growth and Development..146–151

    10.1   Economic Growth versus Economic Development

    10.2   A Comparative Study of Indian and Chinese Economies

11. Sustainable Development..152–160

    11.1   Economic Development and Environment

    11.2   Sustainable Development—Meaning

    11.3   Global Warming

12. Introduction to Statistics...161–164

    12.1   Meaning and Definition

    12.2   Steps Involved in Statistical Analysis

    12.3   Scope of Statistics

    12.4   Limitations of Statistics

13. Data Collection and Presentation...165–178

    13.1   Introduction

    13.2   Types of Data

    13.3   Methods of Collecting Primary Data

    13.4   Organisation of Data

    13.5   Presentation of Data

14. Measures of Central Value 179–199

    14.1   Meaning

    14.2   Arithmetic Mean (AM)

    14.3   Median

    14.4   Mode

    14.5   Relationship between Mean, Median and Mode

    14.6   Geometric Mean (GM)

    14.7   Harmonic Mean (HM)

15. Measures of Dispersion 200–220

    15.1   Concept of Measures of Dispersion

    15.2   Methods of Studying Variation

16. Correlation 221–236

    16.1   Introduction

    16.2   Measures of Correlation

17. Index Numbers 237–244

    17.1   Meaning

    17.2   Types of Index Numbers

    17.3   Purpose of Index Numbers

    17.4   Methods of Constructing Index Numbers

    17.5   Problems Involved in Constructing a Price Index Number

18. Mathematical Tools Used in Economics 245–248

    18.1   Concept

    18.2   Function

    18.3   Equation of a Straight Line

    18.4   Slope of a Line

- ➢ Project Work 249–269
- ➢ Model Test Paper-1 270–272
- ➢ Model Test Paper-2 273–275

1   Definition of Economics

1.1. Introduction

Economics is a subject that has intrigued humanity from time immemorial. Yet, every day we make decisions and choices that belong within the realm of economics. We all participate in the economy as consumers, as workers and also as producers, we pay taxes, we deposit our savings in a bank account, all these activities (and many more) belong to the arena of economics. Also, if economics is used to analyse human behaviour and the world around us, then we find that the principles of economics can be applied to many different areas of life. The scope of economics is, thus, very broad. Consequently, many economic thinkers have tried to explain various aspects of this subject. To provide an insight into the discipline, this chapter seeks to introduce you to four basic definitions of economics as given by Adam Smith, Alfred Marshall, Lionel Charles Robbins and P.A. Samuelson.

1.2. Wealth-Oriented Definition—Adam Smith

Adam Smith (1723–1790), also known as the Father of Economics, was a Scottish economist. He is famous for his work titled "An enquiry into the nature and causes of the wealth of nations". In short, this book is also called "Wealth of Nations". As the name suggests, Adam Smith focused on the concept of wealth. He defined economics as "the science of wealth". He assumed that wealth is the most important factor in the human society as it can fulfil all the desires of human beings. He also assumed that all the efforts of human society were directed towards earning more and more wealth. Adam Smith, in his book, stated that **"The great object of political economy of every country is to increase the riches and power of that country."**

1.2.1. Features of Smith's Wealth Definition

1. According to Adam Smith, economics largely deals with the wealth of nations. He believed that economic prosperity of any nation depends only on the accumulation of wealth. Hence, the main focus of nations is on acquiring and amassing wealth.

2. In his definition of economics, he gave first priority to wealth and the second priority to mankind. He also believed that wealth and only wealth can give higher satisfaction to all mankind. According to him, the wealthier a nation is, the happier are its citizens. Thus, implicitly Smith associated wealth with economic prosperity.

3. His definition shows that economics also deals with an enquiry into the causes behind the creation of wealth. He believed that wages earned by active human resources is the most important source of income of a nation and concluded that apart from wages, there is nothing else which can be regarded as a source of wealth of a nation. Hence, wealth of a nation could only be increased by raising the level of production.

4. His definition indicated that wealth of a nation includes only material goods, that is, different manufactured items. Non-material goods or services were completely excluded from his definition.

5. He focused on the role of economic man in the production of wealth of a nation. He claimed that economics studies the behaviour of those human beings who have only one objective of earning more and more wealth at any cost and by any means. Human being of such a nature, in his words, was called an "Economic Man".

1.2.2. Criticism of Smith's Wealth Definition

1. Smith gave undue importance to wealth in economic life. He assigned primary role to wealth and only secondary place to mankind. Critics, however, point out that human life cannot be sacrificed for wealth. Rather, wealth should be used as a means to improve the welfare of the mankind.

2. According to Smith, wages earned by active human resources is the most important source of income of a nation. Critics, however, are of the view that natural resources, human resources and capital resources of a nation, if utilized efficiently, can yield maximum wealth.

3. Adam Smith considered that economics is a science of wealth and material goods. He, however, did not consider the role of services in the production of wealth and in the welfare of human beings. Critics are of the view that services of doctors, teachers, lecturers, engineers, etc., also fulfil human wants and therefore, these services should also be regarded as a part of wealth.

4. Adam Smith assumed that economic man is the man whose objective is to earn more and more wealth, at any cost and by any means. Critics of the definition, however, point out that almost all human beings have qualities such as feelings of trust, love, respect, friendship, empathy, etc., which they value more than wealth in their lives and which may provide them with greater satisfaction than wealth.

5. During late 1770's, when Smith published his book, people were very religious and extolled spiritual values. Thus, the notion that economics is a science of wealth was not fully accepted. The critics dubbed economics as the "Bread and Butter Science", "Dismal Science"(as called by Thomas Carlyle), etc., and such contempt for economics was because Adam Smith sidelined humanistic aspect in his definition of economics.

However, the criticisms leveled against Adam Smith were a little harsh because by wealth, he meant the production of commodities. He did not preach worshipping of wealth. What he meant was that by utilizing resources efficiently and by increasing production, nations can grow. Hence, by studying the production process, he meandered into crucial concepts within economics such as income, wages, employment and growth. Thus, for Adam Smith, the meaning of wealth was material wealth that accrues via the production process.

1.3. Welfare-Oriented Definition—Alfred Marshall

Alfred Marshall (1842–1924) was an English Economist who has contributed to a large extent in broadening the understanding of this unique discipline of Economics. In 1890 A.D., he published his book entitled, "Principles of Economics", which is said to have protected the existence of economics by emphasising that human welfare is more important than wealth. He is credited with removing the bias that people had towards economics when they classified it as a dismal science or pig science and when they considered it to be solely dealing with wealth. In fact, he is responsible for laying the foundation of welfare economics. Marshall, therefore, shifted the focus of economics from wealth to welfare at the end of the 19th century.

In his words, Economics is defined as **"the study of mankind in the ordinary business of life; it examines that part of individual and social action which is most closely connected with the attainment and with the use of the material requisites of well being"**.

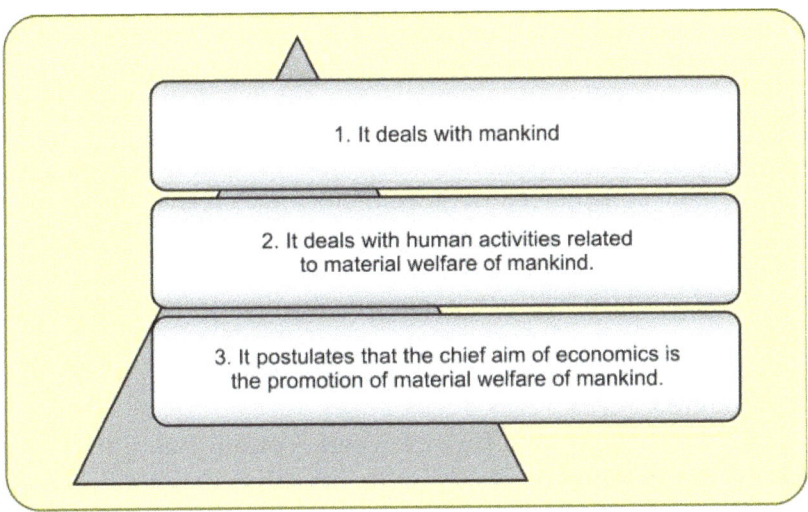

Fig. 1.1 : Three Main Aspects of Welfare Definition of Alfred Marshall

1.3.1. Features of Marshall's Welfare Definition

1. According to Marshall, wealth is not an end in itself, but it is the means by which man acquires material well being. Hence, wealth is not the end but the means to an end.

2. Further, he does not agree with the concept of amassing wealth. The classical economists like Adam Smith, David Ricardo, John Stuart Mill, etc., have always centered their arguments around the decisions made by an economic man. An economic man works selfishly to collect wealth. Marshall, as a Neoclassical economist, on the other hand, shifted the focus of economics from being a wealth-centered subject to being a discipline that highlights the objectives of social betterment (welfare).

3. Marshall gave primary importance to mankind and regarded wealth as secondary. According to him, economics deals with the study of man in the ordinary business of life and it also enquires how an individual gets his income and how he uses it. Thus, it is on one side, the study of wealth and on the other and more important side, a part of the study of man. He emphasizes the role of man in the creation of wealth and income. He also included social actions besides individual actions in his definition and hence, made his definition more inclusive than his predecessors.

4. He also emphasizes in his definition that human beings cannot be studied in isolation, for they form the very fabric of the society.

In short, we can state what Marshall meant diagrammatically.

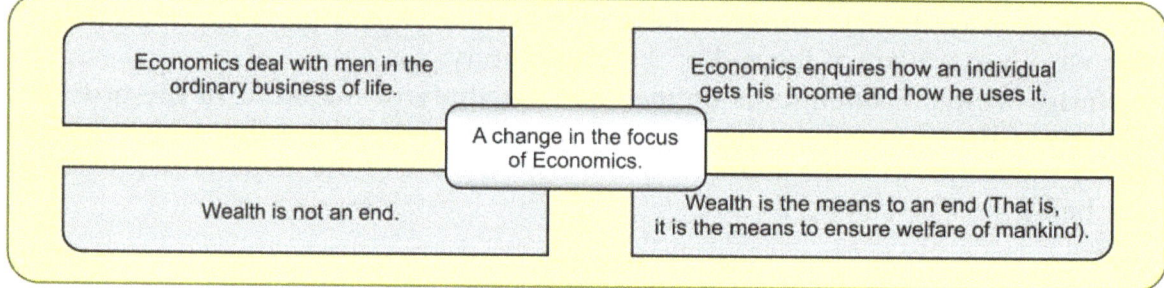

Fig. 1.2 : A change in the focus of Economics

1.3.2. Criticism of Marshall's Welfare Definition

1. Lionel Robbins criticizes Marshall's definition because he concentrated only on material well being and completely neglected non material well-being. Non material well-being is equally important for the holistic welfare of human beings. On this ground, therefore, Marshall's definition is incomplete.

2. The concept of welfare has not been specifically defined. Marshall's definition aimed at measuring human welfare in terms of wealth. But, welfare is not amenable to measurement, since welfare is a subjective concept. Strictly speaking, wealth can never be a measure of welfare.

3. Marshall could not establish a link between economic activities of human beings and human welfare. There are various economic activities that are detrimental to human welfare. The productions of war equipments, alcohol, opium, etc., are considered as economic activities but these do not promote human welfare.

4. Finally, Marshall's definition ignores the fundamental problem of scarcity in an economy. It was Lionel Charles Robbins who later gave the scarcity definition of economics.

1.4. Scarcity-Oriented Definition—Lionel Charles Robbins

Lionel Charles Robbins (1898–1984) was a British Economist, who gave the most accepted definition of economics in his book 'An Essay on the Nature and Significance of the Economic Science', published in 1932. According to him, **"Economics is the science which studies human behaviour as a relationship between ends and scarce means which have alternative uses."** Through this definition, he widened the scope of economics by including every sphere where scarcity of resources prevailed.

1.4.1. Features of Robbins' Scarcity Definition

1. Robbins' scarcity definition of economics has a wider scope because it includes not just those human activities that deal with wealth (as postulated by Adam Smith) or material well being (as claimed by Alfred Marshall) but it includes under its ambit, all kinds of human activities. Further, when economics is defined in this manner, it can no longer be considered as a dismal science because its focus has shifted away from wealth.

2. His definition states that the human wants are unlimited and the nature of these unlimited wants is such that when one want is satisfied, another want crops up. Therefore, there is no end of wants.

3. Though wants or ends are unlimited, the means or resources to satisfy these wants are limited or scarce. Had resources been plentiful, there would not have been any economic problems. Thus, scarcity of resources is the fundamental economic problem of any society.

4. The means have alternative uses which makes it necessary to utilize each of these resources judiciously. Same resource can be used for the satisfaction of different types of human wants. For example, a piece of land can either be used for the cultivation of wheat or for the production of cars.

5. Since wants are unlimited and the means are scarce and have alternative uses, wants have to be ranked in order of priorities. On the basis of such priorities, resources have to be allocated in an efficient manner for the satisfaction of these wants.

6. Since human wants are unlimited, an economy will have to decide which wants are to be satisfied immediately and which wants are to be postponed for the time being. This is the problem of choice in an economy. Thus, the problem of scarcity of resources gives rise to the problem of choice.

Robbins definition can be presented in a nutshell here.

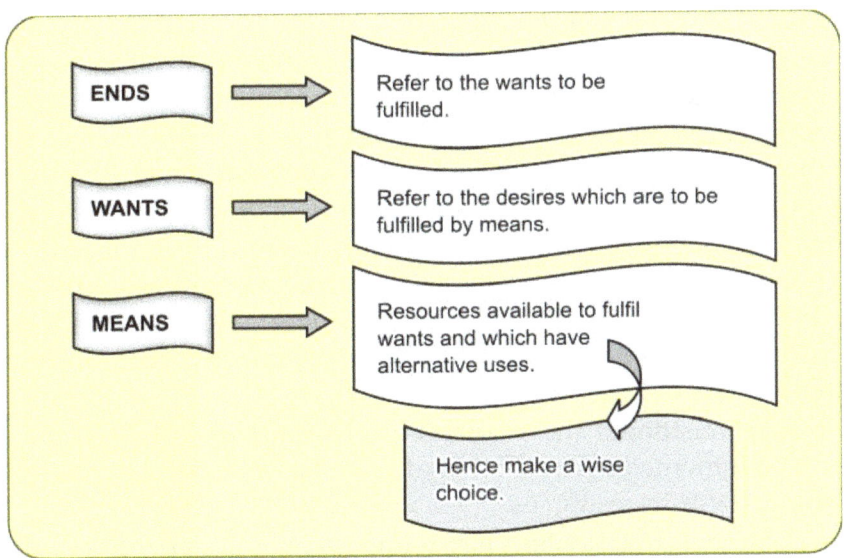

Fig. 1.3 : Lionel Robbins' Definition in a nutshell

Robbins gave humanistic aspect to economics by bringing in the concepts of wants, means and choices. He also catapults the discipline to the level of science by making it an analytical subject and locating the basic problems of economics—the problems of scarcity and choice. Robbins does not qualify the ends or wants as good or bad. He steers clear from passing any kind of value judgments and hence defines economics as a positive science and not as a normative one. He emphasizes on the concept of scarcity. Since scarcity and choice go hand in hand in each and every economy, the concept of choice also gets included in the economic theory. When choices are included, the question that arises is who makes these choices ? Economic theory assumes that these choices are made by a rational human being, also called the homoeconomicus agent, who wants to maximize his utility or profits. Robbins refers to this kind of agent as a decision-making individual.

Scarcity is always referred to in relative sense and not in absolute terms. Absolute means independent or solely in quantity or numbers while relative means in comparison to something else and in ratio or percentage of something else. Scarcity in economic sense always means in relation to. For example, consider rotten tomatoes in the basket of a vegetable seller, such tomatoes are not scarce as no individual wants them. The good tomatoes with the vegetable vendor may be in absolute abundance, but if demand for them exceeds the availability or supply of the tomatoes, then in economics, they will be considered scarce. Hence, in Robbins definition, allocation of resources becomes crucial. In fact, economics is an allocation science. It deals with optimum rational decisions made by agents who may be producers, consumers, or distributors. These agents could also be an institution, or even a country. The choices they make will define how resources are allocated between various uses.

1.4.2. Criticism of Robbins' Scarcity Definition

1. Robbins has been criticized for the fact that he assumes the ends to be given. However, in reality, ends are chosen by men.

2. Also, some ends may lead to further ends as they themselves become means to that end. For example, a person may want a job to earn an income to buy a house. Here, the wanting of a job is a means to acquire the end, that is, income, which itself becomes the means to acquire a house. So, an end may become a mean for some other end. Robbins has not mentioned any such phenomena.

3. Another criticism leveled against Robbins definition is that all the economic problems may not occur due to scarcity of resources. Sometimes economic problems may also occur due to excess of resources. For example, excess wheat production may lead to a sharp fall in its price, which may not cover even the cost of production, causing huge losses to the farmers.

4. Robbins has considered the availability of resources to be static. However, the resources may be augmented over a period of time. So Robbins' definition does not take into account the growth in resources.

5. Another criticism is that Robbins has defined economics merely as a microeconomic theory. Other important aspects of economics like national income, employment, banking system, taxation system, etc., had been ignored by Robbins.

6. In an attempt to raise economics to the status of a positive science, Robbins downplayed the importance of economics as a social science. Being a social science, economics must study social relations. However, Robbins emphasized too much on 'individual' choice. Scarcity problem, in the ultimate analysis, is a social problem—rather than an individual problem. Social problems give rise to social choice. Robbins could not explain social problems as well as social choices.

1.5. Growth-Oriented Definition—Paul Anthony Samuelson

Paul Anthony Samuelson (1915–2009), was a Neo-Keynesian American Economist, who has defined economics with respect to the modern concept of growth. According to him, **"Economics is a study of how men and society choose, with or without the use of money, to employ scarce productive resources which could have alternative uses, to produce various commodities over time, and distribute them for consumption, now and in the future, among the various people and groups of society. It analyses costs and benefits of improving patterns of resource allocation"**. With this definition, Samuelson elaborated the concept of production and scarce resources.

1.5.1. Features of Samuelson's Growth Definition

1. Samuelson has given a dynamic aspect to the definition by mentioning a time span for production, distribution and consumption. Hence, his definition is not static but is growth oriented.

2. Samuelson also broadens the definition to include choices with respect to distribution and consumption, both in the present and in the future. By doing so, he has intuitively brought in inter-generational choices related to use of resource base in a sustainable manner and thereby, making choices not to use up all resources in the present, for, future production resource base cannot be left totally depleted.

3. Though he did not explicitly state this, his definition can be extrapolated to include sustainable development and to make prudent use of non-renewable resources. It also leaves room to accommodate the choices made for the use of renewable resources so that the posterity of nations is taken care of.

1.5.2. Criticism of Samuelson's Growth Definition

1. Even though Samuelson has placed requisite emphasis on production, consumption and distribution of goods, scarce resources, money and men, he did not take into account certain socio-economic and political factors which affect the well-being of human beings. He has underplayed the importance of development in the welfare of the society. Development indicators such as Human Development Index, Multidimensional Poverty Index, Gender Development Index, Gender Inequality Index, Physical Quality of Living Index, etc., have been totally ignored in his definition.

2. He has also neglected the role of service sector in the growth trajectory of a nation. There is no mention of services as being a want or an end in his definition.

In a dynamic world, we cannot continue with a static definition that is frozen in time. Therefore, it is imperative that the definitions change with changing economic scenarios and ideologies across nations and within nations.

Summary

1. **Definitions of Economics**
   (i) **Adam Smith :** Adam Smith defined economics as "the science of wealth". He assumed that wealth is the most important factor in the human society as it can fulfil all the

desires of human beings. He also assumed that all the efforts of human society were directed towards earning more and more wealth.

(ii) **Alfred Marshall :** He defined economics as "the study of mankind in the ordinary business of life; it examines that part of individual and social action which is most closely connected with the attainment and with the use of the material requisites of well being."

(iii) **Lionel Charles Robbins :** According to him, Economics is the science which studies human behaviour as a relationship between ends and scarce means which have alternative uses.

(iv) **Paul Anthony Samuelson :** According to Paul Samuelson, Economics is a study of how men and society choose, with or without the use of money, to employ scarce productive resources which could have alternative uses, to produce various commodities over time, and distribute them for consumption, now and in the future, among the various people and groups of society. It analyses costs and benefits of improving patterns of resource allocation.

Exercise

◆ Short Answer Questions (2 marks)

1. State the definition of economics that focuses on wealth.
2. What did Marshall mean by 'ordinary business of life' ?
3. What are wants ?
4. Explain the meaning of means.
5. What is scarcity ?
6. Why does choices arise ?
7. Samuelson's definition is dynamic in nature, explain why ?
8. Name the title of the book Adam Smith wrote.

◆ Long Answer Questions (3-6 marks)

1. What is the relationship between ends and means ?
2. Explain the concept of relative and absolute scarcity.
3. Why does the issue of choice arise in case of Lionel Robbins' definition ?
4. Explain the definition of economics as given by the Father of Economics.
5. Compare the definitions of Alfred Marshall and Paul Samuelson.
6. Compare Adam Smith's and Lionel Robbins' definition of economics.
7. Critique P.A. Samuelson's definition of economics. What has he left out ?
8. Explain Robbins' definition of economics by giving an example of use of time in a day of a student like you.

Micro and Macro Economics : Concepts

2.1. Introduction

Economics covers the study of human activities. It studies men in his ordinary business of life. Human wants are unlimited and therefore, economic activities such as production, exchange and consumption are needed in order to satisfy those wants. Production of goods and services requires various factors such as land, labour, capital etc. Investment is needed to acquire these factors to carry out production smoothly. Investment is the result of past savings and the amount of savings determines the level of investment. Goods and services are consumed because of their utility and utility is created through various production processes. All produced goods are available for sale at a given price. Money is needed to avail these goods for consumption. Thus, economics is a subject of great depth and breadth. To understand the discipline, it is imperative that certain important concepts are clearly understood. The concepts range from across economics-from microeconomics and macroeconomics to welfare economics. This chapter is a lucid exposition of basic concepts and terminologies that are relevant for us to understand this wonderful discipline.

2.2. Microeconomics : Meaning and Features

The study of economics is divided largely into two parts which are, microeconomics and macroeconomics. Micro means a small part. Hence, in microeconomics, the whole economy is not studied. What are examined are small components of the whole economy. Hence, we study an individual consumer and her or his choices or a producer and his or her profit maximizing decisions in the market. Microeconomics suffers from the limitation that it does not mirror what happens in the economy as a whole; because it concentrates on the decisions made by individual consumers, firms and industries.

2.2.1. Features of Microeconomics

1. It deals with small parts of the economy.
2. Hence, it looks at individual consumers, firms and industries.
3. It deals with individual income, consumption and savings.
4. It studies the determination of price of any product or factors of production.
5. It deals with the working of the market via the price mechanism, which is nothing but the determination of price and quantity of a commodity, by the forces of demand and supply.

Hence, it deals with the demand of the consumer, supply of the producer and the equilibrium of market forces in the short run and the long run under different types of market. Microeconomics, therefore, includes the study of market structures and the behaviour of individual firms and industries.

It also looks into the flow of economic resources from the owners of these resources to the business units via the service sector. Microeconomics has an important place in the study of economics. It majors in efficiency and allocation of scarce resources, governed by optimum choices at the micro level. It does not, however, deal with macro variables nor does it reflect upon the working of the entire economy.

2.3. Macroeconomics : Meaning and Features

Macroeconomics, on the other hand, studies the economy as a whole. It is concerned with aggregates and depicts the entire picture of the economy. If in microeconomics, we study individual animals, in macroeconomics, we look at the entire jungle with its wild life. Macro variables that are dealt with in this aspect of economics are national income, aggregate investments, aggregate consumption, aggregate savings, aggregate output, national employment, economic growth and development. Macroeconomics deals with how an economy grows over time and examines the determinants of development. Macroeconomics is, thus, crucial to understanding economics and fills the gaps left by microeconomics in its inadequacy in explaining the working of the economy as a whole.

2.3.1. Features of Macroeconomics

1. It deals with the study of the economy as a whole.
2. It is concerned with the study of aggregates.
3. National income, aggregate savings and aggregate investments are major concepts dealt with in macroeconomic analysis.
4. It studies the determination of general price levels.
5. It investigates into the problem of unemployment and the achievement of full employment.
6. It studies the aspect of decision making at the aggregate and national levels.

It includes all growth theories, whether related to developed or developing economies. It also includes the study of economic systems and the working of the economy under different systems.

Macroeconomics, hence, helps in understanding the working of complicated economic systems and provides an overall view of world economies. It also lends itself to the formulation of useful policies for the economy. It includes the entire study of the budget and all variables such as taxes, public expenditure, public debt etc. In short, macroeconomics is a deep and vast discipline and encompasses the entire gamut of the economy. Macroeconomic analysis of the economy also provides urgent solutions for problems faced by the economy. It deals with the economy wide phenomena and deals with variables such as aggregate demand, aggregate supply, prices, inflation, income, employment, economic growth etc.

2.4. Differences between Micro and Macro Economics

Microeconomics	Macroeconomics
1. It studies economic aspect of an individual unit.	1. It studies the economy as a whole.
2. It deals with individual income, consumption and savings.	2. It deals with national income, aggregate consumption and aggregate savings.
3. It facilitates determination of price of any product or factors of production.	3. It facilitates determination of general price level in an economy.
4. Its scope is narrow and restricted to an individual unit.	4. Its scope is wide as it deals with economic units on the national level.
5. Its alternative name is price theory.	5. Its alternative name is income theory.

2.5. Human wants — classification

All the desires and aspirations and motives of humans are known as human wants in economics. The human wants that can be satisfied with goods and services of any kind are economic wants like for example food, shelter, clothing, etc.

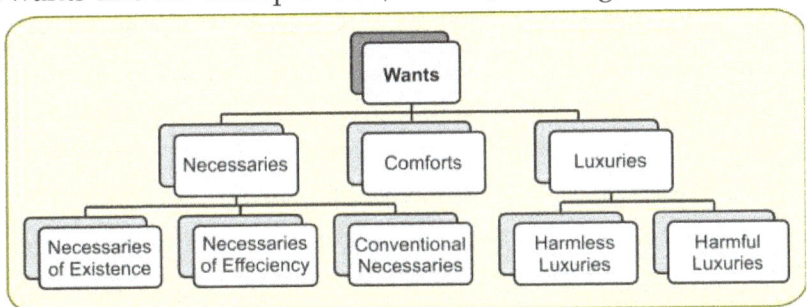

Fig. 2.1

2.5.1. Human Wants can be broadly classified as under

1. **Necessaries** : Bare essentials required universally for subsistence or survival, or for maintaining a certain minimum standard-of-living. Necessaries again can be sub-divided as

    (i) Necessaries of existence: Things without which we cannot exist. For example, water, food, clothing, shelter, etc.

    (ii) Necessaries of efficiency: The things which increase our efficiency. For example, fruits, vegetables, etc.

    (iii) Conventional necessaries: The things which we are forced to use by social customs. For example, dowry, parties, etc.

2. **Comforts** : After satisfying our necessaries we desire to have some comforts. For example, electric cooker, refrigerator, etc.

3. **Luxuries :** Luxury means excessive consumption. After getting comforts, man desires for luxury. Luxury articles are those which are not needed. For example, gold and silver, costly furniture, etc.

2.6. Utility Analysis : The Marginal Concepts

The marginal concept is the unifying glue in the entire microeconomics and hence, it is important that it is well understood. Marginal refers to an additional unit. Due to the fact that resources are scarce, their usage has its own benefits and costs. The objective of the economic agents is to maximize the net benefit or utility or revenue they get from the usage of these resources. The net benefit is nothing but the total benefit (or utility) minus the total cost.

Net Benefit = Total Benefit – Total Cost

As long as the addition to total benefit is larger than the addition to total cost, the net benefit will increase. If the addition to total cost is greater than the addition to total benefit then, the net benefit will decrease. If the addition to the total benefit is the same as the addition to total cost then, the net benefit will remain the same. The addition to total benefit is nothing but the marginal benefit and the addition to total cost is nothing but the marginal cost. Another way of explaining this is that the marginal benefit is the benefit obtained from the additional unit of resource used and the marginal cost is the cost of this marginal unit. For example, if you take the case of an employer employing labourers, each additional labourer to be hired due to a growing demand will be termed as the marginal labourer. The marginal concept is therefore very important in economics. It measures the rate of change in utility or cost or wage or resource use.

Table 2.1 Relationship between Marginal Values and Net Benefit

CONDITION	NET BENEFIT
If MU > MC	Increase
If MU < MC	Decrease
If MU = MC	Remains the same

2.7. Utility : Meaning

Goods and services are desired because they have an ability to satisfy human wants. This feature of being able to satisfy human wants is termed as utility. For example, we derive utility from WiFi services as it gives us satisfaction by connecting us to our friends and family through social media. Mangoes give us satisfaction since we enjoy the fruit and it satisfies our want to relish it. In the same way, a house gives us satisfaction as it fulfils our wants for a safe and clean residence. In all these cases, therefore, the consumer is deriving utility from the WiFi service, from mangoes and from a house.

2.7.1. Features of Utility

Some important features of utility are given below :

1. Utility is the amount of satisfaction a person derives from some commodity or some service without any reference to the usefulness of the good to the person. It has an important influence on the demand for a commodity or a service.

2. Initially, it was assumed that utility can be measured exactly. Hence, economists assigned definite numbers to this abstract concept. They assumed that utility can be quantified. For example, it was assumed that one can say that we derive say 2 units of utility from the first unit of an item and 1 unit of utility from the second unit of an item. This, however, is not true as abstract concepts like satisfaction, utility etc., cannot be cardinally measured.

3. We know fully well that we do not desire all items equally. There is some kind of a priority list in the mind of the consumer. When the consumer ranks the items in the list according to his or her preference (that is, some item may be marked as the first preference, another item could be marked as the second preference and so on), it then brings into economics, the ordinal measure of utility and satisfaction. Many economists believe that utility is an abstract entity and hence, cannot be measured with numbers but can be ranked as an order of preference. Hence, ranks of preference can be assigned like 1st, 2nd, 3rd etc.

4. Utility is a psychological factor. It plays an important role in behavioural economics. What is meant by psychological factor is that what utility a consumer gains from the good or service depends on his or her social cognitive and emotional underpinnings. For example, a student of 16 years will assign different weights to the utility of a dosa in north India as compared to the student in south India. Hence, utility is a complex term.

5. Utility of a good is more if the good is scarce. Hence, utility is relative in nature. If the good is in abundance, its utility will drop. If it is scarce, its utility will rise and so will its price or value. Take the example of sand and diamonds. Diamonds have relatively greater utility to a consumer than sand and are also, way more costlier than sand.

6. Further, utility does not always give pleasure. It is the concept that describes the satisfaction obtained from consuming a good or a service. A polio vaccine is not a pleasurable service but it brings in utility of assuring good health.

7. Utility is created in a number of ways. It can also be derived from consumption of services. For example, when one consumes the services of a lawyer due to the legal problems, one gets satisfaction.

2.7.2. Total and Marginal Utilities

Economists have defined Total Utility (TU) as the total satisfaction obtained by consuming a given total amount of a good or a service. For example, the total satisfaction obtained from eating 10 mangoes is the total utility of 10 mangoes.

Marginal Utility (MU) is the additional satisfaction derived from each additional unit consumed. In this case, the utility obtained from each mango as it is consumed is the MU of that mango. It is also defined as the addition made to total utility when an additional unit is consumed. Often economists tend to subdivide utility into an imaginary unit called util.

As a consumer increases the consumption of a good over a period of time, the total utility or total satisfaction derived from it increases to a point and thereafter, it decreases. However, as the consumer keeps on consuming the good, the marginal utility or the additional utility derived from it, decreases.

Relationship between Total and Marginal Utility

Marginal utility is the change in the total utility when an additional unit is consumed. It can be calculated with the help of total utility. When change in total utility is divided by change in number of units of consumption, we get MU. The sum of marginal utilities from all units of consumption gives total utility. Both TU and MU are inter-related.

Table 2.2 and Figure 2.2 shows the relationship between TU and MU.

Table 2.2 : Total and Marginal Utilities

Units (No. of Oranges)	Total Utility (TU) (Units of Satisfaction in Utils)	Marginal Utility (MU) (Units of Satisfaction in Utils)
1	20	20
2	36	36 – 20 = 16
3	46	46 – 36 = 10
4	50	50 – 46 = 04
5	50	50 – 50 = 0
6	44	44 – 50 = – 6

In the table, it can be seen that by consuming the first orange, the consumer derives 20 utils of satisfaction. Util is an arbitrary measure of utility or satisfaction. The additional utility (MU) she derives from the first orange is 20 utils and Total Utility (TU) she derives from the first orange is also 20 utils. When the consumer consumes the second orange, she derives an additional utility (MU) of 16 utils and from the two oranges, she derives a total utility of 36 utils (20 + 16). Alternatively, this can be explained as, that she derives 16 utils of satisfaction (36 – 20) from the second orange. That is, the MU of the second orange is 16 utils. From the third orange, she derives an additional or marginal utility of 10 utils (46 – 36). The TU derived from the consumption of three oranges is 46 utils (20 + 16 + 10) or (36 + 10).

It is, thus, seen that as the consumer consumes oranges, the total utility increases till the fifth orange. The MU, however, keeps decreasing. The fifth orange adds zero marginal utility, hence, the TU of consuming 4 oranges and the TU of consuming 5 oranges is the same (50 utils). The figure 2.2 depicts the same feature. The number of oranges consumed are measured on the X-axis and the marginal utility obtained is measured on the Y-axis. It is seen that as the consumer increases the consumption of oranges, the TU rises and finally levels off at the fourth and fifth oranges. The MU curve is a downward sloping curve and at the fifth orange, it touches the X-axis as the MU of the fifth orange equals zero (50 – 50) that is, the utility of 5 oranges (50) minus the utility of 4 oranges (50) is zero. Now, if the consumer is foolish enough to consume the sixth orange, the TU will decrease to 44 utils. The marginal utility becomes a negative numeral. The sixth orange, hence, does not give any satisfaction or utility to the consumer. On the contrary, it gives dissatisfaction or disutility to the consumer (44 – 50 = – 6). In the figure, it is observed that the MU curve has gone below the X-axis into the negative quadrant indicating disutility. Hence, MU moves from being positive to zero to negative, if consumption of oranges is continued.

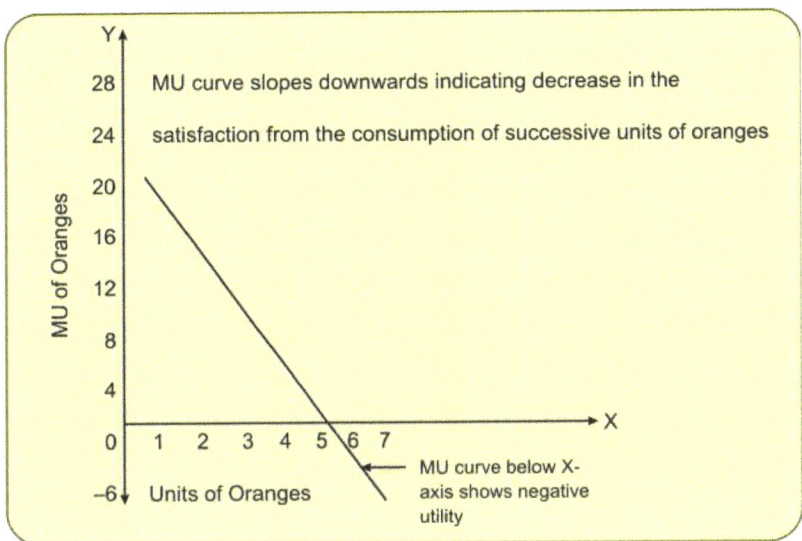

Fig. 2.2

2.7.3. The Law of Diminishing Marginal Utility (LDMU)

Alfred Marshall states the law—"The additional benefit which a person derives from a given increase of his stock of a thing diminishes with every increase in stock that the person already has." The law of diminishing marginal utility explains a common phenomenon experienced by every consumer. If a hungry person has apples to satisfy his or her hunger, the first apple will give the consumer great satisfaction, however, the second apple will not give the same level of satisfaction as the first one and the third apple will give lesser satisfaction than the second apple and so on. Additional utility derived from consuming one more apple or any other item, keeps declining. This is known as the law of diminishing marginal utility. This law can be applied to any item, including cash. If the person goes on eating apples, there will be a point when the marginal utility (that is, utility of the additional apple) will be equal to zero. Beyond this, if apples are consumed, each additional apple will reduce utility or increase disutility. It must be noted however, that the total utility of first apple is less than that of second apple. The total utility of second apple is less than that of the third apple and so forth. This means that the total utility keeps increasing up to the point where MU = 0 (Fig 2.3). After this, TU will drop and MU will become negative (the MU curve lies below the X-axis where utility is negative which implies that utility turns to disutility). As the stock decreases in size, the MU will go on increasing (the reverse of the law of DMU). Hence, one can say that the MU varies inversely with the stock. This law is the reason behind falling marginal utility.

The law of diminishing marginal utility holds true under the following assumptions :

1. Rational consumer aims at maximizing his/her utility.
2. Commodity is consumed continuously.
3. Proper units of a commodity must be consumed by the consumer.
4. Various units of commodity consumed should be homogenous in characteristics.
5. Tastes and preferences of consumer must remain the same during the consumption of the successive units of commodity.
6. Income of consumer remains constant during the operation of the law of DMU.
7. Prices of substitutes do not change.

Table 2.3 : Total and Marginal Utilities

No. of Apples consumed	Total Utility (TU) (Units of Satisfaction in Utils)	Marginal Utility (MU) (Units of Satisfaction in utils)
1	20	20
2	36	36 – 20 = 16
3	46	46 – 36 = 10
4	50	50 – 46 = 04
5	50	50 – 50 = 0
6	44	44 – 50 = – 6

From the table (2.3) and the diagram (Fig. 2.3), we can derive the following relationship between MU and TU :

1. As long as MU remains positive, TU keeps on increasing.
2. When MU becomes zero, TU is maximum. This point is also known as the point of satiety.
3. When MU becomes negative, TU starts declining.

To sum it, TU increases, reaches a maximum point, and then starts falling. MU keeps falling, till it becomes zero and then, it turns negative.

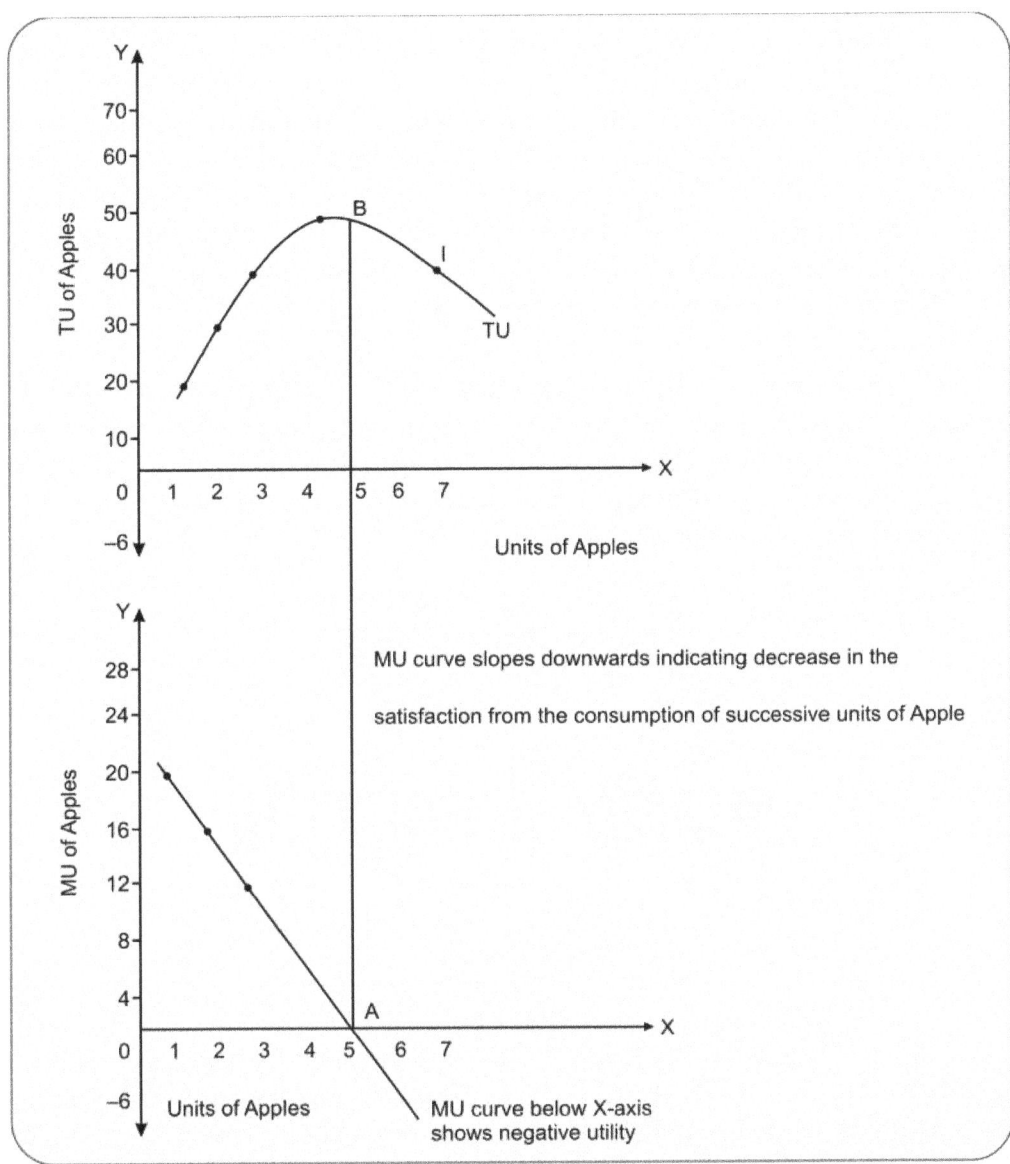

Fig. 2.3

2.8. Price : Meaning and Concepts

The amount of money needed to purchase a unit of a commodity is known as price. If the price of 1 kg of sugar is ₹ 25, it means that 1 kg of sugar can be bought by paying ₹ 25. Therefore, price is the value in exchange for the goods. In a market, prices are signals that guide decisions made by agents in economics. Agents can be consumers, producers, distributors, institutions and countries or anybody that has to make decisions to buy or to sell or to distribute. For example, if the price of butter increases, consumers will decide to reduce its consumption. Instead of butter they may start using margarine.

Prices, therefore, are signal to increase or decrease consumption of an item. However, prices also decide who produces a good and how much of a good is produced. Prices, therefore, are crucial to any decision making as they indicate how much will be bought and how much will be sold. However, it is also true that change in demand and supply leads to a change in price. If Aggregate Demand (AD) is greater than Aggregate Supply (AS), then, there is excess demand and prices will rise. The excess demand pushes prices up. Such a situation of consistent rise in the price is called inflation. The increase in price is an indication to the suppliers to increase supply and to the consumers that it's better to decrease demand. By doing so, AS would become equal to AD and price would be stabilized.

If, on the other hand, aggregate supply is greater than aggregate demand, then in economics this condition is called a glut. This will push the prices down. Such a situation of consistent fall in the price is called deflation. The glut, through a fall in prices, indicates that producers should supply less and consumers should demand more. This then makes AS equal to AD and prices gets stabilized.

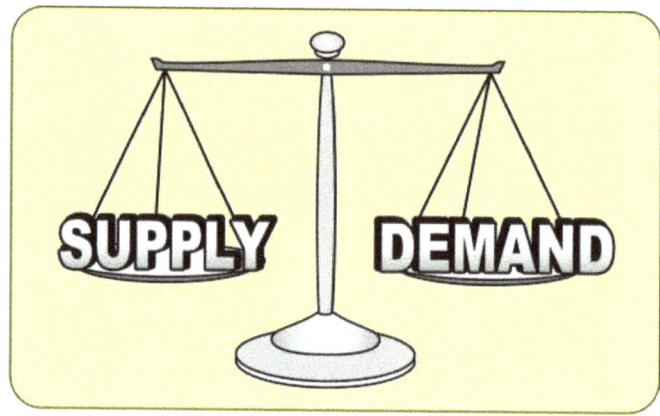

Fig. 2.4

Hence, in a free market economy, when the market forces of AS and AD are balanced, equilibrium is reached. Classical economists like Adam Smith and J.B. Say assumed that this is the best point as at this point, everyone is satisfied.

2.8.1. Inflation

A general rise in the price level is termed as inflation. In other words, there is excess money available to buy goods and services but not enough goods and services are being provided in the market. There is a short imbalance between AD and AS. Hence, the prices of the goods increase which leads to a fall in the value of money. For example, if you could buy 1 kg of sugar for ₹ 25 but now the price of sugar goes up to ₹ 50 per kg, it will not be possible to buy 1 kg sugar for ₹ 25. You will need more cash to buy the same amount of sugar or you can buy only ½ kg of sugar. This means that the ability of ₹ 25 to buy sugar has dropped. In economics, we say that the purchasing power of ₹ 25 has reduced. So, if the prices have risen, it implies that the purchasing power or the power of the currency to buy drops, this is nothing but inflation. In macroeconomics, economists speak about the general rise in prices which means a sustained increase in prices over a period of time. *Inflation, therefore, is an increase in the overall price level in an economy.* A unit of the currency is able to buy less, or in other words, the purchasing power of the currency falls when general prices rise in an economy.

2.8.2. Types of Inflation

Prices may rise when aggregate demand exceeds aggregate supply in the market or due to a rise in the factor prices. Accordingly, inflation can be categorized as demand pull inflation and cost push inflation.

1. **Demand Pull Inflation :** Demand pull inflation occurs when aggregate demand exceeds aggregate supply in the market and supply is unable to match the extra demand. Due to shortage of goods and services, price levels shoot up and purchasing power of the currency falls. Aggregate demand may rise due to expansion of money supply, fall in taxes, rise in population or increase in public expenditure. Consequently, purchasing power of the people increases resulting in excess demand. This causes the price to rise.

2. **Cost Push Inflation :** Factors of production which are land, labour, capital etc., are used to produce a commodity. Cost of production increases when the price of inputs like raw materials' cost, interest, rent or profit margin go up. The cost of production increases and pushes the price up. Naturally, if the producers have to pay more for all the inputs they use to produce goods then they will raise the price of the goods in the market. Such nature of rise in the price due to increase in input costs or profit margin causes cost push inflation. Cost push inflation is caused due to rise in factor prices, higher profit margin or due to rise in indirect taxes by the Government.

2.9. Value

In economics, value bears great importance. Adam Smith differentiated between value-in-use and value-in-exchange. *For e.g.*, water has great value in use but little value in exchange, however, diamonds have great value in exchange but little value in use.

An important concept in economics is real value and nominal value. Real value is a more important measure. It is the value of goods and services minus the rate of inflation or price rise. Or it is the value assuming prices to be constant. The nominal value, on the other hand, is ambiguous as it includes the variations in prices. Hence, if from the nominal value, the impact of rising prices is removed, we are left with the real value. For example, if a person's annual income is ₹ 80,000 in 2015 and if the income is ₹ 90000 in 2016, then we can say that the nominal growth rate is 12.5% {(90000 – 80000) / 80000 × 100)} but if the inflation rate was say 7.5% then, we can say that the real growth rate is 5% (12.5% – 7.5%). Another way to explain this is that nominal value this is the value of a good in terms of cash, while the real value is the value of a good in terms of what it is worth in terms of other goods and services. For example, if it costs ₹ 12 lakhs to study a management course and the cost of a car is also ₹ 12 lakhs, then the real value of the management course is the car that you could buy with those 12 lakhs. In other words, the cost of the management course equals the cost of a car.

2.10. Wealth

Wealth is a stock of goods existing at a particular period of time. For a stock of goods to be considered wealth, it must have the following five characteristics-

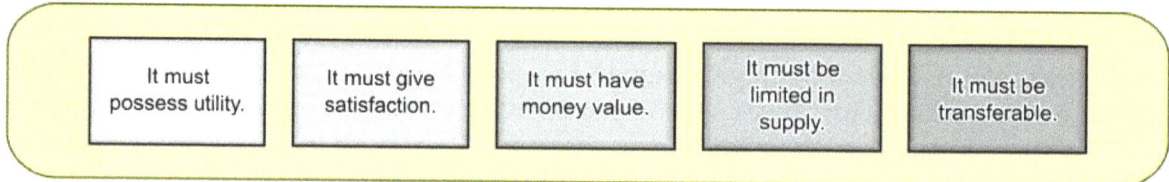

Fig. 2.5 : Features of Wealth

If a stock of good does not have any utility, it is worthless and must be got rid of. It becomes wealth only if there is utility and only if it yields satisfaction. For example, a carriage of the Indian Railways is wealth, but once it becomes obsolete and does not yield utility, it becomes scrap. Further, if a good has no money value, then it is not wealth. For it to have value, it must be scarce. Only then will it be valued. Wealth should also possess the quality of being transferred to others. That is, the ownership should be changeable from one person to another.

There are three kinds of wealth, which are personal wealth, business wealth, and social wealth.

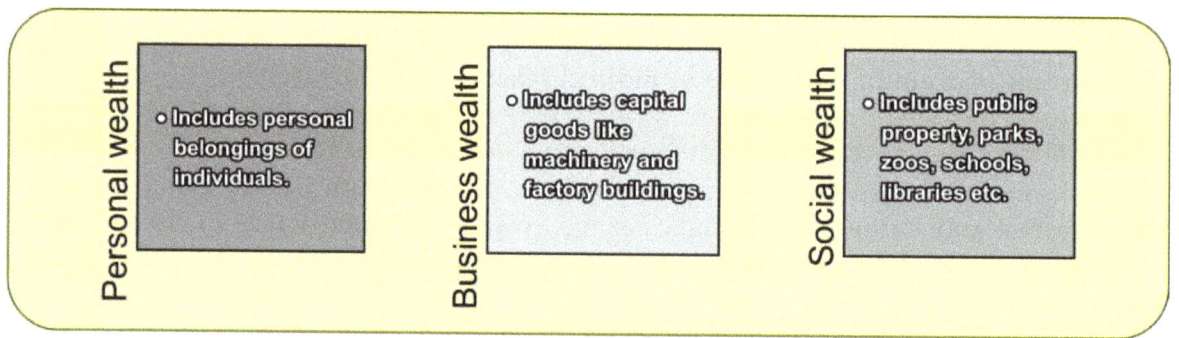

Fig. 2.6 : Types of Wealth

1. **Personal Wealth :** Personal wealth is the wealth a person owns. It may be resources such as property, cash or it could be knowledge and skills. Accumulation of personal wealth is an underlying motive behind working, saving and investing. Further, without personal wealth, a person will not be a productive agent.

2. **Business Wealth :** Business wealth is more like the property of a firm or an enterprise. It is the amount of capital and labour and the combination of the same that helps in producing the output. It includes machinery, factories, industries, oil field resources, mineral deposits etc.

3. **Social Wealth :** Social wealth is the backbone of the economy. It includes all productive units that enhance the human resources and their ability to produce. For example, schools, colleges, centers of higher learning and research, hospitals, parks, zoos, cultural centers etc.

Wealth is the basis of production and is, therefore, extremely important in terms of what it can deliver for individuals and a country at large. Without *personal wealth* individuals will not want nor will they be able to work, invest and save. *Business wealth* plays a major role in the growth of an economy. Only when the business units flourish does the economy become vibrant and grows. Social wealth is the mainstay of an economy. Without *social wealth* nothing can be done. It forms the very backbone of the economic units and is crucial for the well being and welfare of the individuals and the country.

2.11. Welfare

Initially, development and progress of a country was measured in terms of the wealth that the country accumulates. Adam Smith clearly stated this in his writings. In fact, according to him, economic development was measured in term of riches. Hence, a society with riches and wealth was considered developed. However, in essence, it must be stated that a country must also look at the well-being of its people. Thus came in the idea that wealth alone is not important but well-being too plays a major role in determining the development and progress of a nation. Thus, the well-being of a society is referred to as welfare. In fact, money and riches alone do not measure prosperity. Prosperity of a nation is a much deeper concept and includes aspects of life such as reduction of poverty and eradication of large disparities in the distribution of income and wealth. A country can be extremely wealthy but there may exist abject poverty in some pockets and huge income disparities. Once this has been looked into, the focus of attention moves from mere wealth to the welfare of the people of the country. These aspects are now widely recognized by the developing economies.

2.11.1. Relation between Wealth and Welfare

Money is needed to achieve well-being in a society but if people do not have wealth, the government has to play a role in ensuring welfare of its people. A country may be rich with huge amount of wealth but if this wealth is not properly distributed, then, a large section of the society will be very poor and will lack all the basic needs to live a comfortable life. Being a wealthy nation does not necessarily ensure welfare of its people. It is here that a welfare state plays a major role in achieving the well-being of its citizens—especially the poor, the ill, the old, the marginalized like women and the communities that are considered as belonging to the lower castes.

In India, for example, there are a number of schemes that have been launched for providing such amenities to the poor. To name a few, we have *Beti Bachao, Beti Padhao Yojana, Pradhan Mantri Jeevan Jyoti Bima Yojana, Atal Pension Yojana, The Tailored Training of Scheduled Caste and Backward Classes, Widows/Destitute Women/Girls Scheme* in Haryana, *The Amma Canteen* in Tamil Nadu , *Mid Day Meal Scheme, Rani Lakshmi Bai Pension Yojana* in Uttar Pradesh, The *Bhagyashree Scheme for the Girl Child* and the *Welfare Scheme for Domestic Workers* in Maharashtra, *The Integrated Child Protection Scheme* in Nagaland, *The Nirbhaya Scheme for Women and Children* in Kerala, etc.

2.11.2. Difference between Wealth and Welfare

Some important differences between wealth and welfare are as follows :

1. Wealth is objective and can be measured—*e.g.,* cash, income, property whereas welfare is subjective and cannot be measured numerically – *e.g.,* civility, literacy, general decorum, etc.

2. Wealth can be measured in terms of money whereas welfare can be estimated from standard of living, life expectancy, literacy rate and other public amenities.

3. Wealth may be same for many people but welfare is subjective and differs from person to person.

2.11.3. Types of Welfare

Welfare can be categorised as economic welfare and social welfare.

1. **Economic welfare :** Economic welfare is the level of prosperity of individuals or groups of individuals in a country. It includes measures such as GNP, standard of living and the volume and utility obtained from wealth and material goods and services.

2. **Social welfare :** Social welfare, on the other hand, includes factors which affect human welfare in a country other than wealth. It includes besides wealth, the distribution of the same in a just manner, the eradication of unemployment, the assurance of basic amenities to the people of the country such as food, clothing, shelter, health, security, self esteem, freedom etc. If any of these is in short supply, peoples' lives will become miserable.

2.12. Money : Meaning

In the words of Robertson, money is "anything which is widely accepted in payment for goods or in discharge of other kinds of obligations". Money, as a medium of exchange performs a number of functions in the economy. Therefore 'Walker' says "Money is what it does". This definition defines money based on its functions. In a broader sense, money includes all medium of exchange such as gold, silver, bills of exchange, cheques, credit and debit cards etc. Money plays a very important role in guiding economic activity and it has a value. Therefore, money is defined as—"anything that is generally accepted as a means of exchange, acts as measure of value and facilitates store of value". Money, as a medium of exchange, has helped in overcoming the inconveniences of the barter system.

2.12.1. Types of Money

Money is of two types :
1. Standard Money
2. Bank Money

1. **Standard Money :** Money consisting of paper currency notes and coins is called standard money. It is legal tender as no one can refuse to accept it. It functions as money on the instructions of the government.

2. **Bank Money :** All bank deposits which can be withdrawn by means of cheques or demand drafts are known as bank money. Bank money is also known as credit money. Bank money is used against the deposits made by people in the bank. It helps us to transfer money from one person to another person from the deposit maintained in the bank.

2.12.2. Functions of Money

The main functions performed by money are as follows :

1. Primary Functions

(i) **Medium of Exchange :** The most important function of money is to remove the difficulties of barter exchange. In a barter system, there was a need for double coincidence of wants. A person who wants to sell a cow and buy a goat has to look out for a person who wants to sell a goat and buy a cow. There also arises the problem of indivisibility in such goods. But with the invention of money, goods can be exchanged at any time and any place. The problem of indivisibility is also eliminated since money is available in all denominations.

(ii) **Money as a Measure of Value :** Money has now become a common measure of value or a unit of account. Any commodity can be valued in terms of money. Under barter system, each and every good had to be valued against each and every other good. Money can address this difficulty and can be used as a yardstick to value all the goods and services in a common unit.

2. Secondary Functions

(i) **Standard of Deferred Payment :** Money payments can be made after a lapse of time. In the barter economy, lending and borrowing took place in terms of goods. But most of the goods deteriorate in value over time. Money, however, has stable value over time and therefore, it facilitates lending and borrowing, making such activities less risky.

(ii) **Store of Value :** Money can be stored as a liquid asset. Currency notes can be kept at home or in the bank account for withdrawal at any time when the need arises. Thus, income and expenditure do not occur at the same time. For example, an employer may have to pay daily wages to the labourers but he may not receive his income daily. Here, money acts as a store of value and is used whenever required.

(iii) **Transfer of Value :** Money also acts as a means of transferring value. The value of money can be easily transferred from one place to another. Money earned from sale of an asset in one place can be used at another place for purchase of other assets.

3. Contingency Functions

(i) **Distribution of National Income :** Money helps in the optimal distribution of national income among the various factors of production. The remuneration in the form of rent, wages, interest and profits to the factors of production namely, land, labour, capital and entrepreneur can be easily distributed in monetary terms.

(ii) **Liquidity :** Money provides the purchasing power to its bearer. It is the most liquid asset that can be used when required.

(iii) **Basis of Credit :** Banks cannot create credit without money. As a store of value, people store money in the banks in the form of deposits. These deposits can be used to offer loans and create credit.

(iv) **Maximum Satisfaction to the Consumers :** Money helps in maximisation of satisfaction of the producers and the consumers. The producers try to maximise their satisfaction by equating the marginal product of the factor of production to its price while the consumers try to maximize their satisfaction by equating the price of the product to the marginal utility.

2.12.3. Barter Economy versus Money Economy

1. **Barter Economy**

Before the onset of the money economy, human beings used the barter system. In this system, goods and services were exchanged for other goods and services. This system, however, had various drawbacks, which are listed below—

(i) *Lack of Double Coincidence of Wants* : Double coincidence of wants means what one person wants to buy and sell must match with what some other person wants to sell and buy. Thus, a seller had to find a person who wanted to buy seller's good and at the same time, had the good that the seller wanted to purchase. This is called double coincidence of wants and was the main drawback of the barter system. For example—if an individual wanted to exchange one bag of rice for a goat, he had to find another person who needed the bag of rice and had a goat to offer in exchange. This matching of individual wants was very difficult to attain.

(ii) *Lack of Divisibility* : The barter system was based on the exchange of goods with other goods. It was difficult to fix exchange rates for certain goods which are indivisible. Such indivisible goods posed a real problem under barter system. For example, it was difficult to determine how many bags of rice would be sufficient to buy one goat.

(iii) *Lack of Common Measure* : In absence of money, there was no common measure available to measure the value of the goods to be exchanged. It was difficult to understand the proportion in which a commodity could be exchanged for another commodity. For example, if a student needed an exercise book, then the problem was to determine the number of tea bags that should be exchanged for it. Another problem was to ensure that enough small tea bags were available to be able to compensate for the value of an exercise book.

(iv) *Difficulties of Storage and Transfer* : Under the barter system, it was not possible to store goods for a longer period of time due to variant nature of the goods. The quality of goods could deteriorate over the period of time and their storage was a costly affair. It was also not possible to transfer these goods from one place to another due to poor transportation system.

(v) *Lack of Deferred Payment* : Goods do not possess the same quality at all times. The future payment in terms of same goods was not possible. Goods and services lacked the standard for deferred payments. This meant that the goods could not be used for contractual payments in the future as it was very risky for both the parties.

2. **Money Economy**

This is an economic system where exchange is facilitated by the use of money, as distinct from the barter system, where goods and services were exchanged. In such an economy, the legal tender money is the money that is officially designated by the government and every person is bound to accept it as a medium of exchange for goods and services and for the discharge of debts. No one can refuse to accept legal tender money. In November 2016, when the Prime Minister demonetized ₹ 500 and ₹ 1000 currency notes, then overnight ₹ 500 and ₹ 1000 currency notes ceased to be legal tender.

These currencies lost their values overnight as their official status as a medium of exchange was revoked. The 25 paisa coins ceased to be legal tender in India from 30th June, 2011. Legal tender money is of two types :

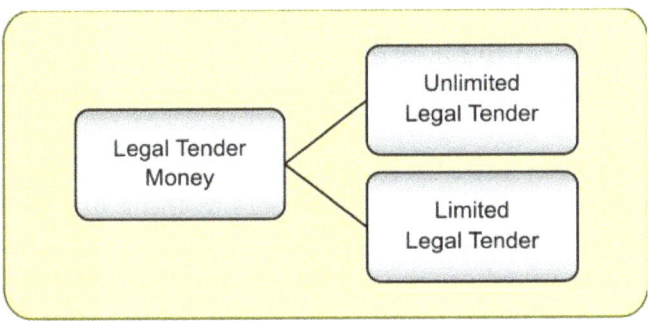

Fig. 2.7 : Types of Legal Tender Money

Unlimited legal tender refers to money that is legal tender up to any amount. In India, rupee notes have unlimited legal tender. They can be used to pay up to any amount of cash. On the other hand, paisa coins in India have limited legal tender and cannot be used to pay huge sum of money. The amount it can be used to pay is fixed. In India, the one rupee note and coins and higher denomination notes and coins are legal tenders for unlimited amounts. This means, any amount of cash can be paid as one rupee notes and coins. However, the 50 paisa coins have limited legal tender. They can be used to pay amounts up to ₹ 10. Any person can and has the right to refuse an amount greater than 10 rupees if paid in the form of 50 paisa coins.

2.13. Market

A market is a place where goods and services are bought and sold. However, this need not be the only qualifying ground for defining a market. In short, the function of the market defines the market. Its function is to enable exchange of goods and services between buyers and sellers. There is no need for a physical place because such exchange can take place online too. If you go to the vegetable market or a cloth store or a book shop, you go to the physical market to buy these goods. However, you could order books on Amazon, purchase clothes from Jabong and buy groceries from Big Basket. In this case, movement of the person to the physical market place is not required. Hence, a market is qualified to be the one where there is exchange of goods and services between buyers and sellers. The place is immaterial to the activity. It may or may not be a physical place per se. Therefore, a market may be defined as a systematic arrangement under which buyers and sellers come in contact with each other, in order to complete their desired transactions.

2.13.1. Size of a Market

The size of a market refers to the volume of demand for any commodity in a particular market. The size of market may be small or large depending on the number of buyers and their purchasing capacity. The development of physical infrastructure like transportation, communication, or banking may have an influential effect on determining the size of a market. There are many factors which determine the size of a market. Some of them are listed below :

1. **Number of Buyers and Sellers** : If there are infinite number of identical buyers and sellers selling homogeneous goods, it is known as perfect competition. This kind of a market structure, however, is hypothetical and does not exist in real life. If there is only one seller, the market structure is called Monopoly. For example, the government has monopoly in Railways in India. If there is only one buyer, it is called Monopsony. This happens when a firm is the only buyer of certain types of inputs including labour. For example, the expertise of a highly renowned doctor. If there are two sellers, it is termed as Duopoly. Besides this, there is Oligopoly where there are few sellers. For example, we have a few internet service providers in India like Vodafone, Airtel, Idea, BSNL etc. The most common form of market structure, however, is Monopolistic competitive market structure where there are large number of buyers and sellers but the products are all different. That is, there is product differentiation.

Table 2.4 : Types of Markets Depending upon the Number of Buyers and Sellers

S. No.	Market Type/ Structure	Number of buyers and sellers	Features
1.	Perfect competition	Infinite buyers and sellers	Goods are all alike or homogeneous and with so many market players, it is impossible for any one participant to alter the prevailing price in the market.
2.	Monopolistic competition	Large number of buyers and sellers	It combines the elements of a monopoly and perfect competition. There is product differentiation. That means, each competitors' product is sufficiently differentiated from the others' product. For example— toothpaste of each seller is different in price and quality from the toothpastes sold by other sellers.
3.	Oligopoly	Few buyers and sellers	They may or may not sell identical goods.
4.	Duopoly	Two sellers	In most cases, the goods sold are not identical.
5.	Monopoly	Only one seller	The firm has the monopoly power to set the price.
6.	Monopsony	Only one buyer	There is only one buyer in the market and therefore, she gets to set the price, *e.g.*, the purchase of labour by only one firm.

2. **Nature of Goods Available for Sale** : The classical economists assumed that the goods are identical and homogeneous. But, in reality, the goods are largely differentiated

in every form and in some cases, even in the quality, *e.g.*, tooth paste. We have many different types of tooth pastes being sold by different sellers in the market and each is distinct from the other. In such cases, a lot of cash is spent by the sellers in selling and advertising the product.

3. **Purchasing Power of a Consumer** : Purchasing power of a consumer is the ability of a consumer to buy goods and services. If prices of commodities are low, the purchasing power of the consumer rises as the same amount of currency can now buy more goods. If there is inflation, the purchasing power of the currency drops. The purchasing power of a dollar is much higher than the purchasing power of a rupee, as a dollar can buy much more goods and services than a rupee.

4. **Availability of Banking Facilities** : In a developed economy, the banking services are well developed and efficient. Internet banking is also very well developed. Availability of banking facilities helps in increasing the number of transactions and hence, helps in enlarging the size of a market. In a country like India, however, this is not the case. Even though there has been a lot of improvement, urban centers still have greater availability of banking facilities than the rural areas.

2.13.2. Free Market and the Doctrine of Laissez Faire

In economics, free market refers to the market where only the forces of demand and supply play a role in determining prices. Further, these forces should be absolutely free to make their impact felt. These forces left to themselves would restore the equilibrium in the market in case of any disruption in the form of rise in the price or a fall in the price. They should not be tampered in any manner, by any form of intervention or disruption. Interventions can take any form such as a subsidy, or a tax, or administered prices, or rationing of goods, or issuing license to sell etc. Any external force that affects the demand or the supply will then interfere with the free market. Classical economists were against any kind of interference. They spoke about a perfect market structure without such interferences. In short, these thinkers were against the role of the government in the business of the country. This doctrine is termed as the doctrine of laissez faire. It simply means that the government (called the state) should not interfere in industry and commerce, their role in these spheres should be kept to the minimum. Adam Smith was a great protagonist of this doctrine.

2.13.3. Market Forces and Determination of Price

Market forces are those forces that determine the price in the market. These are- the demand force and the supply force. Behind these forces are two sets of players – the buyers and the sellers. Hence, in the market, we have the interaction of these two forces. Individual players in the market are free to decide about their actions. By this, we mean that the buyers and the sellers can exhibit free choice.

In a free market, prices are determined by the combined action of buyers and sellers. In fact, the interaction of the forces of demand (action of the buyers) and the forces of supply (action of the sellers) determines the price. Such a price is called the equilibrium price because it comes to settle when the forces of demand match the forces of supply.

Equilibrium price is determined where, D = S at point E (as shown in fig. 2.8).

Where, D stands for Demand and S stands for Supply.

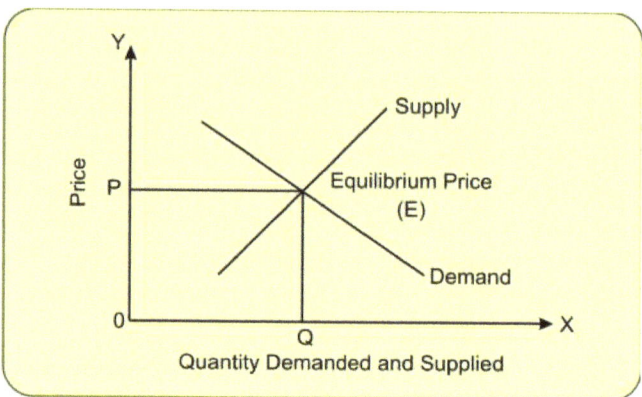

Fig. 2.8 : Determination of Equilibrium Price

2.13.4. Two Market Forces : Demand and Supply

Demand and supply forces together determine the price in the market. Since the market is free, consumers are free to make demand decisions and the firms who are the suppliers, are free to make supply decisions. These decisions of the two parties are conveyed to each other through the impact their decisions have on prices, through what is called the price mechanism. The prices that result are, then, the prices acceptable to both the consumers and the sellers. Changes in demand and supply impact the prices and this then signals change. For example, during the 2015 floods in Chennai, production and supply of goods got interrupted. This led to prices shooting up as the supply of goods was less than the demand. An increase in price is an incentive to the suppliers and hence, they will try and increase the output. An increase in price is also a signal to the consumers who will try and reduce their demand. Hence, the changes in demand and supply acts on prices which functions both as incentives and signals. For elucidating further, we can say that an increase in demand is signaled by a rise in price, this then is an incentive to the seller who increases supply. The increased demand which set in motion the rise in price is then matched by a rise in supply. Demand equals supply and the equilibrium price is set. A rise in supply is signaled by a fall in price, that is, as supply increases, prices will dip. This fall in price is an incentive to the consumers to consume more and so, the demand rises to match the increased supply (as shown in fig. 2.9). This adjustment of supply to demand and demand to supply via signals and incentives is invisible and hence, Adam Smith called it the Invisible Hand. By invisible hand, he meant the functioning of the price mechanism, also known as the market mechanism. Such a mechanism works in the goods and factor markets. The *goods market* is the market where goods and services are bought and sold and the *factor market* is where factors of production (land, labour and capital) are bought and sold. Factor market affects the supply forces and goods market affects both the demand and the supply forces.

The two markets are interdependent. What happens in one market will have an impact on the other. For example, assume that demand for cars increase. This will create the shortage of cars and an increase in their prices. The rise in price will choke some demand off but the increased price will be an incentive to the producers, who will increase their production and hence, will demand more inputs like iron and steel, car parts, capital, land, labour etc. This increased demand of inputs will cause a shortage of these inputs in the factor market and therefore, their prices will rise. A rise in the prices of inputs will reduce some of the demand for the same but will encourage the suppliers of inputs to supply more input bringing about an equilibrium between the demand and supply of inputs (as shown in fig. 2.10).

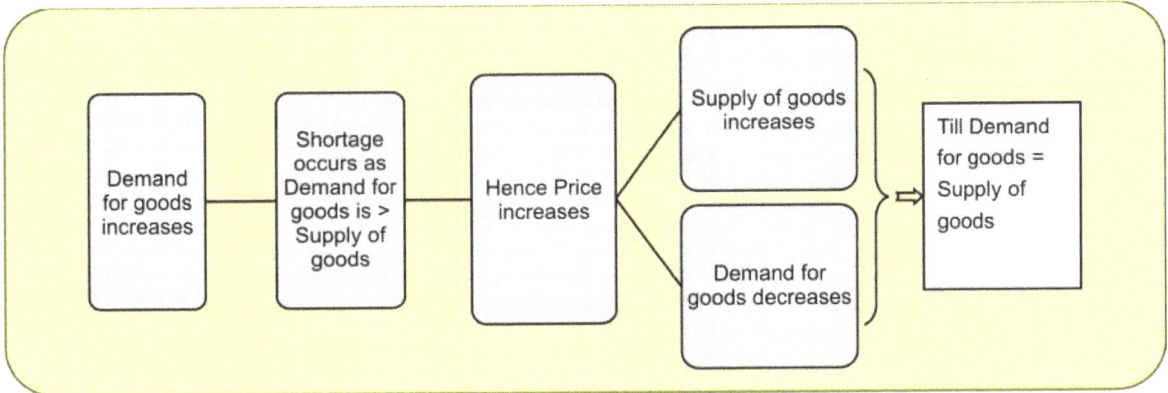

Fig. 2.9 : Goods Market Mechanism

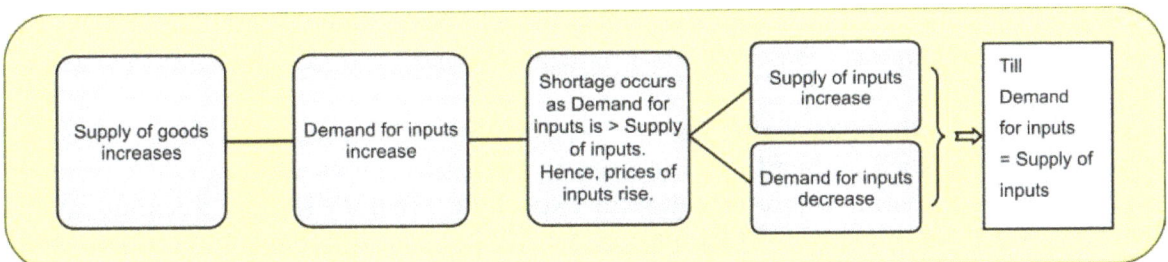

Fig. 2.10 : Factor Market Mechanism

From the two figures, it is clear how the two forces of demand and supply work together to bring about the equilibrium price, be it in the goods market or in the factor market. The invisible hand, therefore, plays a major role in attaining this and according to the doctrine of laissez faire and free market mechanism, no external force is necessary to bring about these adjustments.

2.14. Capital

Capital is the wealth in the form of assets owned by a person or an organisation which is used in the production of goods and services. In other words, capital is a factor of production or an input in the production process. All wealth may not, however, represent capital in the sense of producing more wealth. For example, a country may have lovely buildings built with excellent aesthetic sense, but these may not play the role of capital as machinery, tools, factory buildings, raw materials, industrial plants, means of transport, semi finished goods, etc, would. Such inputs in the production process have also been termed as *physical capital*. Land is also a form of physical capital but is considered as a separate input in production. Capital is also money. For business units, capital is the money raised to buy assets such as tools, machinery, buildings of factories and plants etc. This is nothing but *financial capital*. Another important aspect of capital is *human capital* which is the skills, experience and expertise embodied in the labour force. Such embodiment occurs through education, training, and various types of skill formation. Children going to school, and then graduating to college, doing internships in college to get hands on experience in the work place, are all part of creating human capital. Various types of skill formation, both formal and informal, also add to the process of the formation of human capital. High levels of Research and Development (R & D) also leads to a higher level of human capital formation. A healthy population with high nutrition levels is the base for viable human resources.

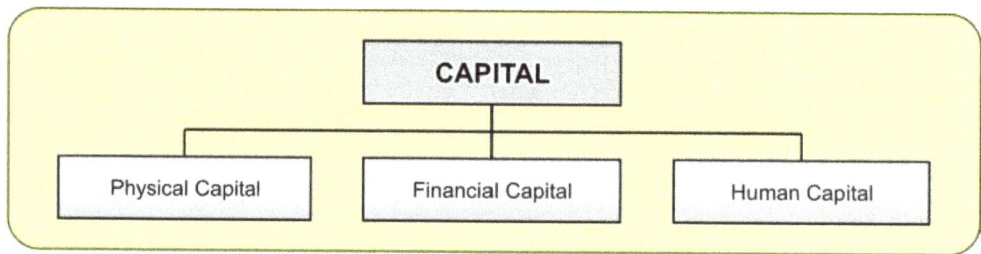

Fig. 2.11 : Types of Capital

1. **Physical Capital** : This includes machinery, tools, factory buildings, raw materials, industrial plants, means of transport, semi finished goods, etc.

2. **Financial Capital** : This includes financial resources raised to buy physical assets. In short, it refers to cash.

3. **Human Capital** : Basically, it is the productivity of labour which is influenced by a host of factors such as health of the population, nutrition of the population, infant mortality rates, maternal mortality rates, life expectancy, literacy levels, education levels, research and development, skill formation, vocational training, happiness index, etc.

A developed country in comparison to an underdeveloped nation normally has a much larger and better capital accumulation in the country. Such a country also has a healthier population. Part of the process of capital formation also includes aspects such as freedom which increases the capabilities of human beings. In fact, the freer the population, the more capacity it possesses to add to production and general well being, as postulated by Amartya Sen. In addition, less gender gap also improves human capital. Countries which have less discrimination against women have a higher GDP in the world, as compared to countries that have a patriarchal backdrop that largely discriminates against women and girls in nearly every walk of life.

2.15. Investment

Investment is the production of items not for immediate consumption but for future use. Investment can also be defined as the creation of new assets or addition made to the capital stock of the country. Investment in economics can mean three things. If there is actual production of real assets like construction of a bridge or a metro rail, then this is called *real investment*. Setting up of schools and colleges, hospitals and farms all come under this type of investment. Investment can also take a financial hue. If securities are bought in the stock exchange market or if individuals buy LIC policies or medical insurance policies or post office savings then they are indulging in financial investments, also known as portfolio investment. If, however, people spend money on education, skill formation, training, and research, then they are investing in human capital. Education is considered to be one of the best forms of investment. From this, it can be seen that investment is crucial in the formation of capital in a country. If there is no investment, there will be no capital and hence, this will affect the production base of the country. The ability of the country to produce will drop and the country will remain underdeveloped. When a country has low levels of investments, it means that the people of that country are saving less because savings translate into investments. People are, therefore, spending on consumption more, rather than spending on building up of physical or human capital. They are not investing in financial assets but are indulging in high levels of consumption. This is common in India. We often see huge expenses on extravagant weddings, other traditional and religious functions, buying of gold and consumer durables. All this is an indication that the individuals are not saving up to the level done in the developed nations. Unproductive consumption pulls down the GDP of a country. Only when the investment rates are high will capital formation increase in a country.

2.15.1. Investment as a Process of Capital Formation

When we deposit money in the bank as a part of our savings, a huge loanable fund is created with the banks. Banks now provide loans from these deposits to the investors who are interested in creation of new capital assets in the country. This process is called mobilization of savings. Now, the producers make investments in the new projects such as acquiring new machines, creation of new buildings or construction of roads, flyovers or airports. This helps in increasing the capital stock of the country or in the process of capital formation. Capital formation, thus, takes place in the following three stages :

1. Creation of savings in the banks
2. Mobilization of savings by the banks, and
3. Investment of mobilized savings by the producers.

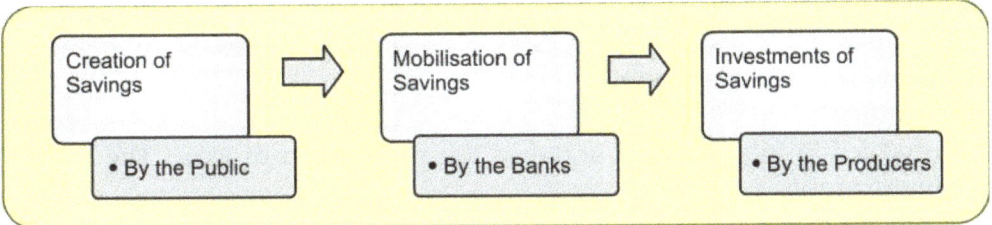

Fig. 2.12 : Stages of Capital Formation

2.16. Income

Income of a person is the amount of cash or goods received by individuals and households for providing factor services in a given year. This is called *personal income*. The sum of the incomes of all the individuals and the households received in a year gives us the *national income* of the country. *Real income* is the amount of goods and services the income can buy. If prices increase, the real income decreases and if prices fall, the real income or the purchasing power of income increases. *Disposable income,* on the other hand, is the income at the disposal of the earner. This is the personal income minus taxes that individual or households have to pay. Tax liability is the amount of taxes an individual has to pay to the government. This tax money does not belong to the individual. It has to go to the government. If an individual or a business unit does not pay the tax, this means that they are evading the tax which is an economic offence.

$$\text{Real Income} = \frac{Y}{P}$$

and, Disposable Income = Y – T

Where, Y = Income, P = Prices, T = Tax Liability

2.17. Production

Production means the creation of goods and services for the purpose of selling in the market. In fact, production involves the transformation of inputs into outputs. Production, in economics, hence, refers to the transformation of raw materials into finished goods and assembling of small parts to make bigger machinery. Production also includes services related to distribution and marketing as for an economist, production is not complete until it reaches the consumer. Hence, transportation, wholesaling, retailing—all form a part of the production process. An increase in production will increase the economic welfare of the consumers and hence, the aim is to raise the production levels of a country.

2.17.1. Factors of Production

Factors of production refers to the resources or inputs needed for producing goods and services. These inputs can be classified as land, labour, capital and entrepreneurship :

1. **Land** : Land consists of all natural resources—some economists consider land as part of the capital. The income land earns is rent.

2. **Labour** : Labour refers to the human effort that needs to be combined with other factors of production for creating an output. The income of labour is wages.

3. **Capital** : Capital is the financial input needed to carry out the production process. Capital also consists of physical capital like factories, machineries, tools and equipments etc. The income of capital is interest.

4. **Entrepreneurship** : Entrepreneurship refers to the ability of a person to bring the factors of production together and organize the production process. The income of an entrepreneur is profit.

When all the factors of production are combined as input, the output or national product is created. By being thus employed, each one earns an income.

Hence, R + W + I + P = National Income.

Where, R is the rent

W is the wage

I is the interest, and

P is the profit.

Since the national income is generated by the employment of all the factors of production that creates the output at the macro level, national employment equals the national product (output) and this equals the national income.

Hence we can say that, NE = NO = NY

Where, NE = National Employment

NO = National Output

NY = National Income

2.17.2. Factor Incomes

The producers use various factors of production in the production process. These factors which include land, labour, or capital are to be procured from the market against payment. The entrepreneur is also required to be paid for his contribution to the production process. Therefore, factor income is the amount paid to the factors of production for their use in the production process. Hence, it includes wages, interest, profit and rent. Income from land is rent, from capital is interest, from enterprise is profits and the labourer earns wages.

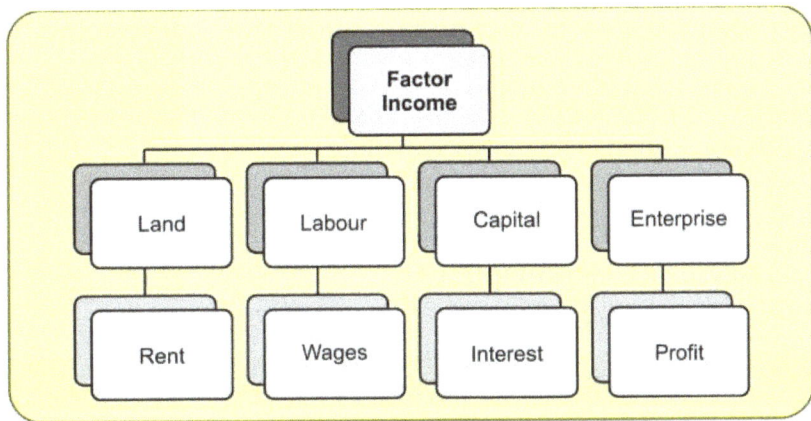

Fig. 2.13 : Factor Incomes

2.18. Consumption

Consumption is the total quantity of goods and services consumed by consumers in a given time period. In other words, it is the total of consumers' demand. Goods and services are consumed because they have the ability to satisfy wants. Consumption plays a major role in the study of both microeconomics and macroeconomics. In macroeconomics, consumption expenditure (C) is one of the components of aggregate demand (AD), the other component being investment demand (I). Consumption depends on the amount of income and savings. It is the excess of income over savings. A higher C pushes up AD and hence, the national income.

Hence, we have,

$$AD = C + I$$

If people in a country have many unsatisfied wants, their propensity to consume will be higher and an increase in income will be reflected in a large increase in C and a small increase in I.

2.19. Saving

Saving is the amount of money not spent on consumption. It is one of the determinants of income and employment. The importance of savings lies in its relationship with investments. All cash saved is invested. Hence, saving is a necessary pre-requisite for investments. If savings are low, investment will also be low. Any decision that leads to a reduction in consumption and helps in the process of production of real capital is viewed as savings. Savings are mainly of two types—individual savings and company savings which are generally ploughed back into the business. There are many reasons why people want to save :

1. For contingencies and emergencies like illness or death, people tend to save some cash.
2. Many save to plan for the future, *e.g.*, people may save for their old age, or for their children's education.
3. Some people save just to accumulate wealth to enhance their status in the society.

Aggregate savings is a macroeconomic concept and represents that part of national income that is not consumed. Hence we can state,

$$Y = C + S$$

Where, Y = National Income
C = Aggregate Consumption
S = Aggregate Savings

2.20. Aggregate Demand and Aggregate Supply

These are very important aggregate variables and play a significant role in determining many macroeconomic variables like prices, income and employment. Aggregate Demand (AD) is the quantity of goods and services that households, firms, and buyers in foreign countries intend to buy at various prices.

$$AD = C + G + I + (X - M)$$

Where, C = Consumption
G = Government Expenditure
I = Investment, and
(X – M) = Net Exports
i.e., X = Total Exports and M = Total Imports

Aggregate supply, on the other hand, is the quantity of goods and services that the firms decide to produce and sell at various given price levels.

In the figure 2.14, we can see that the AS curve is upward sloping – higher the price, more will be quantity supplied and vice versa. The AD curve is downward sloping which means that as prices fall, more will be demanded and vice versa. Equilibrium price is determined when AS = AD at point E.

Micro and Macro Economics : Concepts | 47

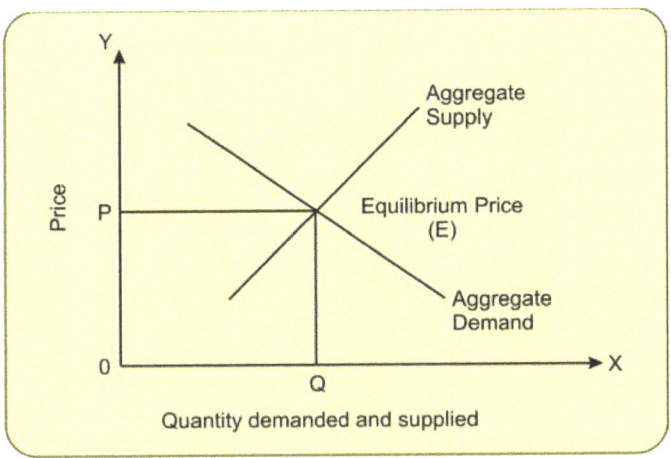

Fig. 2.14 : Determination of Equilibrium Price

AS and AD Compared	Aggregate Supply	Aggregate Demand	Movement of Prices
AS > AD	Over supply or glut	Implies lack of AD	Prices will fall
AS < AD	Under supply	Implies excess AD	Prices will rise
AS = AD	AS matches AD	AD matches AS	Prices will remain in equilibrium

Table 2.4 : Price Mechanism

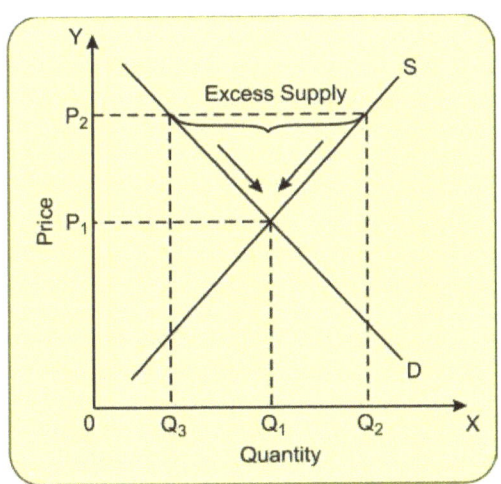

Fig. 2.15 : Excess Supply

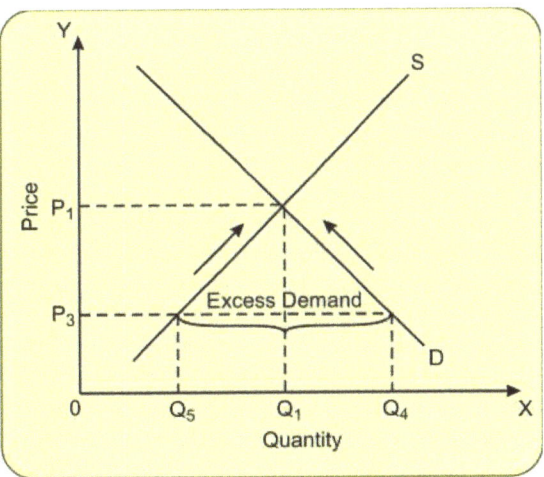

Fig. 2.16 : Excess Demand

2.21. Business Cycles or Trade Cycles

Business activities have a tendency to fluctuate and this gives rise to a regular cycle of booms and depressions. From the end of the 18th century till 1913, booms occurred at intervals of about 7 to 8 years on a global scale. Between each pair of booms, there was a slump or depression. Boom implies an upsurge in economic activity. Depression signifies a down surge in economic activity. After 1913, the regularity of the business cycle was disrupted mainly due to the world wars. In fact, the inter-war period experienced the great depression from 1929 to 1939. This was the longest and the deepest depression and even led to the creation of new economic theories based on the unsolvable nature of the depression. It was at this time that Keynes wrote his theory and emphasised the role of the government in economic activity. He postulated that deliberate efforts had to be taken by the government to avert the depression. (Fig 2.17)

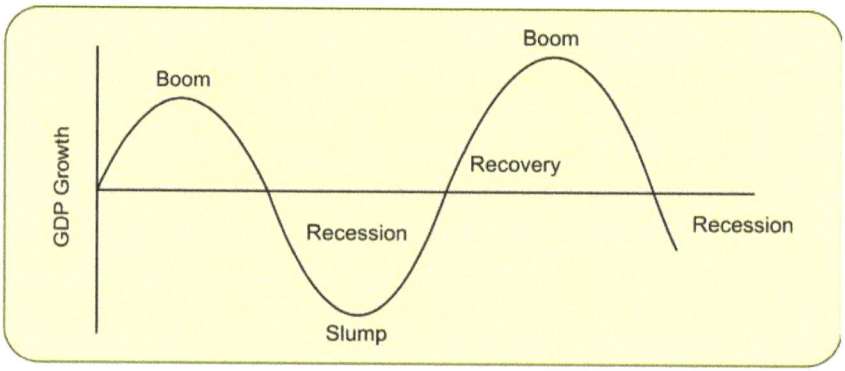

Fig. 2.17 : Business Cycle

2.21.1. Features of a Business Cycle

1. **Slump/Depression** : Depression or slump is marked by a fall in aggregate demand, glut or over supply, fall in prices and profits and hence unemployment, a fall in income and wages and general pessimism. Investments drop reducing production and employment as people do not buy produced goods.

2. **Recovery** : Depression in an economy does not last forever as the government intervenes. The persistent low prices reduce costs and entrepreneurs start to realize more profits. This gives way to business optimism and slowly the economy recovers. Business units start employing more labour and factors of production, this increases income and demand and the economy starts to surge upwards.

3. **Boom** : As the upsurge gathers momentum, profits increase with increasing prices and businesses prosper. More and more investments are undertaken and there is an increase in employment, income and wages. There is business optimism as profits hit a new high due to the soaring prices.

4. **End of the Boom** : Boom does not last forever. The rising prices and wages will push up the cost and slowly profits will start to dip. All idle factors have been employed and may be over employed and over exploited. This will reduce efficiency and hence raise the costs. Once costs increase, profits dip and this then leads to a recession that ends in a depression.

5. **Recession** : Recession is the period in the economy when profits start declining and business suffers. Business contracts are broken and pessimism sets in, leading to depression or slump. In fact, the recession is the progression towards depressed economy,

marked by falling income, falling aggregate demand, declining prices, falling profits, and declining employment.

Summary

1. Micro means a small part. Hence, in microeconomics, whole economy is not studied. What are examined are small components of the whole economy. For example, we study the consumer, the producer, an industry, or a firm. We do not look at the interaction of all these agents in the economy as a whole.

2. Macro means study of the whole. It is concerned with aggregates and depicts the entire picture of the economy. It deals with inflation, price levels, gross domestic product, aggregate income, consumption, investments, savings, aggregate demand, aggregate supply, unemployment and employment. It is that part of economics which concerns itself with large scale or general phenomena.

3. All the desires and aspirations and motives of humans are known as human wants in economics. Human wants can be satified with goods and services such as food, shelter, clothing etc. The human wants are of three types—(i) Necessaries, (ii) Comforts, (iii) Luxuries.

4. Resources are scarce and so their usage has its own costs and benefits attached. Net Benefit = Total Benefit – Total Cost.

5. Utility is the want satisfying quality of goods and services.

6. For the sake of convenience, economists often tend to subdivide utility into an imaginary unit called util.

7. Total utility is the total satisfaction obtained by consuming a given total amount of a good or a service.

8. Marginal utility is the additional satisfaction gained from the consumption or the use of an additional unit of a good.

9. The law of DMU is stated thus, "The additional benefit which a person derives from a given increase of his stock of a thing diminishes with every increase in the stock that he already has."

10. A market is a place where goods are exchanged between buyers and sellers.

11. Free market economy is an economy where all economic decisions are taken freely by individuals, households and firms and the government does not intervene.

12. The invisible hand is a term used by Adam Smith to explain the price mechanism, which is also known as the market mechanism.

13. Wealth is the stock of goods existing at a particular period of time. There are three kinds of wealth—*viz.*, Personal Wealth, Business Wealth and Social Wealth.

14. Welfare is well being of the people of a nation—it is a much deeper concept than wealth of a nation. A country may be wealthy but the welfare needs of its people may not be met. Welfare or well being of the citizens of a nation state will occur if the wealth is equally distributed and people have a decent standard of living.

15. A barter economy is the one where goods and services are exchanged for other goods and services. This system was cumbersome and has now been replaced by money economy.
16. In the money economy, money or a standard of measure is used for exchange of goods and services, for buying and selling and for all trade transactions. Money is, therefore, the legal tender of a country. It is a measure accepted legally as the medium of exchange. Such legal tender can be limited and unlimited.
17. Capital is a factor of production or an input in the production process. Capital, therefore, represents all inputs used in the production process that have themselves been produced. For example, machines, tools, implements, factories etc.
18. Investment is the production of items not for immediate consumption but for future use.
19. Income is what a person earns in a year while adding to the production process. Income of the nation is the earnings of the citizens of the country. National income represents the national output as this output has been created while the income is earned. Both represent the same value.
20. Production is the transformation of inputs into finished goods or outputs. This is done by firms and by doing so, they earn profits.
21. Consumption is the act of using goods and services.
22. Savings represent that part of the income that is not spent on consumption. These savings could be invested or deposited in the banks.
23. Aggregate Demand (AD) is the quantity of goods and services that households, firms, and customers abroad intend to buy at various prices.
24. Aggregate supply is the quantity of goods and services that the firms decide to produce and sell at various given price levels.
25. Glut is oversupply. This situation occurs when there is a lack of aggregate demand. Goods remain oversupplied in the market as demand on an aggregate has fallen.
26. Excess demand is a situation opposite to glut or excess supply. This happens when aggregate demand is more than aggregate supply. This leads to a rise in prices.
27. Prices are signals that help the consumer and the producer take decisions regarding consumption and production in the market.
28. A general rise in price levels is termed as inflation.
29. Demand pull inflation occurs when aggregate demand is so large that it cannot be met by the aggregate supply of output in that time period.
30. Cost push inflation occurs when the costs of inputs spiral up. When producers have to pay more in the form of rising costs, they will not allow the increase in cost to eat into their profits and hence, they will raise the prices causing inflation.
31. Real value is the value of goods and services minus the rate of inflation or price rise.
32. Nominal value includes the variation in price levels.
33. Business cycle refers to the alternative periods of boom and depression.

Micro and Macro Economics : Concepts | 51

◆ Short Answer Questions (2 marks)

1. Define microeconomics.
2. What is macroeconomics ?
3. Define human wants.
4. What are utils ?
5. Define marginal utility.
6. Explain the concept of utility.
7. What is total utility ?
8. What happens to MU when TU is maximum ?
9. Define the term diminishing rate.
10. Explain the law of DMU.
11. Define a market.
12. What is a goods market ?
13. Define the factor market.
14. Explain the doctrine of laissez faire.
15. Define government intervention. Give two examples.
16. Define wealth.
17. What are the types of wealth ?
18. Define welfare.
19. Mention four welfare measures initiated by the Government of India.
20. What is a barter economy ?
21. Define the term legal tender.
22. Explain the meaning of unlimited legal tender.
23. What is limited legal tender ?
24. Define money.
25. What is a money economy ?
26. Mention two problems of the barter economy.
27. Discuss the meaning of the term capital.
28. How many kinds of capital are there ? Name them.
29. What is physical capital ?
30. You as a person form which part of capital ?
31. What is consumption ?
32. Define the term income.
33. What is disposable income ?
34. Define savings.
35. What is real income ?
36. Explain the term investment.
37. What is production ?
38. What are factors of production ?
39. What is personal income and factor income ?

40. What is human capital ?
41. What is the nominal value ?
42. Why is the real value called so ?
43. What is excess demand ?
44. How can you explain the phrase 'too many goods chasing too less cash' ?
45. What pulls prices up ?
46. What pushes prices down ?
47. Explain the terms value in use and value in exchange.

◆ **Long Answer Questions (3-6 marks)**

1. Differentiate between microeconomics and macroeconomics.
2. What do you understand by the term human wants? How human wants can be classified ?
3. Define the concept of net benefit.
4. Delineate the relationship between TU and MU.
5. Elucidate the law of DMU.
6. Write a brief note on the concept of margin.
7. Give a table and diagram to show the behaviour of MU.
8. How are the goods and factor markets inter-related ?
9. Explain the working of the invisible hand.
10. What is government intervention ?
11. Differentiate between real and nominal values.
12. Explain how equilibrium prices are obtained.
13. Explain demand pull inflation.
14. What is cost push inflation.
15. Describe the two concepts of AD and AS. How does these two factors determine price in the market ?
16. Discuss how wealth and welfare are different.
17. What is wealth ? Explain the features of wealth.
18. Write a note on the welfare schemes of the Government of India.
19. What is a barter economy ? Discuss the problems of such an exchange system.
20. What is the money economy ? What role does money play in such a system?
21. Define the term legal tender and explain the difference between limited and unlimited legal tender.
22. Explain all aspects of factor income.
23. What role does savings play in the growth of a country ?
24. "Without investments the country will deteriorate economically"—discuss this statement.
25. Explain the concept of consumption.
26. What is capital ? Explain how human capital is crucial for the development of a country.

3 Basic Problems of an Economy

3.1. Introduction

Human wants are unlimited but the resources available to satisfy those wants are limited. An economy cannot produce goods in an unlimited quantity to satisfy all human wants because no economy has infinite productive resources. This is the problem of scarcity. Scarcity means that people want to consume more than an economy can produce. Why we, as individuals and as a nation, face economic problem is because we cannot have all that we want. And the fact that the resources are scarce relative to the infinite wants of an economy implies that we have to make a choice in the allocation of these scarce resources. This is the problem of choice which means that the choice has to be made in terms of what goods to produce and how much to produce, how to produce and for whom to produce. Thus, economic problem is the problem of scarcity and the problem of choice.

> In short, an economic problem arises because :
> - Human wants are unlimited but the resources available to fulfil these wants are limited.
> - Hence, a rational choice has to be made in order to ensure that these scarce resources are allocated in an optimal manner.
> - For this reason, economic theory assumes that a decision maker is a rational human being who makes optimal choices which results in maximum satisfaction to the consumer and maximum profit to the producer.

3.2. Basic Problems of an Economy

Basic problems of an economy means the problems that are faced by all economies, be it a capitalist economy or a socialist economy or a mixed economy. These problems are discussed below :

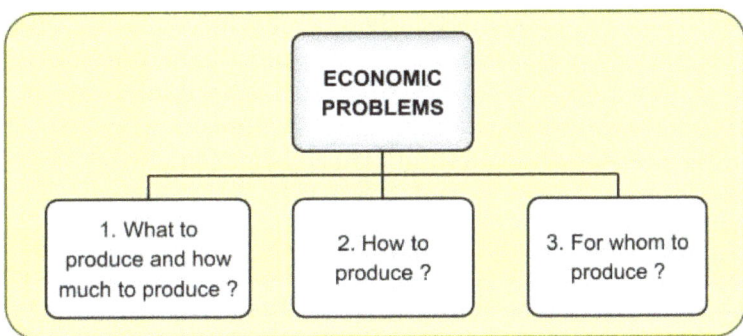

Fig. 3.1 : Basic Problems of an Economy

1. **What to Produce and How Much to Produce** : The problem of 'what to produce and how much to produce' is the problem of determining what goods and services are to be produced and in what quantities. Every economy face the constraint of limited resources. This constraint makes it essential for an economy to choose whether it wants to produce more of consumer goods like butter, clothes, cars, machinery or more of military goods like guns and artilleries, missiles etc.

What goods and services an economy ultimately produces depends on the kind of resources available in that economy and the types of goods demanded by the consumers in that economy. For example, coastal countries will produce and demand more of sea food like salmon, shrimp, crab but the landlocked countries will produce and demand more of food grains like wheat, rice etc.

2. **How to Produce** : The problem of 'how to produce' relates to the choice of technique of production. This choice has to be made because there are alternative methods to produce any kind of good and because the resources to be used in the production process are scarce. Generally, there are two types of techniques of production—labour intensive and capital intensive. Labour intensive technique is the one which employs more of labour and less of capital to produce a given quantity of a good, that is, the ratio of labour to capital is high. Capital intensive technique is the one which employs more of capital and less of labour to produce the same good, that is, the ratio of capital to labour is high.

Whether an economy makes use of labour intensive technique or capital intensive technique depends on two factors :

(i) The kind of resources available in that economy. If an economy has surplus labour, then it would employ labour intensive technique but if an economy lacks human resources then it would make use of capital intensive techniques such as machinery, automated plants etc.

(ii) The level of technical knowledge and skills available in that economy. For example, an economy with skilled labour force will be able to produce goods at a lower cost in comparison to an economy with unskilled labour force.

The primary idea underpinning the choice of techniques of production is that the resources are scarce and should be used in the most economical manner possible.

3. **For Whom to Produce** : The problem of 'for whom to produce' relates to the problem of deciding how goods and services produced in an economy be distributed among its members. Goods are produced for those who have the paying capacity. The capacity of people to pay for goods depends upon their level of income. This problem, in essence, is therefore the problem of distribution of income among the factors of production (land, labour, capital and enterprise), who contribute in the production process. The sum total of the income (rent, wages, interest and profit) of these factors of production is called the national income. Therefore, distribution of national income determines the distribution of goods and services in an economy.

3.3. Opportunity Cost

Scarcity leads to the problem of choice and choice implies making sacrifices. If an economy produces more of consumer goods, it will have to be satisfied with less of military goods. Because the resources available are limited, an economy cannot have more of both consumer goods and military goods. The sacrifice involved in making such choices has been termed as opportunity cost by the economists. The opportunity cost of an action is what you must give up when you make a certain choice. That is, opportunity cost is the value of the next best alternative that is forgone when another alternative is chosen. For example, if a farmland can be used to produce 1 ton of wheat or 4 tons of rice, then we can say that the opportunity cost of producing 1 ton of wheat is 4 tons of rice that are forgone or sacrificed.

3.4. Rational Choice

Choices in economics are made by economic agents who are assumed to be rational. This means that it is assumed that an economic agent weighs the costs and benefits of the alternatives before making a choice and chooses that alternative that gives him the best value for money. In other words, the rational choice is the choice that gives maximum profits to the producers and maximum satisfaction to the consumers. It is held that an economic agent will make a choice that gives him the greatest benefit or satisfaction—given the choices available—and is also in his highest self-interest. There is absolutely no room for social service or altruism in the choice that he makes. It is all based on solipsism or selfish behaviour.

However, it has been argued that economic agents do not always make prudent and logical choices because they are not always able to obtain all the information they would need to make the best possible decision.

3.5. The Production Possibility Curve or the Product Transformation Curve

Since human wants are infinite, an economy, even with its total productive human and non human resources, cannot produce enough goods to satisfy all those wants. The available resources and level of technology always has a limitation on the production of goods in an economy. This implies that increase in the production of one commodity will leave lesser resources for the production of other commodity. When we choose the best combination of two goods that an economy can produce with available resources and level of technology, it is called production possibility. When various combinations of two goods that can be produced with the given amount of resources and level of technology are represented graphically, we obtain a downward sloping curve known as the production possibility curve (PPC). Hence, a production possibility curve is defined as "a curve which depicts all possible combinations of two goods that an economy can produce utilizing available resources and technology".

3.5.1. Assumptions of Production Possibility Curve

Production possibility curve is based on the following five assumptions :

1. An economy produces only two goods and all the resources that an economy has, are exhausted in the production of these two goods.

2. The amount of resources that an economy has, is fixed.

3. The techniques of production and technology do not change.

4. All the resources are fully employed.

5. Resources are not equally efficient in the production of all goods. This means that when a resource is transferred from the production of one good to the production of another good, its efficiency decreases leading to an increase in the cost of production.

Hence, the production possibility curve is a curve that shows the combinations of two goods that can be produced using all the available resources and technology in a specified period of time. A combination on the curve implies that all the resources in an economy are fully employed and there is no unemployment. Any point beyond the curve is unattainable because an economy lacks both resources and technology to achieve that level of production and any point beneath the curve implies unemployment or underutilization of some of the available resources.

3.5.2. Features of Production Possibility Curve

Features of the production possibility curve are as follows :

1. The curve is concave to the origin. Concavity of the production possibility curve implies increasing opportunity cost. Opportunity cost increases because resources are not equally efficient in the production of both the goods. This means that when we produce more of one good, we have to use those resources which were more suitable for the production of the second good. This leads to a decrease in the efficiency of the resources and increase in the cost.

2. The curve starts from a point on the Y-axis and ends at a point on the X-axis.

3. At point A, all the resources are used to produce only sugar and no wheat.

4. At point F, all the resources are used to produce only wheat and no sugar.

5. Any point on the curve indicates a combination of sugar and wheat that is produced.

6. Movement from A to F shows how one good is transformed into the other. Hence, the curve is also called the product transformation curve.

7. The curve also shows the opportunity cost of producing a good. For *e.g.*, at point D, the opportunity cost of producing wheat is the amount of sugar not produced.

8. A point on the curve means that all the resources of an economy are fully employed.

9. A point beneath the curve shows unemployment or less than full capacity utilization of plants, machinery and resources.

10. A point beyond the curve is unattainable in the present time frame. If one must reach for the points beyond the curve, there has to be improvement in technology and labour productivity.

11. An outward shift of the curve indicates economic growth as can be seen in Figure 3.3.

12. The curve can move outwards asymmetrically if better technology is used in the production of any one of the commodities (sugar or wheat) as can be seen in Fig. 3.4 and 3.5.

13. The PPC also shows input-output relationship. It indicates the inputs of factors of production and output as the commodities are produced.

3.5.3. Explanation of Production Possibility Curve

The production possibility curve (PPC) can be explained with the help of the following production possibility schedule and diagram :

Table 3.1 : Production Possibility Schedule

Possible Combinations	Wheat (in Million Tons)	Sugar (in Million Tons)
A	0	15
B	1	14
C	2	12
D	3	9
E	4	5
F	5	0

Assuming that an economy produces only two goods : wheat and sugar. Then, with available resources and technology, it can produce various combinations of the two goods as shown in the table given above. The table shows that if an economy utilizes all its resources to produce only sugar, it can produce 15 million tons of sugar but no amount of wheat. But when it produces 14 million tons of sugar, it also can produce 1 million ton of wheat. As the economy increases the production of wheat, the quantity of sugar that can be produced goes on decreasing. Combination F shows that the economy has

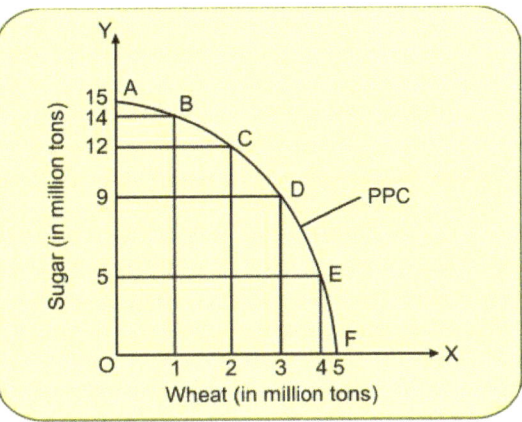

Fig. 3.2

diverted all its resources towards the production of wheat and it produces absolutely no amount of sugar. Therefore, the table shows a total of six possibilities (A, B, C, D, E, and F) of the combinations of two goods. When all these production combinations (A to F) are joined, we get a curve (AF) sloping downwards, known as the production possibility curve. It shows the various possible combinations that an economy can produce using the available technology and given resources, when all the resources are fully and efficiently employed. Hence, a production possibility curve shows that more of one commodity can only be produced by reducing the production of other commodity. An economy decides to produce any such possible combination as is demanded by its people. The production possibility curve functions under the assumption that innovation or technological change remains constant.

3.5.4. The Role of Technology and Shift in the Production Possibility Curve

When innovation or technological changes take place in an economy, they may have their impact on the growth of the economy. If better and improved technology is used to produce both sugar and wheat, it may lead to an increase in their production level. In such a situation, production possibility curve (PPC) shifts outwards from QP to Q_1P_1 (that is, away from the origin) as shown in the following diagram :

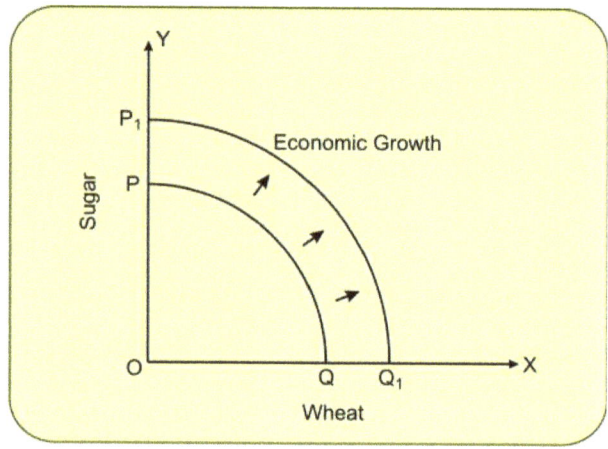

Fig. 3.3 : Diagram showing use of Technology in the Production of both goods-Sugar and Wheat

Use of Improved Technology to Produce Sugar

When better and improved technology is used to produce sugar but not wheat, its production will increase without any change in the production of wheat. In such a situation, production possibility curve (PPC) will move upwards from QP to QP_1 on Y-axis, as shown in the following diagram :

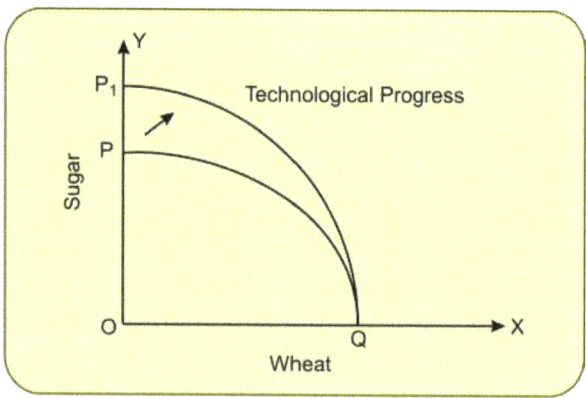

Fig. 3.4 : Diagram showing use of Technology in the Production of Sugar only

Use of Improved Technology to Produce Wheat

When better and improved technology is used to produce wheat but not sugar, its production will increase without any change in the production of sugar. In such a situation, production possibility curve (PPC) will move rightwards from PQ to PQ_1 on X-axis, as shown in the following diagram :

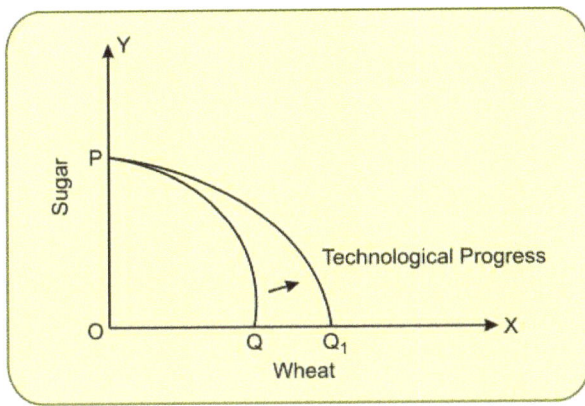

Fig. 3.5 : Diagram showing use of Technology in the Production of Wheat

Hence, over a period of time, with increased investments in machineries and plants, use of new raw materials, innovation in the method of production, the production possibility curve of an economy can shift outwards. Use of technology, thus, makes it possible for an economy to reach to the point beyond the curve by accelerating its rate of economic growth. Advancements in technology enables an economy to produce more goods with the same stock of natural resources, thereby, reducing the rate of depletion of resources. Thus, it is rightly said that the economic growth is a race between depletion and invention.

3.5.5. Absence of Innovation or Technology

When an economy produces different combinations of two goods in the absence of innovation or technological advancement, its natural resources gets depleted. Consequently, an economy can now only produce less of both goods. Under such a situation, production level absolutely depends on the supply of labour force. Absence of technology may, thus, retard the economic growth as production level decreases. It leads the production possibility curve (PPC) to shift inwards from QP to Q_1P_1 (that is, towards the origin), as shown in the following diagram :

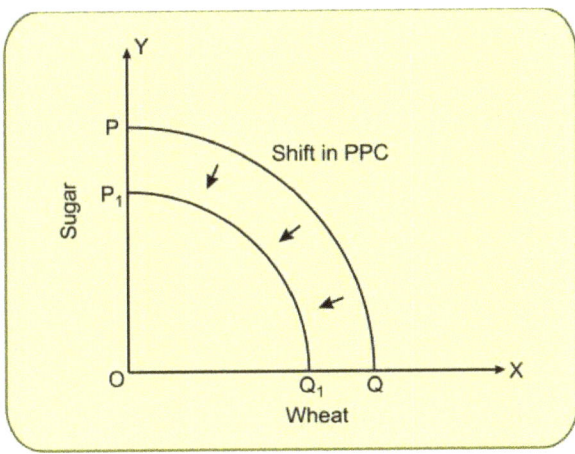

Fig. 3.6

3.5.6. Criticism of the Production Possibility Curve

Though the production possibility curve has provided us a very sound analytical tool to understand the basic problems of what to produce, how much to produce and how to produce in an economy, some economists have criticized it on the following grounds :

1. A country produces a number of goods and not just two goods, hence, the curve is an oversimplification.

2. It is assumed that the amount of resources is fixed. This is not the real picture though. It is not a static world and resources are definitely not fixed.

3. It is assumed that there is no improvement in technology. This is not what we see. There has been tremendous improvement in technology over the years. In this respect, the curve represents a picture far from reality.

4. The production possibility curve assumes efficient production. This means that there is zero wastage in the production process. This also is an incorrect assumption for every production process has some wastage included.

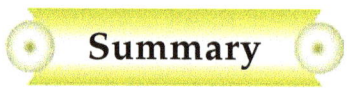

Summary

1. Since resources are limited and wants are unlimited, choice becomes crucial.
2. Economic agents are assumed to be rational, that is, it is assumed that they will make optimum choices. An optimum choice will maximize profit for the producers and utility for the consumers.
3. Basic problems of an economy are :
    (i) What to produce and how much to produce ?
    (ii) How to produce ?
    (iii) For whom to produce ?
4. The problem of 'what to produce and how much to produce' is the problem of determining what goods and services are to be produced and in what quantities.
5. The problem of 'how to produce' is related to the techniques of production, *e.g.*, should sugar be produced with more capital or more labour ?
6. The problem of 'for whom to produce' relates to the problem of deciding how goods and services produced in an economy be distributed among its members. It is related to making choices as to how the national product should be distributed among all the stakeholders of production.
7. The opportunity cost of an action is what you must give up when you make a certain choice. That is, opportunity cost is the value of the next best alternative that is forgone when another alternative is chosen.
8. Rational choice is when any decision is made keeping in mind the benefits of the activity against the opportunity cost.
9. The PPC is a curve depicting all possible combinations of two goods that a country can produce within a given time period, with full employment of the available resources and given technology.

◆ Short Answer Questions (2 marks)

1. Mention three basic problems of an economy.
2. What is meant by 'For whom to produce'?
3. When does the PPC move outwards?
4. What is meant by producing beneath the PPC?
5. What is a rational choice?
6. Define opportunity cost.
7. What is the next best alternative? Give an example to elucidate the concept.
8. What does movement on the PPC imply?
9. What is meant by choice?
10. Why is the production possibility curve also called product transformation curve?
11. Why do economic problems arise?
12. What happens to the production possibility curve when the technological progress is absent?

◆ Long Answer Questions (3-6 marks)

1. Explain in detail the three basic problems of an economy.
2. Explain the concept of the opportunity cost.
3. Define the PPC and list its various assumptions.
4. Define the PPC and enumerate its features.
5. How and why does the PPC move outwards over a period of time?

4. Types of Economies

4.1. Economy : Introduction and Meaning

Human wants are unlimited and no economy can produce every type of good in an unlimited quantity to satisfy all those wants because of the constraints imposed by limited resources. Further, economic resources are not equally distributed. The types of goods produced by an economy depend on the kind of resources it has been endowed with. People are engaged in various types of economic activities to fulfil their needs. The production of goods, distribution and consumption are some of the major economic activities which depend on efficient utilization of the available resources. Therefore, a systematic arrangement has been made in every country to redress the central problems faced by an economy in order to provide livelihood to the people. Hence, an economy is defined as a system in which people earn a living to satisfy their wants through the process of production, consumption and distribution of goods and services. Economic system, on the other hand, refers to how countries control and use inputs in the production process to create the output. The manner in which a country harnesses factors of production such as land, labour, capital, entrepreneurship and knowledge to bring about production is defined by the economic system that is prevalent in that country.

4.2. Types of Economies

Economies have been classified on the following basis –
1. On the basis of nature
2. On the basis of economic development
3. On the basis of ownership of resources

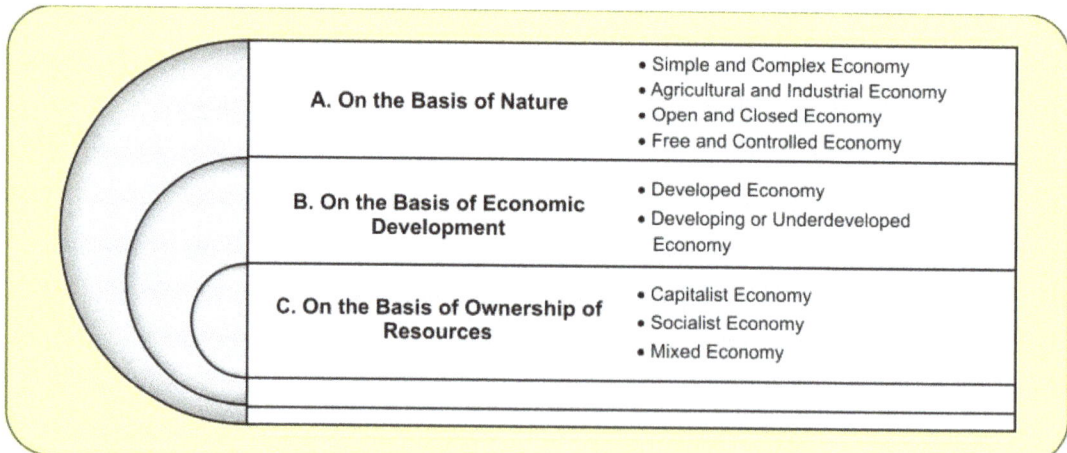

Fig. 4.1 : Types of Economies

4.2.1. Types of Economies : On the Basis of Nature

1. **Simple Economy** : An economic system where production, consumption and exchange of goods is carried out on a limited scale is referred to as simple economy. This economic system operates with limited population which has limited needs. However, in the contemporary world, such an economy does not exist.

2. **Complex Economy** : An economic system where production, consumption and exchange of goods is carried out on a larger scale is referred to as complex economy. In this economic system, production of goods is carried out with the help of modern technology and by taking the help of auxiliary services like transport, banking, warehousing etc. Such an economy produces surplus goods which promote domestic and foreign trade.

3. **Agricultural Economy** : Agricultural economy refers to an economy where a large proportion of the population depends on agriculture for their livelihood. The production, distribution and consumption largely revolve around the agriculture and its allied activities. Some small scale and cottage industries are also found but they are also dependent on agriculture for the supply of raw material.

4. **Industrial Economy** : Industrial economy refers to an economy where a large proportion of the population depends on trade, industry and commerce for their livelihood. The production of goods is carried out on a larger scale using advanced level of technology. In such an economy, gross domestic product (GDP) of the country is largely determined by trade, industry and commerce.

5. **Open Economy** : Open economy is the one that allows exchange of goods and services between countries without any restrictions. Such an economy promotes international trade by permitting export of surplus goods and import of deficit and better quality goods from abroad. Today, open economies all across the world have intertwined into a 'Global economy'. This implies that any positive or negative event in one economy has spillover effects on all the economies with which it has trade relations.

6. **Closed Economy** : Closed economy is just the opposite of an open economy. It is defined as an economy having no trade relations with the rest of the world. Such an economy produces goods for its own domestic needs and believes in self reliance. Therefore, international trade is completely absent in such an economic system.

7. **Free Economy** : It refers to an economic system where production, consumption, distribution and price determination of goods and services and other economic activities are carried out without state intervention. Usually, prices are not regulated by the state and are determined with the help of the market forces of demand and supply.

8. **Controlled Economy** : It refers to an economic system where production, consumption, distribution and price determination of goods and services and other economic activities are controlled by the State or Central Government. Usually, prices are regulated by the state and are not determined with the help of the market forces of demand and supply. In such an economic system, the government plays a role of regulatory authority and decides on all matters pertaining to an economy.

4.2.2. Types of Economies : On the Basis of Economic Development

Economies all over the world are in different stages of the developmental trajectory. Some are developed and some are still considered as underdeveloped economies. A country that has a low Human Development Index (HDI) and a smaller industrial base as compared to other countries is termed as a less developed or an underdeveloped or a developing economy.

Developed Economy

Industrialized economies, also called More Economically Developed Countries (MEDC) are those economies that have advanced technologies and higher standards of living. Their HDI indices are also much higher. Such countries are also called the First World Countries. The erstwhile Communist countries including Soviet Union are termed as the Second World Countries. The common measures used to judge the developmental stages of an economy are per capita income, gross domestic product, amount of infrastructure, general standards of living, and the Human Development Index which includes per capita income, literacy rate and life expectancy.

HDIs of some of the countries as per the UNDP's Human Development Report, 2016, are given below :

Table 4.1 : Human Development Index Values

RANK	COUNTRY	HDI VALUE
VERY HIGH HUMAN DEVELOPMENT		
1	Norway	0.949
2	Australia	0.939
3	Switzerland	0.939
4	Germany	0.926
5	Denmark	0.925
6	Singapore	0.925
7	Netherlands	0.924
8	Ireland	0.923
9	Iceland	0.921
10	Canada	0.920
11	United States	0.920
12	Hong Kong	0.917
13	New Zealand	0.915
14	Sweden	0.913
15	Liechtenstein	0.912

16	United Kingdom	0.909
17	Japan	0.903
18	Korea (Republic of)	0.901
19	Israel	0.899
20	Luxembourg	0.898
MEDIUM HUMAN DEVELOPMENT		
121	Iraq	0.649
124	Nicaragua	0.645
125	Guatemala	0.640
131	India	0.624
132	Bhutan	0.607
144	Nepal	0.558
147	Pakistan	0.550

As is evident from the table given above, India, with the HDI value of 0.624, does not fall into the category of developed nations. India is still a developing economy and has a long way to go to achieve the status of a developed economy.

Main Features of Developed Economies

1. **High GDP :** Developed economies register a very high rate of economic growth due to the use of modern technology and efficient use of factors of production and other resources. Service sector and industrial sector are well developed and contributes the most to the GDP in such economies.

2. **High Per Capita Income :** These economies experience high per capita income due to high growth rate and high national income. High per capita income increases the purchasing power of the people which accelerates the productive capacity within the economy. This promotes the standard of living of the people.

3. **High Rate of Literacy :** Developed economies allocate huge amount of resources on education and promotion of skills and knowledge. Consequently, literacy rate is very high in these economies.

4. **Developed Infrastructural Base :** High rate of economic growth in these economies also promote the development of physical infrastructure. The communication system, transportation system, power generation etc., are well developed in these economies.

5. **Use of Modern Technology :** Developed economies allocate a substantial amount of resources on research and development. Consequently, they use modern technology in the production process. Use of modern technology enhances productivity and provides the benefits of economies of large scale production.

6. **High Rate of Life Expectancy :** Developed economies allocate huge amounts of funds on the development of health care services. This, in turn, brings down the mortality rate, resulting in increase in life expectancy in these economies.

7. **High Standard of Living :** Well developed health care system, comprehensive learning opportunities and strong infrastructural base in developed economies promote high standard of living.

Underdeveloped or Developing Economy

According to the United Nations *"an underdeveloped country is one in which per capita real income is low when compared to the per capita real income of the United States of America, Canada, Australia and Western Europe. In this sense, an adequate synonym would be poor country"*. Hence, the characteristic feature of an underdeveloped economy is poverty. It must be noted, however, that such countries do have a potential to develop. As Jacob Viner has described: An underdeveloped country is one *"which has good potential for using more capital or labour or more available natural resources, or all of these to support its present population on a higher level of living or if its per capita income level is already fairly high to support a larger population on a not lower level of living"*. Hence, there is a potential to develop. It is for this reason that such underdeveloped countries are now referred to as developing countries. The developing countries are also called Third World Countries.

Main Features of Underdeveloped Economy

1. **Low Per Capita Income :** Such countries have low per capita income indicating poverty. However, this is not the only indicator of poverty. Unequal distribution of the national income also intensifies poverty levels in the country. Poverty also persists due to stagnation in growth and low capital formation. Technology used is generally obsolete and natural resources are not tapped properly. All these factors lead to mass poverty in underdeveloped countries, where a substantial proportion of the population is deprived of the basic necessities of life.

2. **Low Capital Formation :** Third world countries are capital poor. In other words, there is a deficiency of capital. The capital stock is low and capital formation is extremely slow. This happens because the saving rate in such countries is low due to low per capita income. Because of low per capita income, demand for goods is also low and hence, the size of the market is small.

Small market size acts as a deterrent to the producers who are reluctant to expand production and undertake more investments. The methods of production, therefore, remain inefficient and obsolete, resulting in low productivity and slow economic growth.

3. **Agrarian Economy :** In underdeveloped countries, a majority of the population is dependent on agriculture for income and sustenance. This is because the non agricultural sectors such as the industrial sector and the service sector are not developed enough to provide employment opportunities to the ever growing population. The pressure of population thus, falls on agriculture. The agricultural farms become fragmented and the ratio of labour to land rises, resulting in low agricultural productivity and low income to the workers. Thus, the contribution of agriculture to the national income remains low.

4. **Unequal Distribution of Income and Wealth :** Another feature of an underdeveloped economy is that there is a vast difference in the income and wealth of the rich and the poor. Such income inequalities are widespread in the urban as well as the rural areas of an economy. Such inequalities manifest themselves in the form of

unequal access to the means of production and concentration of economic power in the hands of a few individuals. This is the major cause of poverty and underdevelopment in these economies.

5. **Large Population and Disguised Unemployment :** Such countries have a high growth rate of population and the density of population is also extremely high. Such teeming millions of people naturally exert tremendous pressure on land. There are too many people to too few plots of land. This leads to falling farm sizes. Further, since there are too many people to land, this leads to disguised unemployment. In other words, even though it seems that the labour is employed on the farm, it actually is unemployed. The evidence of this is the marginal output of labour which is either very low or equal to zero. In other words, more people are employed in agriculture than what is actually required. A reduction in the number of workers will lead to an increase in the total output of the farm. This happens when the labour to land ratio is very high and when the capital to labour ratio is very low.

6. **Economic Backwardness :** In underdeveloped countries, people are economically backward. In general, there is a shortage of clean water, minerals, forest cover, power, skilled labour force, capital etc. This shortage results in the underutilization of resources, inaccessibility of people to the factors of production, primitive methods and techniques being adopted and a small market size. All this shows that there is a potential for growth if the resources are efficiently utilized.

7. **Backwardness in General :** In underdeveloped economies, people are less literate and generally believe in superstitions and fate. This attitude impacts growth and development adversely. Sidelining of women from the development process is rampant in such economies. There are huge gender inequalities and gender empowerment is not taken seriously. Women in general are denied freedom and lack the access to resources, space, time and mobility. There is a lack of drive and entrepreneurship. General lethargy slows the economy down. Hygienic conditions are poor. People live in filth and squalor and this leads to spread of infectious and contagious diseases.

8. **Dualistic Economies :** In underdeveloped economies, there is a huge divide in terms of development. Some areas are highly developed while other areas do not experience much development. A typical example of dualism is the Audi car and a bullock-cart moving on the same road together in an underdeveloped country.

Table 4.2 : Differences between Developed Economies and Developing Economies

S. No.	Basis of difference	Developed Economies	Developing Economies
1.	National Income	Such economies have high national income.	Such economies have low national income.
2.	Standard of Living	People maintain high standard of living in such economies.	Low standard of living is the main feature of such economies.
3.	Literacy Rate	Literacy rate is very high.	Such economies experience lower literacy rate.
4.	Life Expectancy	Life expectancy is high.	Life expectancy is low in such economies.

5.	Sectorial development	Service sectors and industrial sectors contribute the most to the GDP.	Agriculture sector contributes the most to the GDP.
6.	Infrastructure	Strong infrastructural base.	Poor infrastructural base.
7.	Use of Technology	Use of modern technology for the production.	Use of outdated technology for the production.

4.2.3. Types of Economies : On the Basis of Ownership of Resources

Scarcity is a fundamental problem of all economies. However, each economy deals with it differently. Economies are different from each other based on the extent of government control. Based on the extent of ownership of resources, there are three main kinds of economies. These are capitalist economy, socialist economy and mixed economy.

At one end of the spectrum lies a fully planned economy, where the government takes all the decisions pertaining to an economy. On the other end lies a free market economy, where the market decides what to produce, how much to produce, how to produce and for whom to produce.

Capitalist Economy

It represents a free market economy. Under capitalism, all individuals and firms have the right to own private property. They are free to use it and earn profits. The central problems of what to produce, how much to produce and for whom to produce are all resolved by the market forces of demand and supply. This means that the price mechanism or what Adam Smith called as the invisible hand operates freely and is the main deciding force in such economies.

However, no country in the world today is fully free with respect to economic decision making—not even countries like the US, UK or Germany.

Table 4.3 : Features of a Capitalist Economy

S. No.	FEATURE	EXPLANATION
1.	Right to Private Property	People and organizations can own private property and there is little or no restriction on the amount of wealth they can amass. They have the right to use their private property to trade and earn profits. The aim of the individuals and institutions in such an economy is not social welfare but to maximize their private profits.
2.	Freedom of Enterprise	An individual is free to take up any occupation. He can enter into trade and production contracts or he can use his property to harness more profit or he can set up firms and plants for production. There is little or no restriction. But, it must be stated that total or

		absolute freedom is not possible in any economy and some controls do exist even in the most capitalistic economies of the world.
3.	Consumer is the King	What the consumer demands is produced through the signals of the price mechanism. If demand of a commodity is greater than its supply, its production is increased. Hence, consumers freely express their desire for goods and services. Their likes and dislikes go a long way in deciding what is produced, and for whom and in what quantities.
4.	Profit and Satisfaction Driven	The main aim of individuals in the economy is to derive satisfaction and to maximize profits. People are driven by selfish motives and not by altruism. It is always the 'I' that matters when economic decisions are taken. What the other has or does not have is not the concern of the individual rational agents in such an economy.
5.	Risk Takers must Control	This is the golden rule of capitalism. The ones who own the capital and the ones who risk their money in business must alone control its operations. If not, it will lead to irresponsible choices and chaos.
6.	Competition	A capitalist economy is characterized by free competition because producers compete for getting the highest profit. Producers compete with one another to attract the consumers and they use methods such as a price cut or advertisement or different kinds of rebate and sale offers to achieve this objective.
7.	Inequalities	Due to the fact that there is stiff competition, there is also the rule of the jungle that prevails *viz.* survival of the fittest. The logic is that the best alone can survive and this leads to a widening gap between the haves and the have nots. Those who have wealth can obtain resources and start big enterprises. The propertyless classes have only their labour to offer. Profits and rents are high but wages are much lower. Thus, the property holders obtain a major share of national income.

8.	Role of Price Mechanism or the Philosophy of Laissez Faire	In capitalism, price mechanism plays a major role. Price mechanism means the free working of the forces of supply and demand, without any intervention of the state. Producers are helped by the price mechanism in deciding what to produce, how much to produce, when to produce and where to produce.

Merits of Capitalist Economy

1. The entire economy works automatically as minimum government control is required. Any kind of control brings in imperfection and slows the system; hence automaticity is good for the economy. As explained earlier, the system works automatically through the working of the invisible hand or the price mechanism.
2. It is a just and rewarding system for hard working individuals, prudent investors and risk takers who are enterprising. Laid back workers, however, are not rewarded. Hence, the system is considered just and fair.
3. Since the consumers are the kings of the market and they are the ones making the major decisions, there is a democratic flavour that creeps into this system.
4. Another important merit is that it encourages the risk taker, the innovator and the creative producer to step out and produce. It gives room for creativity and enterprise and hence, is good for the economy. Due to this, the economy grows and develops, accompanied by technological growth.
5. The capitalistic system adapts well to calamities. Economic history of the capitalist countries of the world can easily bear witness to the fact that this system, though has been buffeted by all kinds of pressures, has always come out victorious. It is hence, extremely acclimatized to the forces of the market.
6. The capitalistic system is efficient in all ways. The system guarantees efficiency as only the best survives. There is no room for mediocrity in this kind of a system.

Demerits of Capitalist Economy

1. Competition is wasteful and leads to a lot of environmental damage along with a wastage of resources and time. Due to cut throat competition, firms and industries waste a lot of money on advertisements, selling, packaging and marketing. All this does not really benefit a society, especially if the country is not a very rich economy. Also, since there is rampant competition, there will be a variety of products created and this will impact the resource base of an economy. Tremendous environmental damage results from such production. The problems of global warming and ozone hole, all emanate from such unprecedented levels of competition.
2. With stiff competition and a mad race to be at the top, the concept of human welfare is completely ignored. In fact, in the face of such competition, economic decisions are based on selfish profit seeking motive and not on human welfare. There is also a minimum role of the government and no one really exists to support the poor and the ones who do not own capital. This leads to widespread income inequality and class conflicts.

3. Such economies are susceptible to economic trade cycles. The great depression of 1929 to 1933 is an example of how unstable capitalistic economies are and how depression can lead to unemployment and pessimism. The recent economic crisis of 2008 also underlined the fact that due to the nature of such an economic system, any kind of disturbance in one sector of the economy has spillover effects on the other sectors, leading to loss of jobs and a drop in income levels. Only the government can rescue the economy from such a situation.
4. In a capitalistic system, political instability can emerge based on class conflict. With some individuals being super rich and others being poor, this kind of conflict can emerge and disturb the political fabric of the nation state. The widening gap between the haves and the have nots can lead to lockouts and strikes and this impact the output levels of the country.
5. This system also brings along social injustice and economic inequities. It leads to the emergence of monopolies, especially when some individuals who own capital gets richer and richer. Sometimes, these monopolies buy or eliminate the smaller firms to establish their supremacy in particular lines of production. They charge high prices and do not have any compulsion to improve efficiency of the production processes.
6. Another bane of this system is the emergence of corruption and immense malpractices. There is nepotism and red tapism which increases levels of bribery in the country.
7. Resources are misallocated in such a system. Since individuals work with the profit motive in mind, they seldom produce items of mass consumption. They indulge in the production of those goods which yield them highest profits. For example, they will not be interested in the distribution of polio vaccine at a discounted price as it will not be lucrative. The poor, however, may not be able to afford such vaccines.

Socialist Economy

In this kind of economy, the resources are largely owned and controlled by the government. In short, private property is restricted. In this sense, socialist economy is just the opposite of capitalist economy. Karl Marx is known as the 'Father of Socialism'. He was absolutely against the ownership of private property and considered capitalism as the cause of class conflicts.

Table 4.4 : Features of a Socialist Economy

S. No.	FEATURE	EXPLANATION
1.	Ownership	Ownership of the means of production is not in the private hands. Land, factories, railways, mines etc., are all owned and operated by the government.
2.	No Private Enterprise	Only the government initiates and controls production. No private individual or institution is involved in this process. There are no land lords and co-operative farming in such a system.

3.	Economic Equality	Economic equality is not guaranteed but there are no glaring disparities in the distribution of income and wealth under this system. In fact, no system can vouch for full equality. It has been proved that inequality in the distribution of income raises the saving and investment rates and this allows the economy to grow. If there is absolute equality in the distribution of wealth and income, the national output will drop.
4.	Equal Opportunity	Under this system, individuals do get equal opportunity to training, obtaining education and skills, employability etc. This is definitely guaranteed to the poor unlike in the capitalistic system. The poor are supported by various social security measures and are, in fact, looked after by the state. Hence, the poor and underprivileged too have a chance to try and move upwards to the higher classes in society.
5.	Planning is Involved	Since the government plays an active role in monitoring the economy with respect to consumption, production, and distribution decisions, the economy needs to be planned very well. Planning, hence, forms an integral part of the socialistic system. Price mechanism is not allowed to guide the decisions. In its place, it is planning and the budget mechanism that takes precedence. Only an increase in production is not enough under socialism, rather it works towards a fair and equitable distribution of the national output.
6.	No Class	This system believes in a class less society. No individual is allowed to be super rich and the poor are given many opportunities and support to try and become better off. This system advocates total annihilation of the gap between the haves and the have nots.
7.	Social Welfare and Social Security	Since everyone cannot face stiff competition, the poor, the marginalized and the downtrodden are supported by social security cover. The public distribution system ensures that they get their quotas of sugar, rice, oil etc. This is practiced in India by issuing each poor family a ration card. There are various schemes

		for the distribution of polio vaccines, subsidized health care, education, polytechnic and other forms of skill formation. In India, every state has its own schemes and then, there are centrally controlled schemes. All these are traits of a socialistic economy.

Merits of a Socialist Economy

1. The system works towards social justice. Under socialism, inequalities of income are reduced and this is its chief merit.
2. There is a more humane allocation of resources. The needs of the society are considered before allocating resources for various schemes where production is undertaken.
3. This system aims at improving efficiency by bringing the fruits of development to majority of the residents of the country. This system enables the marginalized to be included in the development paradigm. Production is undertaken with the motive of welfare of the society in mind and not just the profit of individuals. New techniques of production and research and development are undertaken with the government sponsoring and this leads to greater efficiency.
4. Social security cover is a large arm of this system. There are many schemes supporting the old, the women, the poor and the children. It is important that no one is ignored in the development process and this is possible not by stiff competition but by the support of the government in terms of guiding and directing the economy in such a manner that there is inclusive growth.
5. Socialistic systems are supported by the government and are not subject to the vicissitudes of the market. Hence, they are more stable and do not get affected by trade cycles adversely.

Demerits of a Socialist Economy

1. Business is not as successful as under capitalism. Since the government is responsible, slack enters the system as individuals are not really held accountable. Profit too is not the motive and incentives are non-existent. Hence, individuals have no drive to work hard and their efficiency drops.
2. Bureaucracy is the biggest bane of a socialistic system. Every decision has to pass through various levels and this, in turn, slows the system and in addition, encourages red tapism, nepotism and corruption.
3. There is always the problem of lack of resources. The government is normally unable to consolidate huge amount of capital required for production and hence, shortages creep into the system.
4. Under this system, there is rampant misallocation of resources. Since the price mechanism is controlled and tampered with by government decisions, the most efficient solution is not obtained. This means that resources are not allocated according to their productivity. This happens due to the fact that the system advocates social welfare and not individual profit.

5. Further, consumers and producers are regimented and lack freedom to take risks and innovate. Individuals are discouraged from taking bold steps as the system is slow and sluggish and controlled by bureaucracy. A lot of time is wasted in the process of production and the consumers are not kings in the market. They are in fact advised/told what to consume. Thus, freedom is sacrificed in this system.
6. Lack of incentives, especially for the hard work, is a characteristic feature of the system. A creative assiduous worker receives the same pay packet as the lazy ones. This kills the incentive to work and hence, the production process slows down.

Table 4.5 : Difference between Capitalist and Socialist Economies

S. No.	Basis of Difference	Capitalist Economy	Socialist Economy
1.	Ownership of Resources	Private individuals own the resources of the country.	Government owns the resources of the country.
2.	Objectives of Economy	Such economy aims at profit maximization.	It aims at social equity and welfare.
3.	Income Distribution	Income inequality exists.	The state aims at equal income distribution.
4.	Price Determination	Price mechanism operate. Market forces determine the price.	In such an economy, price mechanism does not operate. State uses regulated price system.
5.	Role of State	The government does not play any role in production. It just takes care of law and order within the country.	The government plays a major role in production and consumption. It may regulate production, consumption and distribution of goods.
6.	Production Decision	Producers take their own decisions regarding productions. State has no interference in it.	All production decisions are taken by the central planning authority.
7.	Consumption Decisions	Consumption decisions are taken by consumers freely.	State may influence consumption decisions by its policies.

Mixed Economy

An economy may not be fully socialistic or fully capitalistic. In the case of a mixed economy, there is a deliberate mix of the public and private activities. Decisions are taken by both the government and the private individuals. It is a system where the public and the private sectors co-exist but the private sector is not allowed to be fully free. The price mechanism is interfered with by the government and controls are used to monitor the private sector. India is a mixed economy and now, even countries like the US and UK have become mixed economies.

Table 4.6 : Features of a Mixed Economy

S. No.	FEATURE	EXPLANATION
1.	Public and Private Sectors Co-exist	Entire production is shared by these two sectors. Normally, the more crucial and basic heavy industries are controlled by the government. It is very important to understand that the public and the private sector generally do not compete with each other. They co-ordinate and work together for the common goal of the country. In India, ports, railways, oil and petroleum, highways are under the control of the government.
2.	Decision Making	The price mechanism operates in the private sector and the budget mechanism operates in the public sector. However, the prices in the private sector, in some cases, may be controlled by the public sector. For example—Indian Government may impose a price ceiling on the prices of certain essential medicines manufactured by the private companies, for the welfare of the poor.
3.	Control of the Private Sector	The government clearly regulates the private sector in a mixed economy. The private sector is supposed to function with the good of the nation in mind and not with the vested interests of few rich owners of capital. The government uses various techniques such as administered prices, price floors, price ceilings, subsidies, taxes and public distribution system to control prices.
4.	Consumer Sovereignty	Consumer sovereignty is not destroyed in a mixed economy. In fact, the government protects the interests of the consumers. Price control is one way of protecting the consumers.
5.	Bridging Class Gaps	The mixed system aims for the reduction in income disparities. Various kinds of schemes are implemented for the poor and hapless so that they can improve their standard of living.

| 6. | Monopoly Power is Destroyed | The government controls the monopolist. Monopolist tends to make huge profits by curtailing the output and raising the prices. The government in a mixed economy looks into all these issues. |

Merits of a Mixed Economy

1. Unlike the socialistic system, in a mixed economy, producers and consumers experience freedom in most decisions. In this system, the initiative of the private sector is always encouraged.
2. The state makes an effort to ensure maximum welfare of its citizens. All kind of support is provided to increase the welfare of the people through various social security measures.
3. A lot of importance is given to the Research and Development (R & D)—both in the private and public sectors. The government encourages individuals to undertake projects and research which leads to the use of modern technology.
4. Allocation of resources is the best in this system. Careful attention is paid to the poor and the rich. Resources, therefore, are optimally used.

Demerits of a Mixed Economy

1. Foreign investors may be reluctant to invest in an economy where there is nationalization of resources and interference from the government.
2. The public sector is inefficient and full of corrupt practices, nepotism and red-tapism.
3. The constant fear of nationalization nags the private sector and they do not have a free atmosphere to invest and grow.
4. At times, the private sector is controlled too much by the government which stifles growth.

4.3. Solution to the Basic Economic Problems

Uneven distribution of natural resources, lack of human specialization and technological advancement etc., hinders the production of goods and services in an economy. Every economy has to face the problems of what to produce, how to produce and for whom to produce. More or less, all the economies use two important methods to solve these basic problems. These methods are : (a) Free price mechanism and (b) Controlled price system or State intervention.

Price mechanism is defined as a system of guiding and co-ordinating the decisions of every individual unit within an economy through the price determined with the help of the free play of market forces of demand and supply. Such system is free from state intervention.

Price of goods and services are determined when quantity demanded becomes equal to the quantity supplied. Price mechanism facilitates determination of resource allocation, determination of factor incomes, level of savings, consumption and production. Price mechanism basically takes place in a capitalistic economy.

On the other hand, *Controlled price mechanism is defined as a system of state intervention of administering or fixing the prices of the goods and services.* In a socialist economy, the government plays a vital role in determining the price of the goods and services. The government may introduce *'ceiling price'* or *'floor price'* policy to regulate prices. However, how a capitalist, a socialist and a mixed economic system solve their basic problems is given below :

1. **Solution to Basic Problems in a Capitalistic Economy** : Under capitalistic economy, allocation of various resources takes place with the help of market mechanism. Price of various goods and services including the price of factors of production are determined with help of the forces of demand and supply. Free price mechanism helps producers to decide what to produce. The goods which are more in demand and on which consumers can afford to spend more, are produced in larger quantity than those goods or services which have lower demand. The price of various factors of production including technology helps to decide production techniques or methods of production. Rational producer intends to use those factors or techniques which has relatively lower price in the market. Factor earnings received by the employers of factors of production decides spending capacity of the people. This helps producers to identify the consumers for whom goods could be produced in larger or smaller quantities. Price mechanism works well only if competition exists and natural flow of demand and supply of goods is not disturbed artificially.

2. **Solution to Basic Problems in a Socialistic Economy** : Under socialistic economy, the government plays an important role in decision making. The government undertakes to plan, control and regulate all the major economic activities to solve the basic economic problems. All the major economic policies are formulated and implemented by the Central Planning Authority. In India, Planning Commission was entrusted with this task of planning. The Planning Commission of India has now been replaced by another central authority—NITI Ayog (National Institution for Transforming India). Therefore, the central planning authority takes the decisions to overcome the economic problems of what to produce, how to produce and for whom to produce.

The central planning authority decides the nature of goods and services to be produced as per available resources and the priority of the country. The allocation of resources is made in greater volume for those goods which are essential for the nation. The state's main objectives are growth, equality and price stability. The government implements fiscal policies such as taxation policy, expenditure policy, public debt policy or policy on deficit financing in order to achieve the above objectives.

The methods of production or production techniques are also determined or selected by the central planning authority. The central planning authority decides whether labour intensive technique or capital intensive technique is to be used for the production. While deciding the appropriate method, social and economic conditions of the economy are taken into consideration.

Under socialistic economy, every government aims to achieve social justice through its actions. All economic resources are owned by the government. People can work for wages which are regulated by the government as per work efficiency. The income earned determines the aggregate demand in an economy. This helps the government in assessing the demand of goods and services by different income groups.

3. **Solution to Basic Problems in a Mixed Economy** : Practically, neither capitalistic economy nor socialistic economy exists in totality. Both the economic systems have limitations. Consequently, a new system of economy has emerged as a blend of the above two systems called mixed economy. Therefore, *mixed economy is defined as a system*

of economy where private sectors and public sectors co-exist and work side by side for the welfare of the country. Under such economies, all economic problems are solved with the help of *free price mechanism* and *controlled price mechanism (economic planning)*.

Free price mechanism operates within the private sector, hence, prices are allowed to change as per demand and supply of goods. Therefore, private sector can produce goods as per their demand and their price in the market. The government may control and regulate production of the private sector through its monetary policy or fiscal policy. On the other hand, controlled price mechanism (economic planning) is used for the public sector by the planning authority. The goods and services to be produced in the public sector, hence, are determined by the central planning authority.

Private sector determines the production technique or production method on the basis of factor prices, availability of technology etc. On the other hand, production technique or production method for the public sector is determined by the central planning authority. While determining the production technique for the public sector, national priority, national employment policy and social objectives are major considerations.

Private sector allocates its resources to produce those goods which are demanded by people who command high purchasing power. Although, production by the private sector is sometimes controlled and regulated by the government through various policies such as licensing policy, taxation policy, subsidy etc., the price determined by free price mechanism may go beyond the purchasing power of low or marginal income group. Therefore, the government may undertake production of certain goods in its hands. The rationing policy is also introduced to provide essential goods at reasonable price to the poor people. The government, thus, ensures social justice by its actions in the mixed economy.

4.4. The Development of India and China

A brief comparison between Chinese and Indian economy on the development indicators of growth, population and sectoral development is presented here. The detailed comparison on other parameters has been presented in chapter number 10.

1. **Growth** : The average GDP growth of China between 1980 to 2014 was around 9.8 percent whereas that of India during the same period was only about 6.2 percent. With demonetisation announced by the Prime Minister Narendra Modi on 8th November, 2016, the IMF has further slashed India's growth estimate for the current fiscal year to 6.6 percent from 7.6 percent while raising China's growth estimate to 6.7 percent from 6.5 percent. Thus, there has been a widening gap between India and China in terms of growth rate in the recent years.

In 2015, China's per capita GNI was $14320 and it was placed on 107th rank while India's GNI per capita was $6030 and it was placed on 152nd rank in the list on Gross National Income Per Capita 2015 released by the World Bank.

According to the Asian Development Bank, the largest economies of Asia—India and China will maintain the growth rate of the region at 5.7% in 2016 and 2017.

2. **Population** : The two most populated countries of the world are India and China. China is the most populated country with approximately 1.36 billion people in 2014.

During 2017, China's population is projected to increase by 7396347 people and reach 1389891171 in the beginning of 2018. Population density in China is 144 people per square kilometer as of May 2017. India is the second most populated country in the world with a population of approximately 1.27 billion people in 2014. In both the countries, the population of women is lower than that of men. China's population and its yearly growth rate have been given in the table 4.7.

Table 4.7 : Population of China (2001-2017)

Year	Population	Growth Rate
2001	1,267,430,000	0.76 %
2002	1,276,270,000	0.70 %
2003	1,284,530,000	0.65 %
2004	1,292,270,000	0.60 %
2005	1,299,880,000	0.59 %
2006	1,307,560,000	0.59 %
2007	1,314,480,000	0.53 %
2008	1,321,290,000	0.52 %
2009	1,328,020,000	0.51 %
2010	1,334,500,000	0.49 %
2011	1,340,910,000	0.48 %
2012	1,347,350,000	0.48 %
2013	1,354,040,000	0.50 %
2014	1,360,720,000	0.49 %
2015	1,367,820,000	0.52 %
2016	1,375,137,837	0.53 %
2017	1,382,494,824	0.53 %

India has greater density of population than China. In India, the density of population is 383 persons per square kilometer as compared to 144 persons per square kilometer in China. The life expectancy in China is 74.7 years. Male life expectancy is 72.7 years and female life expectancy is 76.9 years. As per the United Nations report, it is higher than the global life expectancy rate which is 71 years. Life expectancy in India for male is 66.9 years, for female is 69.9 years and overall life expectancy is 68.3 years as per the latest data published by WHO in 2015. Literacy rate in China is 96.36% whereas in India, it is 74.04 %.

Table 4.8 : Population and its Growth, India : (1901-2011)

Census Years	Population	Decadal growth		Average annual exponential growth rate (percent)	Progressive rate over 1901 (percent)
		Absolute	Percentage		
1901	23,83,96,327	—		—	—
1911	25,20,93,390	1,36,97,063	5.75	0.56	5.75
1921	25,13,21,213	– 7,22,177	(0.31)	– 0.03	5.42
1931	27,89,77,238	2,76,56,025	11.00	1.04	17.02
1941	31,86,60,580	3,96,83,342	14.22	1.33	33.67
1951	36,10,88,090	4,24,27,510	13.31	1.25	51.47
1961	43,92,34,771	7,81,46,681	21.64	1.96	84.25
1971	54,81,59,652	10,89,24,881	24.80	2.20	129.94
1981	68,33,29.097	13,51,69,445	24.66	2.22	186.64
1991	84,64,21,039	16,30,91,942	23.87	2.16	255.05
2001	1,02,87,37,436	18,23,16,397	21.54	1.97	331.52
2011	1,21,01,93,422	18,14,55,986	17.64	1.64	407.64

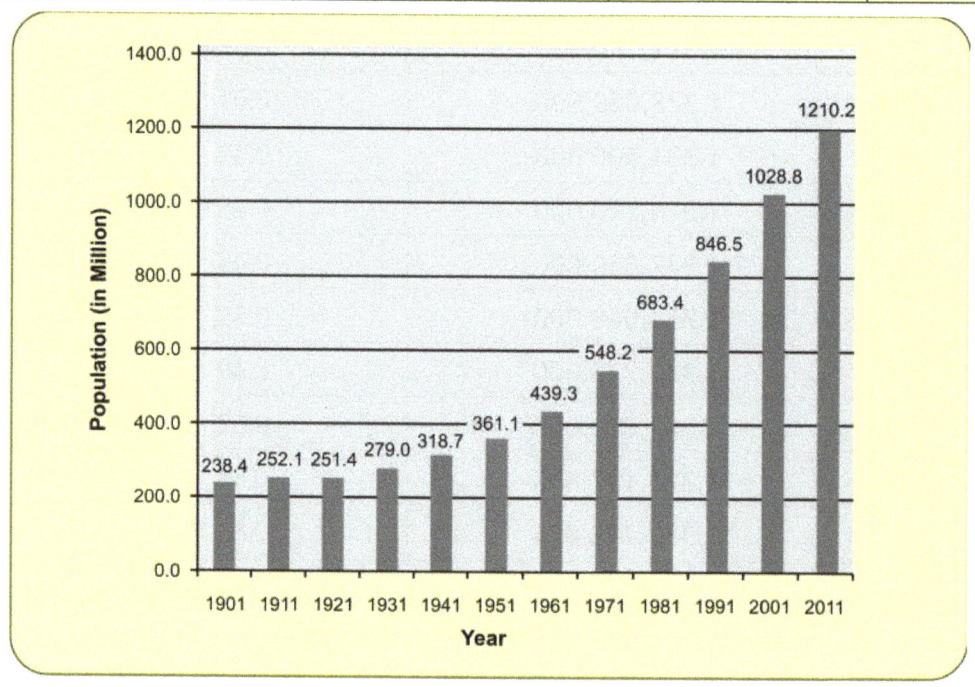

Fig. 4.2
Source : Census 2011 : Provisional Population Total—India

Since the rate of growth of population in India is higher, the difference in population in the two countries is gradually coming down. It has been estimated that in 2028, India will emerge as the most populated country in the world surpassing China. It is shown in the following graph :

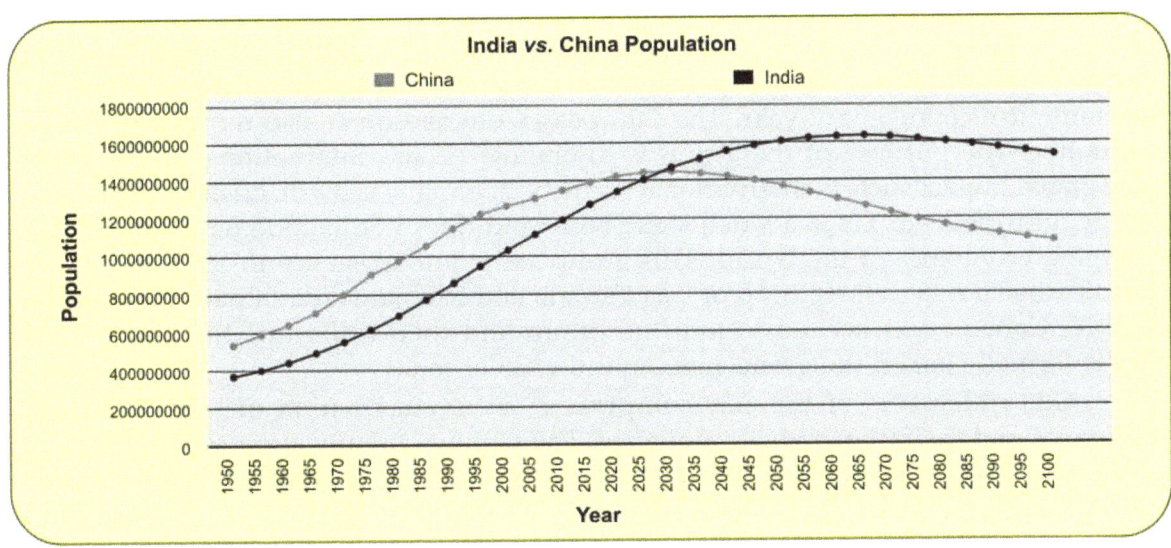

Fig. 4.3 : Projected Population of Two Countries : India and China

3. **Sectoral Growth** : Sectorwise GDP composition of India in 2014 was as follows—Agriculture (17.9%), Industry (24.2%), and Services (57.9%). Sectorwise GDP composition of China in 2014 was—Agriculture (9.7%), Industry (43.9%), and Services (46.4%). Clearly, it is seen that India is more agrarian than China and China has a stronger industrial base. Industrial sector is the major contributor to the GDP in China whereas in India, service sector contributes the most to the GDP.

Table 4.9 : Contribution of Various Sectors to GDP (2014)

Country	Agriculture	Industry	Services
India	17.9%	24.2%	57.9%
China	9.7%	43.9%	46.4%

4.5. Regional and Global Economic Groups

Every country of the world promotes international trade to create jobs, attract investments, attract new technology and to provide a wider choice in products and services to the consumers. They also focus on the free flow of foreign funds and on the movement of factors of production freely to get benefits of specialization. For this purpose, these countries form regional groupings or associations to facilitate free trade among these groups by removing trade barriers. These groups work to promote co-operation among the member countries, to facilitate trade and to resolve various inter-country issues. Some of the important groups formed by the countries are given below :

1. **SAARC** : South Asian Association for Regional Cooperation (SAARC) was founded on 8th December, 1985 in Dhaka, Bangladesh. SAARC is a regional intergovernmental organization and a geopolitical union of nations in South Asia This organization promotes development and regional integration in economic affairs. The members are Afghanistan, Bangladesh, Bhutan, India, Nepal, Maldives, Pakistan and Sri Lanka. Headquarter of SAARC is in Kathmandu in Nepal.

2. **G8** : Group of Eight is a regional organization comprising of 8 industrialized nations, which are Canada, France, Germany, Italy, Japan, Russia, United Kingdom and the United States. This group meets for conferences throughout the year but has one summit meeting every year. The European Commission is also represented in the committee. The purpose of the group is to openly discuss international issues which have global impact such as international security, economic growth, crisis management, energy, terrorism etc. G8 is a small static body and does not include newly developed emerging economies of the world. This group came into existence in 1975 and at that time, it was known as the Group of 6 as Canada and Russia were not part of the group. In 1976, Canada was invited to join the group and then it became the G7. In 1998, Russia formally joined the group making it the G8 of today.

3. **G20** : Members of the G20 comprise of an amalgamation of large advanced economies and the fast growing economies. The regional organization represents $2/3^{rd}$ of the world population. The 20 members are Argentina, Australia, Brazil, Canada, China, France, Germany, India, Indonesia, Italy, Japan, Republic of Korea, Russia, Saudi Arabia, South Africa, Turkey, UK, USA and the European Union. It was founded in 1999 with the objective of examining and reviewing policy issues related to international finance and economic stability. The group has a summit every year and each year the theme varies.

4. **ASEAN** : Association of South East Asian Nations (ASEAN) is a regional organization comprising of countries in the South East Asian region. The member countries are Indonesia, Malaysia, Philippines, Singapore, Thailand, Brunei, Cambodia, Laos, Myanmar, and Vietnam. The aim of the group is to accelerate economic growth and social progress and strive for regional stability and also help the member nations to resolve differences peacefully. It was formed on 8th August, 1967.

5. **EU** : The European Union (EU) consists of 28 members and the member states have to agree in one accord for the EU to adopt policies related to defense and foreign affairs. The European Economic Community (EEC) was formed in 1957 and consisted of 6 core states which are Belgium, France, Italy, Luxembourg, Netherlands and West Germany. The EEC was the predecessor of the EU. For any country to join EU, there must be an approval of all the existing member countries. To be a part of the EU, the country should be a democratic country with a free market. On 1st July 2013, Croatia became the newest member of EU. Any country can withdraw from the union. In fact, UK has recently withdrawn from the union. In June 2016, UK held a referendum related to the membership in the EU. The result was 51.89% of the people being against EU membership. On 29th March 2017, the British Prime Minister, Theresa May invoked Article 50 to formally initiate the process for withdrawal from EU.

Summary

1. Types of Economies : The economies can be classified on the following basis :
   (i) On the basis of nature,
   (ii) On the basis of economic development,
   (iii) On the basis of ownership of resources.

2. On the basis of nature, the economies can be classified as :
   (i) Simple economy,
   (ii) Complex economy,
   (iii) Agricultural economy,
   (iv) Industrial economy,
   (v) Open economy,
   (vi) Closed economy,
   (vii) Free economy,
   (viii) Controlled economy.
3. On the basis of economic development, the economies can be classified as :
   (i) Developed economy,
   (ii) Developing or underdeveloped economy.
4. On the basis of ownership of resources, the economies can be classified as :
   (i) Capitalistic economy,
   (ii) Socialistic economy, and
   (iii) Mixed economy.
5. The basic problems of what to produce, how to produce and for whom to produce are solved with the help of price mechanism in a capitalist economy, controlled price system in a socialistic economy and by the use of both in selected sectors in a mixed economic system.
6. A brief comparison of Indian and Chinese Economies has been presented on the following parameters :
   (i) Growth,
   (ii) Population, and
   (iii) Sectoral growth.
7. Regional and Global economic groups :
   (i) SAARC
   (ii) G8—Group of Eight
   (iii) G20
   (iv) ASEAN—Association of South East Asian Nations, and
   (v) EU—the European Union

Exercise

◆ Short Answer Questions (2 marks)

1. Define dualism.
2. What is disguised unemployment ?
3. Define the HDI ?
4. What is a third world economy ?
5. Expand MEDC.

6. What is an agrarian economy ?
7. Give the expansion for SAARC.
8. Which are the member countries of the group of 8 developed nations ?
9. Name the 20 countries of the G20.
10. Is EU a part of the G8 grouping ?
11. Is EU a part of the G20 grouping ?
12. Name the members of the ASEAN.
13. What is the purpose of the ASEAN ?
14. In terms of GDP which country is better off—India or China ?
15. Is India a member of the ASEAN ?
16. Give another name for the price mechanism.
17. What is the invisible hand ?
18. Who introduced the concept of the invisible hand ?
19. What are the three major questions that an economic system faces ?
20. What is an economic system ?

◆ Long Answer Questions (3-6 marks)

1. What is dualism ? Explain.
2. Discuss three features of an underdeveloped country.
3. Explain how under developed countries have the potential to increase production and standard of living.
4. How do you classify economies on the basis of economic development ? Explain.
5. Compare the sectoral growth patterns in India and China.
6. Write a short note on the ASEAN.
7. Compare the G8 and G20.
8. Explain the population changes in China and India. What has been projected regarding this ?
9. Explain how does the mixed economy work ?
10. Explain how does the capitalistic system work ?
11. Explain how does the socialistic system work ?
12. What are the merits of the mixed economy ? Discuss.
13. What are the demerits of the mixed economy ? Discuss.
14. What are the merits of the capitalistic economy ? Discuss.
15. Explain briefly the demerits of the capitalistic economy.
16. Discuss the merits of a socialistic economy.
17. What are the demerits of a socialist system ? Explain.
18. Compare and contrast the capitalistic and socialistic economies.
19. Compare and contrast the mixed and socialistic economies.
20. Compare and contrast the capitalistic and mixed economies.

Introduction to Indian Economic Development

5.1. Indian Economy – Post Liberalisation

In 1919, the government of India initiated a series of economic reforms to pull the economy out of the crisis of 90's which came to be known as New Economic Policy.

One of the component of this new economic policy was liberalisation.

Liberalisation of the economy means freedom of the producing units from direct or physical controls imposed by the government.

The main features of liberalisation policy were as follows :
(i) Abolition of industrial licensing
(ii) Removal of restrictions
(iii) Relaxation of MRTP Restrictions
(iv) Encouragement to foreign investment
(v) Foreign technology

All these measures improved the performance of the industrial sector and domestic industries were forced to become efficient to face foreign competition.

5.2. Indian Economy — Post Liberalisation Positive/Negative Impact

Positive Impact

1. Vibrant Economy : Indian economy has become vibrant economy after liberalisation which was indicated by GDP growth. Post liberalisation, GDP increased to 8% per annum.

2. Stimulant to Industrial Production : Liberalisation Policy worked as a strong motivator for industrial production in the indian economy.

3. Control on Inflation : Rate of inflation has been lowered due to greater flow of goods and services in the economy. It is estimated to be 2.9% for 2017-18 which was 6 – 9% for 2012 – 14.

4. Flow of Private foreign investment : Private foreign investment had a good jump after the adoption of liberalisation policies. It was a great relief to the government as domestic economy was not generating enough surplus and technology was getting obsolete.

Negative Impact

1. Neglect of Agriculture : GDP growth has mainly been inereased due to secondary and tertiary sectors. Due to liberalisation policy, economy ignored agricultural sector and more than 50% population is dependent on this sector. This has increased the gap between rural and urban economies.

2. Urban Concentration of Growth process : Liberalisation policies have resulted in the concentration of growth process in urban areas which has again widened the 'rural - urban gulf'.

3. Economic Colonialism : India suffered nearly 200 years of political colonialism during the British rule, Now MNCs are expanding their economic control on the under develop and developing countries.

4. Lopsided growth process : This policy's growth process is lopsided as it is not an inclusive growth process. It does not include all the sectors of the economy.

It is clear that economy has improved in a significant manner after liberalisation policy but it is not free from demerits. So with due care, Keeping in mind the negative effects, if this policy is applied we would definetely get much better results for economy.

5.3. Agricultural Sector in India—Problems and Steps taken by the Government

Agriculture is considered as the backbone of the Indian economy since more than 60 percent of the population is dependent on agriculture for its livelihood. During 1950-51, share of agriculture and allied activities was about 59 percent of the total national income. However, the share of the agriculture in national income gradually declined to 40 percent in 1980-81 and is just about 15 percent currently. Agriculture is a source of food supply and is also a supplier of raw materials to the industries. Industries like cotton, jute, edible oil, tea, coffee, rubber, etc., are all dependent on agriculture for their raw material. Indian agriculture also contributes to foreign exchange earnings. Agricultural commodities like tea, coffee, spices, tobacco, sugar, etc., are some of India's principal exports. Agricultural sector, thus, plays a predominant role in the Indian economy.

5.3.1. Problems of Indian Agriculture

Agriculture is the primary occupation and family occupation for many households in India. A large number of farmers in India practice subsistence farming. The sector is highly unorganised and there is still a use of primitive methods for cultivation of crops. The agricultural sector in India has been plagued by several problems which have ultimately reduced its contribution to the national income. Some of the problems faced by the agricultural sector are as follows :

1. **Fragmentation and Inequality in the Distribution of Land :** In India, about 85 percent of the land is held by small and marginal farmers who individually own less than 2 hectares of land. The size of the land holding is highly uneconomic for the use of machines and other farm equipments. Rapid growth in the population and break-up of the joint family system has resulted in fragmentation and sub-division of land. The distribution of land is also unfair with concentration of large land holdings in the hands of rich landlords. Small landholdings increase the cost of production and prevent the use of machines and other farm equipments, therefore, reducing productivity. Many small farmers in India cultivate on lands owned by absentee landlords and therefore, they lack the incentive to increase production and adopt measures to maintain soil fertility.

2. **Land Tenure System :** In India, three types of land tenure systems prevailed in the pre-independence period—the Zamindari system, the Ryotwari system and the Mahalwari system. The Zamindari system developed a class of parasitic Zamindars

who acted as intermediaries between the farmers and the landlords and exploited the tenant farmers. In Ryotwari system, the ownership rights were handed over to the peasants and the British Government collected taxes directly from the peasants. Though, the land reforms have been successful in abolishing the intermediaries, they have not been successful in achieving an equitable distribution of land. Insecure tenancy and eviction still prevail in parts of the rural areas. The land tenure system determines the ownership rights over the land which is important for agricultural development.

3. **Cropping Pattern** : The cropping pattern reflects the area under different crops at a specific point of time. Food crops and cash crops are the two types of crops produced by the agricultural sector. With the increased commercialisation and higher prices of cash crops, they are becoming more attractive and the production has turned to be in their favour. This has led to the shortage of food grains in the country and has increased the dependence on food imports.

4. **Instability in Production** : The production of the agricultural sector is highly instable and the sector continues to depend on monsoon for irrigation. As a result, agricultural production fluctuates every year leading to uncertainty in the sector.

5. **Poor Condition of the Agricultural Labourers** : A large proportion of the population dependent on agriculture is illiterate and is exploited by the landlords. Bonded labour is still prevalent in some parts of the country. The agricultural sector is highly unorganised and the labourers in the sector are paid very low wages. Surplus labour and disguised unemployment in the sector further pushes down wages.

6. **Inadequate Infrastructure** : The agricultural sector suffers from the lack of supply of adequate inputs like fertilizers, HYV seeds, and irrigation facilities. Most of the farmers are still dependent on rainfall and small size of land holdings prevent the implementation of any irrigation facility in the farm. The absence of organised markets also results in low level of earnings from the farm products. Many farmers fall into the clutches of the middlemen for quick sale of their crops due to unavailability of adequate storage infrastructure.

7. **Instability in Prices** : Due to huge fluctuations in the production, the prices of agricultural products are not stable. A surplus production reduces the prices of the commodities which, in turn, affects the income earned by the farmers. Indian government has, therefore, initiated the policy of minimum support price , under which the government purchases food grains from the farmers at some pre-determined price to ensure adequate income to the farmers.

5.3.2. Steps taken by the Government for the Development of Agriculture in India

The Government of India has adopted several measures for the development of Indian agriculture. Some of these measures are as follows :

1. **Land Reforms** : Introduction of land reforms by the Government of India in the post-independence period abolished the intermediaries like Zamindars. The reforms also included regulation of rent, conferment of ownership and imposing a ceiling on land holdings. These measures relieved the farmers from the clutches of the exploitative

landlords and provided them ownership rights and security of tenure. However, land reforms in India could not achieve much success due to various administrative deficiencies.

2. **Consolidation of Landholdings and Encouraging Co-operative Farming** : Consolidation of landholdings and encouraging co-operative farming were measures introduced to prevent sub-division of landholdings and to enable the use of modern agricultural practices on farms.

3. **Agricultural Price Policy** : To ensure that the farmers receive a remunerative price for their products, the Indian government announced the minimum support price and procurement price for various agricultural products. However, these practices have been benefiting the large farmers more who have huge marketable surplus.

4. **Agricultural Credit and Marketing** : The Government had also initiated various policy measures for the provision of institutional credit to the farmers through co-operative and commercial banks. The National Bank for Agricultural and Rural Development (NABARD) was set up as an apex development bank in 1982 to ensure smooth flow of credit to the agricultural sector. Further, the government has also made provisions for the development of regulated markets by introducing the measures for grading and standardization of output and standardization of weights and measures. The co-operative marketing structure has also been strengthened to provide a smooth marketing facilities to the farmers.

Beyond these measures, the government has also made provisions for storage facilities by constructing warehouses and has extended irrigation facilities by developing major and minor irrigation projects. It is also promoting research in agriculture by setting up agricultural universities and Indian Council of Agricultural Research (ICAR). Green revolution has been extended to various parts of the country and measures have also been taken to develop dryland farming.

5.4. Industrial Sector in India—Problems and Policies

During 200 years of British rule, no efforts were taken to develop Indian industries. India shifted its focus to the industrial sector from the second five-year plan. Since then, the government has been taking various initiatives to build a strong industrial base in the country. Industrial growth helps in capital formation and lead to an increase in the national income. It creates employment opportunities and reduces the pressure on agriculture. The industrial sector supports the agricultural sector by supplying agricultural equipments and by creating the market for agricultural commodities. It further enables the economy to reduce imports and become self-reliant. The share of industrial sector is about 26 percent of the GDP and it provides employment to about 22 percent of the total workforce in India. Post globalisation, however, the Indian industries, both private as well as public, are facing stiff competition from international producers. Industrial sector in India is under threat due to cheap Chinese imports, rising cost, new technology, etc. Some of the problems faced by the Indian industries include :

1. **Poor Capital Formation** : Industries require huge amount of investments for rapid expansion. Low level of savings in the country has led to poor rate of capital formation

which has reduced the rate of industrial growth in India.

2. **Infrastructural Inadequacies** : High growth rate of industrial sector can be achieved only with the availability of sound infrastructural facilities. Due to poor network of roads, railways, and communication facilities in many parts of the country, industrial development could not take place in these areas.

3. **Lack of Human Capital** : Indian industries also face the problem of dearth of skilled and efficient labour force. Handling sophisticated computerised machines requires skilled and trained labour. India has been losing many skilled professionals to other countries due to the high levels of wages paid in those countries.

4. **Change in Production Pattern** : There has been an increasing trend in the production of elite goods such as refrigerators, air conditioners, etc., which has slowed down the production of commodities of mass consumption. This has created a distortion in the output structure.

5. **Poor Performance of Public Sector Enterprises** : Due to lack of innovation and faulty pricing policies, many public sector industries have been incurring heavy losses. Therefore, the public sector enterprises have failed to generate the required surplus, resulting in the wastage of resources.

6. **Regional Imbalance** : As industries require excellent transport infrastructure, most of the industries are located in the developed regions and states of India. Western regions like Gujarat and Maharashtra have attained maximum industrial growth whereas states like Odisha and Bihar continue to remain industrially backward due to poor infrastructure. This has resulted in an imbalance in the growth between states.

7. **Industrial Sickness** : Inefficient management has resulted in growing number of strikes and lockouts dampening industrial production. Further, competitive markets and lack of investments in research and development have also turned many industries into sick units. Growing industrial sickness is a threat to industrial growth.

5.4.1. Industrial Policy in India

The industrial policy refers to the comprehensive package of measures aimed at tackling various issues of the industrial sector in the country. The Government of India adopted its first industrial policy on April 06, 1948 which laid emphasis on the development of cottage and small scale industries. The industrial policy resolution of 1956 made provisions for expansion of both private and public sector industries in a coordinated manner with flexible and industry-friendly policies.

The government led by Late Mr. P.V. Narasimha Rao on July 24, 1991, announced the New Industrial Policy introducing a number of liberalisation and privatisation measures. This new industrial policy is also known as LPG (Liberalisation, Privatisation and Globalisation) Policy. The major initiatives taken under the New industrial policy were :

1. **Abolition of Industrial Licensing** : The new industrial policy abolished the compulsory licensing for many industries except for the industries which had security and strategic concerns such as hazardous chemical industries, cigarettes and tobacco manufacturing industries, industrial explosive industries and other industries producing goods that could raise environmental concerns.

2. **Restructuring of Public Sector** : The government under the new policy reduced the list of industries reserved for the public sector and committed to strengthening and making profitable those public sector units that were in the reserved list. The industries in the reserved list included :

(i) Arms and ammunition and allied defence equipment

(ii) Atomic energy

(iii) Coal and lignite

(iv) Mineral oil

(v) Mining of iron ore, manganese chrome, gypsum, sulphur, gold and diamond

(vi) Mining of copper, zinc, lead, tin, molybdenum and wolfram

(vii) Minerals specified in the schedule to the atomic energy, and

(viii) Rail transport

Private sector participation was also invited to raise the competitiveness of these industries. The Board of Industrial Finance and Reconstruction (BIFR) was set up for rehabilitation and reconstruction of sick industries.

3. **Amendment to Monopolies and Restrictive Trade Practices (MRTP) Act** : The MRTP act was amended to remove the restrictions on the assets held by the companies. It also made provisions to remove pre-entry restrictions and restrictions on amalgamations, mergers and expansion. Emphasis was rather shifted to controlling and regulating monopolistic behaviour and restrictive and unfair trade practices.

4. **Foreign Investments** : Provisions were made for automatic approval of Foreign Direct Investment (FDI) in almost all the sectors except for a few sensitive ones. Foreign equity up to 51 percent was allowed in export oriented companies. The Foreign Investment Promotion Board was set up to negotiate with international firms for investments. Further, automatic permissions were given to foreign technology agreements in high priority industries to the extent of $2 million. In other industries, automatic permission was provided if no foreign exchange was required for any payments.

Thus, the new policy brought about a transformation in the industrial sector in India. Delicensing, scrapping of limits on assets holdings and privatisation were critical decisions taken by the Government which gave a boost to the industrial sector. However, the absence of a suitable policy for technological innovation and absence of measures to address imbalanced regional development were some of the drawbacks of the new industrial policy of 1991.

Industrial policy should strive to create a competitive environment for business enterprises. The policy should be transparent and non-discriminatory. Successful implementation of policies also requires efficient administrative machinery. The policy, thus, had a long way to go with respect to these aspects.

5.5. Foreign Trade : Problems and Policies

Foreign trade refers to the exchange of goods and services between countries. It is very important to expand the market for commodities produced within a country and to provide domestic consumers with a wide range of choices and quality goods at low prices. Foreign trade enables the countries to access those products and commodities that cannot be produced domestically due to resource constraints and other reasons. The following are some of the important features of international trade :

1. **Immobility of Factors of Production** : The factors of production mainly labour and capital cannot be easily transferred from one country to another country due to various restrictions on immigration of workers and procedures and restrictions involved in the movement of capital. Due to the immobility of factors of production between countries, the commodities are traded to reap the benefits of comparative advantage and to provide the domestic consumers with a wide range of choices.

2. **Differences in Currencies** : When goods are imported from a foreign country, the payment has to be made in the currency of that particular country from which goods are imported. Thus, the exchange rate plays an important role here. As the currency value of the importing country depreciates, the imports become more expensive and exports become cheaper. But when the currency of the importing country appreciates, the imports become cheaper and the exports become expensive.

3. **Diversity of Markets** : Foreign trade provides the producers an opportunity to cater to the consumers with diverse nature and different tastes and preferences. The socio-economic background of the consumers also varies widely between nations than within the nation.

4. **Differences in Political Framework** : In international trade, exchange of goods and services take place between countries of varied political systems. Each country is more concerned about the welfare of its people, even at the expense of welfare of people in other countries. Hence, a number of rules and regulations are framed by the various governments which regulate the flow of goods and services between their country and rest of the world.

5. **Trade Restrictions** : The restrictions on trade also varies from one country to another. Since every country is more concerned about its own welfare and growth, it imposes various restrictions on trade in the form of tariffs and quotas. Countries may also subsidise their products to promote exports. Thus, the policy adopted by the government towards foreign trade has a significant impact on the volume of goods it trades.

5.5.1. Foreign Trade Policy

India's Foreign Trade Policy is also known as Export Import Policy (EXIM) in general. Developing export potential, improving export performance, encouraging foreign trade and creating favourable balance of payments position are the main objectives of the EXIM policy of India. Foreign Trade Policy or EXIM Policy is a set of guidelines and instructions established by the DGFT (Directorate General of Foreign Trade) in matters related to the import and export of goods in India. It is prepared and announced by the Central Government (Ministry of Commerce).

Objectives of Foreign Trade Policy

The main objectives of foreign trade policy are as follows :

1. To accelerate the economy from low level of economic activities to high level of economic activities by making it a globally oriented vibrant economy and to derive maximum benefits from expanding global market opportunities.

2. To stimulate sustained economic growth by providing access to essential raw materials, intermediate components, consumables and capital goods required for augmenting production.

3. To enhance the technological strength and efficiency of Indian agriculture, industry and services, thereby improving their competitiveness.

4. To generate employment opportunities and encourage the attainment of internationally accepted standards of quality.

5. To provide quality consumer products at reasonable prices.

In the light of the above mentioned objectives, there are two broad aspects of the foreign trade policy—the import policy which is concerned with regulation and management of imports and the export policy which is concerned with the promotion and regulation of exports. The main objective of the government's EXIM Policy is to promote exports to the maximum extent. Exports should be promoted in such a manner that the economy of the country is not affected by unregulated exportable items especially needed within the country. Export control is, therefore, exercised in respect of a limited number of items whose supply position demands that their exports should be regulated in the larger interests of the country.

5.5.2. Trade Policy Reforms since 1991

The year 1991 was a turning point in the Indian economy as during this year, the economic reform policies were implemented. The time period after 1991 is known as post liberalisation period. Economic reforms focused mainly on the trade policy reforms, that is, on opening Indian economy to the rest of the world. Under the trade reforms policy, new initiatives were taken to create an environment for the promotion of foreign trade. The new policy made provisions for reducing the degree of regulation and licensing control on foreign trade. The 1991 economic reforms were focused primarily on the formal sector, and as a result, we have seen significant development in those areas that were liberalized. Telecom and civil aviation are some important sectors that have benefited greatly from deregulation and subsequent reforms. However, liberalisation and economic reforms still have a long way to go, especially for the informal sector including the agricultural sector and Micro, Small and Medium Enterprises (MSMEs).

Steps Taken for the Promotion of Exports and Imports

The main features of the new trade policy as it has evolved over the years since 1991 are as follows :

1. **Removal of Restrictions from Imports and Exports :** During the pre-liberalisation period, imports were regulated by means of a positive list of freely importable items in

India. Since 1992, imports were regulated by a limited negative list. The trade policy of 1 April 1992, removed restrictions from the imports of almost all intermediate and capital goods. Only 71 items remained restricted. This led India's foreign trade to reduce its balance of payment deficit. The government has also introduced a number of measures to promote exports such as free trade zones, special economic zones (SEZs), development of ports, quality check of exports, setting up of commodity boards to promote the export of traditional commodities such as tea, rubber, coffee, etc.

2. **Reduction of Tariff Rates :** A rational reduction in the import duty rate was recommended by the Chelliah Committee in its report. The report had suggested a peak rate of 50 percent. Following the suggestion, the 1991-92 budget had reduced the peak rate of import duty from more than 300 percent to 150 percent. This process of cutting down the customs tariffs was even carried further in successive budgets.

3. **Provision of Trading Houses :** The export houses and trading houses were permitted to import a wide range of goods according to the new reform policy of 1991. The government also permitted the setting up of trading houses with 51 percent foreign equity for the purpose of promoting exports. During post liberalisation period, in the first trade policy (1992-97), export houses and trading houses were provided the benefit of self-certification under the advance license system, which permits duty-free imports for the purpose of exports.

Steps Taken for the Promotion of Foreign Investment

The reforms in foreign trade are not realistic without the promotion of foreign investment. Consequently, during the post-reform period, the government took several measures to promote foreign investment in India. Some of the important measures are given below :

1. **Raising Foreign Equity :** At the first move in the direction of promoting foreign investment, the government announced a specified list of high technology and high-investment priority industries wherein automatic permission was granted for foreign direct investment (FDI) up to 51 percent of foreign equity during 1991. The limit was raised further to 74 percent and subsequently to 100 percent for many of these industries. Moreover, many new industries have also been added to the list over the years.

2. **Establishment of Foreign Investment Promotion Board :** To promote foreign direct investment (FDI), a Foreign Investment Promotion Board (FIPB) has been set up to negotiate with international firms and approve direct foreign investment in selected areas. All kind of foreign direct investments are regulated by FIPB.

3. **Promotion of Foreign Institutional Investment :** The trade reform policy also felt the need of promoting foreign institutional investment. The government had taken numerous steps from time to time to promote Foreign Institutional Investment (FII) in India.

Rationalization of Exchange Rate

Rationalization of the exchange rate was needed for the success of trade policy. The following steps were taken in this direction :

1. In July 1991, the rupee was devalued by around 20 percent.

2. Liberalized Exchange Rate Management System (LERMS) was announced during 1992-93 in which a dual exchange rate was fixed. It allowed the exporters to convert 40 percent of the foreign exchange earnings at the official exchange rate and the remaining 60 percent at the market determined exchange rate.

3. In 1993, a unified exchange rate was adopted in which 100 percent conversion at market determined rate was allowed. India, thus, adopted market determined exchange rate in 1993.

Steps Taken to Improve Balance of Payments

One of the important measures undertaken to improve the balance of payments situation was the devaluation of rupee. In the very first week of July 1991, the rupee was devalued by around 20 percent. To promote foreign investments in high-priority industries, automatic permission was granted for foreign direct investment upto 51 percent of foreign equity, which was subsequently raised to 74 percent and to 100 percent in many industries. Foreign Investment Promotion Board was set up to facilitate smooth flow of foreign investments. This resulted in improving balance of payment situation in favour of India. The purpose was to bridge the gap between the real and the nominal exchange rates that had emerged on account of rising inflation and hence, to make the exports competitive.

5.5.3. Latest Foreign Trade Policy of India (2015-2020)

On 1st April, 2015, the new Foreign Trade Policy (FTP) for the period 2015-20 was announced which replaced the Foreign Trade Policy of 2009-14, which expired on 31st March, 2014.

Features of Foreign Trade Policy (2015-2020)

1. **Merchandise Exports from India Scheme (MEIS) :** (i) One of the important features of the new trade policy is that all the existing schemes for rewarding merchandise exports such as Focus Product Scheme, Market Linked Focus Product Scheme, Focus Market Scheme, Agricultural Infrastructure Incentive Scrip, VKGUY have now been merged into a single scheme to be known as 'Merchandise Export from India Scheme (MEIS)'. There would be no conditions attached to the scrips issued under the new scheme.

(ii) Another important feature is that proposed trade policy has made the provisions for rewards for export of notified goods to notified markets under 'Merchandise Exports from India Scheme (MEIS)' and will be payable as a percentage of realized Free on Board (FOB) value.

2. **Introduction of 'Service Exports from India Scheme (SEIS)' to Promote Exports of Services :** (i) To promote service exports from India, the existing scheme 'Served from India Scheme (SFIS)' and all other schemes have been replaced by 'Service Exports from India Scheme (SEIS)' in the new trade policy. This new scheme will benefit all services exporters in India.

SEIS will apply to those service providers which are located in India. It will not apply to 'Indian Service Providers'. Thus, the new scheme, SEIS provides for rewards to all service providers of notified services, who are providing services from India, regardless of the constitution or profile of the service provider.

(ii) The new trade policy proposed that the rate of reward under SEIS would be based on net foreign exchange earned by the service providers. The earlier scheme of rewards, such as duty credit scrip, will no longer be with actual user conditions and will no longer be restricted to usage for specified types of goods but would be freely transferable and usable for all types of goods and services.

3. Provision of Incentives for Special Economic Zones (SEZs) : The new trade policy also proposes to extend incentives (MEIS and SEIS) to units located in SEZs. Such incentive policy may encourage the industries located in these zones to increase their productivity and to undertake more investments.

4. Use of Credit Scrips for Payment of Various Duties : (i) The new trade policy has made the provision for transfer of duty credit scrips freely. Such credit scrips may also be used for payment of custom duty, excise duty and service tax.

(ii) New trade policy also made the provision of free transfer of scrips, received under MEIS and SEIS schemes and from the import of goods.

(iii) All those scrips issued under 'Exports from India Scheme' can only be used for the following purposes :

(a) Payment of customs duty for import of inputs or goods including capital goods, except those goods listed in Appendix 3A of the new trade policy.

(b) Payment of excise duty on domestic procurement of inputs or goods, including capital goods as per Department of Revenue notification.

5. Use of e-Commerce for Filing Taxes : As part of Digital India vision, mobile apps would be created to ease filing of taxes and stamp duty. Automatic money transfer using internet banking has also been proposed. Online procedure to upload digitally signed document by a Chartered Accountant or Company Secretary or Cost Accountant is to be introduced.

6. Provisions for Agricultural and Industrial Goods : Agricultural and village industry products are to be supported across the globe at the rates of 3% and 5% under MEIS. A higher level of support is to be provided for processing and packaging of agricultural and food items under MEIS.

7. Self Certification : Manufacturers, who are also status holders, will be allowed to self-certify their manufactured goods as originating from India. Tax and duty on the goods manufactured by the Indian manufacturers has been reduced to boost Make in India vision of the government.

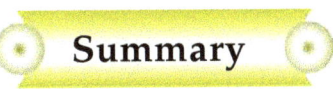

Summary

1. **Features of Indian Economy— Post liberalization**
    (i) Abolition of Industrial licensing.
    (ii) Removal of restrictions.

(iii) Relaxation of MRTP restirictions.
   (iv) Encouragement to Foreign investment.
   (v) Foreign technology.
2. **Per Capita Income**—Average income earned per person in a country in a particular year. It is obtained by dividing the national income of the country by the population of that country.
3. **Problems of Indian Agriculture**—
   (i) Fragmentation and inequality in the distribution of land
   (ii) Land tenure system
   (iii) Cropping pattern
   (iv) Instability in production
   (v) Poor condition of the agricultural labourers
   (vi) Inadequate infrastructure
   (vii) Instability in prices
4. **Land Tenure**—Land tenure refers to the institutional structure that determines the nature of individual's ownership over the land. It also specifies the relationship between the land holder and the state.
5. **Cropping pattern**—Cropping patterns refers to the proportion of area under various crops at a specific point of time.
6. **Steps taken by the Government for the development of agriculture in India**–
   (i) Land Reforms
   (ii) Consolidation of landholdings and encouraging co-operative farming
   (iii) Agricultural price policy
   (iv) Agricultural credit and marketing.
7. **Land Reforms**—Land reforms refer to the changes in the rules and regulations governing ownership of land.
8. **Consolidation of landholdings**—Consolidation refers to bringing together fragments of land in order to increase the productivity of land.
9. **Agricultural price policy**—This is a policy formulated by the Government to provide remunerative prices to farmers for agricultural commodities.
10. **Problems of the Industrial Sector in India**—
    (i) Poor capital formation
    (ii) Infrastructural inadequacies
    (iii) Lack of human capital
    (iv) Change in production pattern
    (v) Poor performance of public sector enterprises
    (vi) Regional imbalance
    (vii) Industrial sickness

11. **Human Capital**—It refers to the knowledge, experience, skill and health possessed by an individual.
12. **Industrial Sickness**—Industrial sickness is a phenomenon in which an industrial unit incurs heavy losses that is equal to or exceeds its net worth.
13. **Initiatives under the Industrial Policy**—
    (i) Abolition of industrial licensing
    (ii) Restructuring of public sector
    (iii) Amendment to MRTP Act
    (iv) Foreign investments
14. **MRTP Act**—Monopolies and Restrictive Trade Practices Act was enacted in 1969 and it aimed at preventing concentration of economic power by controlling the acts of the monopolists and unfair trade practices that could harm consumer welfare.
15. **Foreign Trade : Problems and Policies**—India's Foreign Trade Policy is also known as Export Import Policy (EXIM). Developing export potential, improving export performance, encouraging foreign trade and creating favourable balance of payments position are the main objectives of the EXIM policy of India.
16. **Trade Policy Reforms since 1991**—
    (i) Steps taken for promotion of exports and imports
    (ii) Steps taken for promotion of foreign investment
    (iii) Rationalization of exchange rate
    (iv) Steps taken to improve balance of payments
17. **Features of Foreign Trade Policy (2015-2020)**—
    (i) Merchandise Exports from India Scheme (MEIS)
    (ii) Introduction of new Scheme 'Service Exports from India Scheme (SEIS)' to promote service exports
    (iii) Provision of incentives for SEZs
    (iv) Use of credit scrips for payment of various duties
    (v) Use of e-commerce for filing taxes
    (vi) Provisions for agricultural and industrial goods
    (vii) Self certification

Exercise

◆ Short Answer Questions (2 marks)

1. State any five features of Indian economy post liberalization.
2. State the Positive impact of liberalization.
3. State the negative impact of liberalization.
4. Define per capita income.

5. List out the problems faced by the agricultural sector in India.
6. What is land tenure system ?
7. What do you understand by cropping pattern ?
8. What are land reforms ?
9. State the purpose of agricultural price policy.
10. What is human capital ?
11. What is industrial sickness ?
12. Expand MRTP.
13. Give two features of Foreign Trade Policy (2015-20) of India.

◆ Long Answer Questions (3-6 marks)

1. Explain the features of Indian economy post liberalization.
2. Discuss the positive and negative impact of liberalization on the economy.
3. Discuss the problems faced by the Indian agriculture.
4. Explain the steps taken by the government for the development of agriculture in India.
5. Analyse the challenges faced by the industrial sector in India.
6. Examine the various initiatives taken by the government under its industrial policies.
7. State the features of Foreign Trade Policy (2015-20) of India.

6. Parameters of Development

6.1. Introduction

The concept of 'Development' has fascinated many economists around the world, from Adam Smith, Marx and Keynes to Amartya Sen and Devraj Ray. The wealthy nations across the world and international organisations such as the United Nations and World Bank are all showing great interest in resolving the developmental challenges confronted by the underdeveloped and developing countries of the world. While the rich nations are now focussing on sustainable development, the poor countries are striving towards achieving economic development. Economists have developed various measures to assess the development of a nation like Gross National Income, Per Capita Income, Human Development Index, Physical Quality of Life Index and so on.

One of the most important and a simple measure of economic development among them is per capita income.

6.2. Per Capita Income

Per capita income refers to the average income earned per person in a given region or country during a specified year. It is obtained by dividing the country's national income by its population.

$$\text{Per Capita Income} = \frac{\text{National Income or Gross National Product}}{\text{Population of the country}}$$

Per capita income is generally treated as the indicator of development of a country. The basic idea behind this is that development is based on the level of income of the residents of a country. Higher the income, higher is the standard of living and development. Though, national income can also be used as an indicator for economic development, it has numerous drawbacks. It fails to take into account the growth rate of population and changes in price level. Failure to distinguish between final and intermediate goods may be misleading while calculating the national income. To overcome these challenges, per capita income has been suggested as a measure to assess the economic development. However, even per capita income cannot be considered as an adequate measure of economic development due to the following reasons :

1. Development refers to an increase in the standard of living of the people. Welfare and standard of living of the people improves only with an increase in consumption expenditure. An increase in the per capita income does not necessarily mean development because people may be increasing the rate of savings with increase in the income and therefore, the consumption may remain the same or it may even fall.

2. When the government spends the increased income on acquiring military goods or on other non-developmental expenditure which does not result in increased welfare of the people, the per capita income figure may be misleading.

3. The per capita income estimates do not take into account the distribution of income. It is only a simple average.

4. It fails to measure the changes in output due to changes in price level.

5. The cost of living varies across the countries and consumers' needs and preferences also differ in each country. Thus, the per capita income of different countries cannot be compared. Further, international comparison may become misleading and inaccurate when per capita income figures of different countries are converted to a common currency.

6. Per capita income also does not reflect the development in social infrastructure such as basic nutrition, health, housing infrastructure, sanitation facilities, education, etc. These facilities are essential for improvement in the living standards of the people.

Despite these limitations, per capita income is still a popular measure of development due to its simplicity and ease of calculation. And, it is also a known fact that countries that have a low per capita income are generally underdeveloped with poor social and economic infrastructure and low standard of living.

6.3. Quality of Life Index (QLI)

Quality of Life Index, popularly known as the 'where-to-be-born-index', measures which country provides the best opportunity in terms of health, safety and a prosperous life. The index is based on the factors which assess quality of life. These factors include :

1. Material well-being, as measured by GDP per capita.
2. Health, as measured by life expectancy at birth.
3. Quality of family life, as measured by divorce rates.
4. Political freedom.
5. Job security which is measured by the unemployment rate.
6. Gender equality.
7. Climate.
8. Quality of community life, which is based on membership in social organisations.
9. Physical security which is based on crime rates, terrorism and homicides, and
10. Governance, as measured by the prevalence of corruption.

When a survey was carried out among 80 countries in 2013 on the above indicators, India ranked 66th with a score of 5.67 out of 10 and China ranked 49th with a score of 5.99 out of 10. The top rank was secured by Switzerland (8.22 out of 10) followed by Australia (8.12 out of 10) and Norway (8.09 out of 10).

6.4. Physical Quality of Life Index (PQLI)

The PQLI, developed by Morris D. Morris, measures the quality of life in a country based on three indicators namely, life expectancy, infant mortality rate and literacy rate. Each of these indicators is measured on a scale of 1 to 100, where 1 indicates worst performance and 100 indicates best performance. The country with the highest life expectancy is rated 100 and the one with the lowest is rated 1. The other countries fall in between 1 to 100. For example, if Norway has the highest life expectancy of 90 years it is given a rating of 100 and if Sudan has the lowest life expectancy of 25, it is given a rating of 1. If in Saudi Arabia, life expectancy is, say 57 years, this is exactly in between 90 and 25 and therefore, it would be given a rate of 50. The final index is the average of the three indices considered for computing the PQLI. The PQLI was, however, subjected to severe criticism from economists as it failed to include many other social and psychological factors. Further, the index gives equal weightage to all the three indicators which is unrealistic.

6.5. Human Development Index (HDI)

Human Development Index was developed by Mahbub-ul-Haq and Nobel Laureate, Amartya Sen and was incorporated by the United Nations Development Program (UNDP) in their first Human Development Report in 1990. HDI was developed as a composite statistic that considers three social indicators—life expectancy, education and per capita income of the countries. It measures the achievement of the country in these three basic dimensions.

1. **Life Expectancy at Birth** : Life expectancy has been considered as an important indicator due to the value that people attach to living a long and healthy life. People can survive for very long if they are well nourished, healthy and educated. Life expectancy at birth measures the number of years a new-born infant would live if prevailing patterns of mortality at the time of its birth continues to remain throughout its life.

2. **Literacy Rate** : Literacy rate measures the percentage of population aged 15 years and above, who can with understanding, read and write simple statements in daily life. The literacy rate reflects people's access to education. A literate person can lead a productive and quality life.

3. **Per Capita Income** : Per capita income assesses the standard of living of the people and is another important indicator of economic development. The per capita income reflects one's command or claim over resources.

Before calculating the HDI, an index is created for each of these dimensions called—Life expectancy index, education index and income index. The goal posts are used to calculate the dimension index. The performance of the country in each of the dimension is expressed as a value that ranges between 0 and 1. The following formula is used to calculate each of these indices :

$$\text{Dimension Index} = \frac{\text{Actual value} - \text{Minimum value}}{\text{Maximum value} - \text{Minimum value}}$$

HDI is now calculated as a simple average of the three dimension indices. The HDI value ranges from 0, which is the minimum value to 1, which is the maximum value. Countries which have a HDI value of less than 0.5 are considered as countries with low human development. Countries with HDI value between 0.5 to 0.8 are considered as countries with medium level of human development and countries with HDI value of more than 0.8 are considered as countries with high level of human development.

According to the UNDP's Human Development Report of 1990, India's HDI value was 0.428.

6.5.1. The Education Index

Before 2010, education index was calculated by taking into consideration adult literacy rate along with combined primary, secondary and tertiary gross enrolment ratio. The Gross Enrolment Ratio (GER) is a statistical measure used to determine the number of students enrolled at elementary, middle and high school. It is expressed as a ratio of number of students who live in the country to those who qualify for that particular grade. For instance, if a country has 1,00,000 people enrolled in school during the academic year 2008 and the total number of school age individuals are 1,50,000, then GER is calculated as follows :

GER = 100000 / 150000 = 0.66

However, since 2010, the education index is calculated based on the mean years of schooling and expected years of schooling.

1. Mean years of schooling refers to the average years of formal education received by people aged 25 years and above, during their lifetime.

Formula to calculate Mean Years of Schooling Index (MYSI) is—

$$\text{Mean Years of Schooling Index} = \frac{\text{Mean years of schooling} - \text{Minimum value}}{\text{Maximum value} - \text{Minimum value}}$$

2. Expected years of schooling refers to the years of schooling a child can expect to receive under current enrolment rates.

Formula to calculate Expected Years of Schooling Index (EYSI) is—

$$\text{Expected Years of Schooling Index} = \frac{\text{Expected years of schooling} - \text{Minimum value}}{\text{Maximum value} - \text{Minimum value}}$$

Education index is then calculated as—

$$\text{Education Index } (I_{\text{Education}}) = \frac{(MYSI \times EYSI)^{1/2} - \text{Minimum value of combined education index}}{\text{Maximum value of combined education index} - \text{Minimum value of combined education index}}$$

6.5.2. The Income Index

$$\text{Income Index } (I_{\text{Income}}) = \frac{\text{Log GNI per capita} - \text{Log (Minimum value)}}{\text{Log (Maximum value)} - \text{Log (Minimum value)}}$$

Where, GNI stands for Gross National Income.

The income index would be 1, if per capita income is the highest and 0, if it is the lowest, that is, USD 100.

6.5.3. The Life Expectancy Index

$$\text{Life Expectancy Index } (I_{\text{Life}}) = \frac{\text{Life Expectancy of a country} - \text{Minimum value}}{\text{Maximum value} - \text{Minimum value}}$$

6.5.4. Calculation of Human Development Index

HDI is calculated as the geometric mean of the three indices.

$$\text{HDI} = (I_{Life}^{1/3} \cdot I_{Education}^{1/3} \cdot I_{Income}^{1/3})$$

The Goal Posts for Human Development Report of 2010 were as follows :

Dimension	Observed Maximum	Minimum
Life expectancy (years)	83.2 (Japan, 2010)	20.0
Mean years of schooling (years)	13.2 (United States, 2000)	0
Expected years of schooling (years)	20.6 (Australia, 2002)	0
Combined education index	0.951 (New Zealand, 2010)	0
Per capita income (PPP $)	108, 211 (United Arab Emirates, 1980)	163 (Zimbabwe, 2008)

The example given below shows the calculation of Human Development Index for China based on its performance in HDI indicators.

Indicator	Value
Life expectancy at birth (years)	73.5
Mean years of schooling (years)	7.5
Expected years of schooling (years)	11.4
GNI per capita (PPP $)	7,263

Life expectancy index = $\dfrac{73.5 - 20}{83.2 - 20}$ = 0.847

Mean years of schooling index = $\dfrac{7.5 - 0}{13.2 - 0}$ = 0.568

Expected years of schooling index = $\dfrac{11.4 - 0}{20.6 - 0}$ = 0.553

Education index = $\dfrac{\sqrt{0.568 \times 0.553} - 0}{0.951 - 0}$ = 0.589

Income index = $\dfrac{\ln(7{,}263) - \ln(163)}{\ln(108{,}211) - \ln(163)}$ = 0.584

Human Development Index = $\sqrt[3]{0.847 \cdot 0.589 \cdot 0.584}$ = 0.663

6.5.5. Limitations of HDI

Human Development Index has evolved over the years, and yet, it has certain limitations :

1. It is a composite index that tries to capture human development in just a single number which is unrealistic.

2. Many vital indicators such as infant mortality, health status, access to drinking water and sanitation facilities etc. are not measured by this index.

3. When all the countries improve their HDI value at the same weighted rate then the countries which had very poor HDI values earlier may not be recognised for their improvement.

4. Equal importance given to all the three indicators may be arbitrary.

5. Prevalence of inequality, unemployment, etc., are not captured by this index.

According to Amartya Sen, the standard of living of a society cannot be judged merely by its per capita income, it should rather be measured by people's capabilities, that is, by what a person can do. Development is, thus, a broad concept that goes beyond income and other material goods. It encompasses a variety of human capabilities such as access to drinking water, health care facilities, education, housing, employment and so on. The HDI, thus, provides only a foundation to the measurement of development of an economy.

6.5.6. India and HDI As per UNDP Report

India was ranked 130 out of 188 countries according to UN Human Development Report, 2018, based on 2017 data with a score of 6.4. In 2010, India ranked 119 out of 169 countries with a score of 0.58. While India's HDI value increased from 0.428 in 1990 to 0.624 in 2016, it still had the lowest rank among BRIC nations. Yet, its annual average growth rate, during the same period, has been higher that of other medium HDI countries. Prevalence of high levels of inequality could be cited as one of the prime reasons for the India's low rank in HDI. However, with several measures taken on the fiscal front by the present government, high hopes have emerged on India's developmental prospects.

Summary

1. **Per Capita Income**—It is defined as the average income earned per person in a country in a particular year. It is obtained by dividing the national income of the country by the population of that country.

$$\text{Per Capita Income} = \frac{\text{National Income or GNP}}{\text{Population of the country}}$$

2. **Quality of Life Index (QLI)**—The Quality of Life Index, popularly known as the 'where-to-be-born-index, measures which country provides the best opportunity in terms of health, safety and a prosperous life.

3. **Physical Quality of Life Index (PQLI)**—The PQLI, developed by Morris D. Morris, measures the quality of life in a country based on three indicators namely, life expectancy, infant mortality rate and literacy rate. Each of these indicators are measured on a scale of 1 to 100, where 1 indicates worst performance and 100 indicates best performance.
4. **Human Development Index (HDI)**—HDI is a composite statistic of life expectancy, education and income to measure the level of human development attained by a country.
5. **Life Expectancy**—Life expectancy measures the number of years a new-born infant would live if prevailing patterns of mortality at the time of its birth continues to remain throughout its life.
6. **Literacy Rate**—Literacy rate measures the percentage of population aged 15 years and above, who can with understanding, read and write simple statements in daily life.
7. **Mean Years of Schooling**—Mean years of schooling refer to the average years of formal education received by people aged 25 years and above, during their lifetime.
8. **Expected Years of Schooling**—Expected years of schooling refer to the years of schooling a child can expect to receive, under current enrolment rates.

Exercise

◆ Short Answer Questions (2 marks)

1. State any two measures of development.
2. How do you calculate per capita income ?
3. What is where-to-be-born-index ?
4. What is HDI ?
5. What is life expectancy at birth ?
6. What do you understand by literacy rate ?
7. State any two limitations of HDI.
8. Write a short note on PQLI.

◆ Long Answer Questions (3-6 marks)

1. Explain any three measures of development.
2. Discuss the limitations of using per capita income as a measure of human development.
3. Differentiate between Physical Quality of Life Index and Human Development Index.
4. Write a note on the indicators of HDI.
5. How is HDI calculated ?
6. What are the limitations of HDI ?

Planning and Economic Development in India

7.1. Concept of Planning

Planning is a continuous process that involves choices and decision making about allocation of available resources with the objective of achieving effective and efficient utilisation and growth of these resources. In India, planning is done both at the centre as well as the state level. Economic planning is done by the central authority after a complete survey of the economic situation. The policy objectives are designed based on the future development goals of the country.

In India, until 2014, planning was the responsibility of the National Planning Commission that was established on March 15, 1950. The first five-year plan was prepared by the Planning Commission for the period 1951-56. The first Prime Minister of India, Pandit Jawaharlal Nehru was the first chairman of the Planning Commission. The Prime Minister was always the ex-officio chairman of the Planning Commission. The Deputy Chairman who was nominated by commission held the rank of a cabinet minister.

In 2014, the government led by Prime Minister Narendra Modi dissolved the Planning Commission and replaced it by the think tank called NITI Aayog. NITI, here, stands for National Institution for Transforming India.

7.2. Objectives of Planning

Planning plays a very significant role especially in a developing country like India. The following are some of the objectives of economic planning in India :

1. **Economic Growth and Development** : Every five-year plan had a growth target that had to be achieved by the end of the planning period. In order to bring about an improvement in standard of living of the people, the per capita income has to rise. A rise in per capita income is necessary to overcome the problems of poverty and its effects.

2. **Increase in Employment** : The developing economies generally suffer from open unemployment and disguised unemployment. India is no exception to it. Slow growth of the agricultural sector and lack of investments in the industrial sector are major causes for high levels of unemployment in the country. Measures have been taken in every five-year plan to create employment opportunities, thereby, increasing labour productivity.

3. **Increase in Investment** : Economic growth cannot be achieved unless adequate investments are made to bring about an increase in output capacity. Investments help in creating employment opportunities. One of the objectives of planning is, thus, to push up the rate of investment to ensure smooth flow of capital to various sectors of the economy.

4. **Social Justice and Equity** : The five-year plans also focused on reducing inequalities in the distribution of income in order to ensure social justice. Prevalence of inequalities in the economy results in exploitation of the poor wherein the rich become richer and the poor become poorer.

5. **Balanced Regional Development** : In India, there exists a wide gap in the development of different states and regions. While Gujarat, Tamil Nadu, Maharashtra etc., enjoy high levels of development, there are states like Bihar, Odisha, Nagaland etc., which remain backward. Planning aims at bringing about a balanced regional development by diverting more resources to the poor and backward regions.

6. **Modernisation** : Modernisation refers to a shift in the composition of output, innovation and advancement in technology. Modernisation helps an economy to advance at a faster pace and compete with the developed nations of the world. The objective of planning is to encourage and incentivise investments into various sectors of the economy, especially the industrial sector, to help them adopt new technologies and thus, increase efficiency.

7.3. An Overview of the Five-Year Plans in India

1. **First Five-Year Plan** : It was formulated for the period 1951-56, when India was confronting the problems of huge influx of refugees, food shortage and severe inflation. The plan, thus, focused on the primary sector, that is, the agricultural sector to increase the food production in India to overcome the crisis. The monsoon was favourable to agriculture in those years and therefore, the production increased. The first five-year plan was quite successful as the targeted growth rate was 2.1 percent and the achieved growth rate was 3.6 percent.

2. **Second Five-Year Plan** : It was formulated for the period 1956-61 and it focussed on rapid industrialisation. The plan aimed at the development of heavy and basic industries and conceived that agricultural sector could be given lower priority as it has been able to achieve its targets in the previous plan. The second plan achieved only a moderate success due to the severe shortage of foreign exchange on account of huge imports to meet the requirements of the industrial sector. The actual growth rate achieved in the plan was 4.3 percent against the target of 4.5 percent.

3. **Third Five-Year Plan** : It was formulated for the period 1961-66. The third five-year plan was prepared with the mindset that India has entered the 'take-off stage' and it is time for it to become a self-reliant and self-generating economy. The plan gave priority to both agriculture as well as the industrial sector. However, the Indo-China conflict in 1962 and the Indo-Pakistan conflict in 1965 made the plan a complete failure as huge amount of expenditure had to be allocated to meet the defence requirements. The actual growth rate achieved in the plan was 2.8 percent as against the target of 5.6 percent.

The failure of the third plan led to the formulation of three annual plans for the years 1966-67, 1967-68 and 1968-69, before the launch of the fourth plan. The period from 1966 to 1969 was, therefore, termed as "Plan Holiday". It was during this period that green revolution was introduced to overcome the food crisis. Green revolution advocated the use of high-yielding variety of seeds, fertilizers, pesticides and extensive use of irrigation.

4. **Fourth Five-Year Plan** : It was formulated for the period 1969-74 and had two basic objectives—growth with stability and progressive achievement of self-reliance. It stressed upon the growth of the agricultural sector and it was during this period that

various family planning measures were introduced to control the rising population. While the plan aimed at a highly ambitious growth rate of 5.7 per cent, it could achieve only 3.3 percent. This failure could be attributed to the huge influx of refugees from Bangladesh and the Indo-Pakistan war in 1972.

5. **Fifth Five-Year Plan** : It was formulated for the period 1974-79 and proposed two main objectives—removal of poverty and attainment of self-reliance. The plan aimed at achieving its objectives by achieving high growth rate, equitable distribution of income and increase in domestic savings. However, the plan was an utter failure due to high levels of inflation. With the Janta Government taking over the power, the plan was terminated in 1978. The growth rate achieved during this period was 4.8 percent as against the target of 4.4 percent.

The Janta Government formulated the sixth five-year plan for the period 1978-83 with the objective of creating employment opportunities. The Janta Government, to its misfortune, lasted only for two years and was replaced by the Congress Government that came up with a different plan. The Planning Commission, in the meanwhile, introduced the 'Rolling Plan' in 1978, which is said to incorporate three kinds of plans—first plan for the current year, second plan for a specific period of 3, 4 or 5 years, according to the needs of the Indian economy and the third plan, for a longer term like 10, 15 or 20 years. The rolling plan was, however, subjected to many criticisms and was later abandoned with Congress Government coming up with the sixth five-year plan.

6. **Sixth Five-Year Plan** : It was introduced by the Congress Government for the period 1980-85. It was based on Nehru's model of growth and aimed at a direct attack on the problem of poverty by creating conditions for increasing employment opportunities. Many employment generation schemes such as Training of Rural Youth for Self Employment (TRYSEM) and Integrated Rural Development Programme (IRDP) were introduced. Though the plan progressed as perceived by the planners during the first four years, a severe famine occurred in the fifth year *i.e.*, 1984-85. Therefore, the agricultural output declined drastically. However, the economy still managed to grow at 5.7 percent as against the target of 5.2 percent.

7. **Seventh Five-Year Plan** : It was formulated for the period 1985-1990 and it aimed at accelerating food grain production, creating employment opportunities and raising labour productivity. The focus of the plan was on 'food, work and productivity'. The plan was quite successful and recorded a growth rate of 6 per cent as against the targeted growth rate of 5 per cent.

8. **Eighth Five-Year Plan** : This plan could not be formulated in 1990 due to uncertain political situation at the centre. Therefore, two annual plans for the years 1990-91 and 1991-92 were formulated. During 1991, India had to face severe balance of payment crisis. The debt burden was mounting and the fiscal deficit was widening. The inflation level was rising and the industrial sector was going through a recession. Because of this crisis and the pressure from International Organisations such as IMF, the government led by P.V. Narasimha Rao introduced the economic reforms in 1991, post which the eighth plan was launched in 1992 for the period 1992-97 reflecting the reforms with various structural adjustment policies. The role of the private sector increased and

several liberalisation measures were introduced. As a result, the growth rate was the highest as compared to the previous plans. The eighth plan achieved a growth rate of 6.8 percent as against the targeted growth rate of 5.6 percent.

9. **Ninth Five-Year Plan** : It was formulated for the period 1997-2002 and its aim was to achieve "growth with social justice and equality". The plan recognised the critical role of the state in the social sectors such as health care, education and infrastructure, since the market forces, by themselves, may not make these areas attractive to the private sector. The plan stressed upon the need for public investment in these areas. The ninth plan aimed at a GDP growth rate of 7 percent. However, due to poor performance of the economy during 1997-98, the growth target was revised to 6.5 percent. Yet, the target could not be achieved and the economy grew only at a rate of 5.4 percent.

10. **Tenth Five-Year Plan** : It was formulated for the period 2002-2007. It was realised that the development goals cannot be achieved by targeting the economic growth alone. Therefore, the tenth five year plan set forth measurable targets on development indicators such as infant mortality rate, literacy, access to electricity, sanitation facilities, sustainable food production and environment. The tenth plan targeted a growth rate of 8 percent. Further, it laid down targets for each state to ensure balanced development. The tenth plan was, however, not successful in terms of poverty reduction, generating employment opportunities and performance of agricultural sector. Many poor states faced decelerating growth. Thus, the plan was not successful in bringing about balanced regional development as well. The plan also failed to achieve its target on infant mortality and maternal mortality rate. The tenth plan recorded a growth rate of 7.6 percent as against the targeted growth rate of 8 percent.

11. **Eleventh Five-Year Plan** : It was formulated for the period 2007-2012 and the plan document was titled "Towards faster and more inclusive growth". With the objective of achieving fast and inclusive growth, the eleventh plan had set targets for various socio-economic indicators. It aimed at achieving a GDP growth rate of 9 percent, agricultural growth rate of 4 percent, generating 58 million employment opportunities, increase in wages of unskilled labourers, reduction in poverty by 10 percent, reduction in drop-out rate, increasing literacy to 85 percent, reducing gender gap, infant mortality rate and total fertility rate, reducing malnutrition among children, provision of safe drinking water, improvement in sex ratio, development of infrastructure and communication. It also had measurable targets for environmental protection such as increase in forest and tree cover by 5 percent, improving air quality and increasing energy efficiency.

The eleventh plan had an ambitious target of achieving a growth rate of 9 percent. Though, the economy took off well achieving a growth rate of 9.3 percent during the first year, it had a drastic fall to 6.7 percent in 2008-09 due to the global financial crisis. The economy, however, managed to achieve a growth rate of 8 percent during this plan due to expansionary measures taken by the government.

12. **Twelfth Five-Year Plan** : It was formulated for the period 2012-2017 and it focussed on achieving faster, inclusive and sustainable growth. It aimed at achieving an inclusive growth by reducing poverty, reducing inequality, empowering people and by bringing in balanced regional development. The goals towards sustainable development

focussed on environmental sustainability, improvements in health and education sector and development of physical infrastructure such as transport, telecommunication, power etc. It had set a growth target of 8 percent and had set monitorable targets for poverty, education, health, infrastructure, environment and sustainability. It also aimed at providing banking services to 90 percent of the households and introduced Adhaar based direct cash transfer of subsidies and welfare payments.

7.4. Achievements of Economic Planning in India

Economic planning in India, formally conceived in 1951, has come a long way in helping the economy to tackle the challenges in various sectors and has enabled it to achieve rapid economic progress. Some of the major achievements of planning in India are as follows :

1. **Economic Growth** : Economic planning in India has been successful in increasing the national income and the per capita income of the country resulting in economic growth. The net national income at factor cost increased from ₹ 4393.45 billion in 1966-67 to ₹ 45,733 billion in 2011-12 (at 2004-05 prices). The per capita income increased from ₹ 8876 to ₹ 38,048 during the same period (at 2004-05 prices). The average growth rate has increased from 3.5 percent during 1950 to 1970 to about 5.5 percent after 1990's. The economy recorded a growth rate of 7.8 percent during the eleventh five-year plan.

2. **Progress in Agriculture** : The first five-year plan focussed on agricultural development. However, agricultural sector did not receive priority in the subsequent plans. Yet, with various initiatives implemented in the agricultural sector such as the green revolution and agricultural pricing policies, there has been a considerable increase in the output of the agricultural sector. The index of agricultural production increased from 85.9 in 1970-71 to 165.7 in 1999-2000 (Base year : 1981-82). The production of major food grains which includes rice, wheat, coarse cereals and pulses has increased from 77.14 million tonnes in 1958-59 to 252.22 tonnes in 2015-16. With the introduction of green revolution, the yield per hectare of food grains has increased from 662 kg in 1959-60 to 2056 kg in 2015-16. Similarly, the production of commercial crops has also recorded an increasing trend. Various reforms in the agricultural sector such as the Rashtriya Krishi Bima Yojana and Kisan credit cards during the ninth plan and National Food Security Mission and Rashtriya Krishi Vikas Yojana during the eleventh plan have been quite successful in improving the performance of the agricultural sector.

3. **Industrial Growth**: Economic planning has also contributed to the progress of the industrial sector. The index of industrial production increased from 54.8 in 1950-51 to 152.0 in 1965-66 (Base year : 1960-61) which is about 176 percent increase in production during the first three five-year plans. It went up from 109.3 in 1981-82 to 232.0 in 1993-94 (Base year : 1980-81). Taking 2004-05 as the base year, the index of industrial production recorded an increase from 108.6 in 2005-06 to 181.1 in 2015-16. The introduction of reforms in 1991 relieved the industrial sector from numerous bureaucratic restrictions that were prevalent earlier. This has led to the rapid growth of the industrial sector in India. India has made remarkable progress in cotton textiles, paper, medicines, food processing, consumer goods, light engineering goods etc.

4. **Public Sector** : The public sector played a predominant role in the economy immediately after the independence. While there were only 5 industrial public sector enterprises in 1951, the number increased to 244 in 1990 with an investment of ₹ 99,330 crores. However, the number of public sector enterprises fell to 217 in March 2010. Yet, the cumulative investment went up to ₹ 5,79,920 crores. The ratio of gross profit to capital employed increased from 11.6 percent in 1991-92 to 21.5 percent in 2004-05. Heavy engineering and transport equipment industries recorded a 117 percent and 111 percent growth respectively in 2006-07 over the previous year. Very high profits were recorded by petroleum, telecommunication services, power generation, coal and lignite, financial services, transport services and minerals and metal industries. The government has eliminated a number of restrictions on the operational and financial powers of the Navaratnas, Miniratnas and several other profit making public sector enterprises.

5. **Infrastructure** : Development of infrastructure such as transport and communication, power, irrigation etc., is a pre-requisite to rapid economic growth and development. Expansion of transport facilities enables easy movement of goods and services and also enlarges the market. Irrigation projects contribute significantly to rural development. Power projects help in meeting the growing demand for power by both industrial and household sector. The total road length increased from about 400,000 km in 1951 to about 4.7 million km in 2011. India has the second largest road network in the world with about 5,472,444 kilometres of road, as on March 31, 2015. The route length of the Indian railway network has increased from about 53,596 km in 1951 to about 64,450 km in 2011. The investment in infrastructure as a percentage of GDP was about 5.9 percent during the tenth plan and increased to about 7.2 percent during the eleventh plan.

6. **Education and Health Care** : Education and health care are considered as human capital as they contribute to increased productivity of human beings. Considerable progress was achieved in the education as well as health sector during the five-year plans. The number of universities increased from about 22 in 1950-51 to 254 in 2000-01. There were about 22 central universities, 345 state universities, 123 deemed universities and about 41,435 colleges in 2016. The number of institutions in higher education has increased to over 100 percent since 2008. With the growth in the number of institutions, the literacy rate in India has increased from 16.7 percent in 1950-51 to 74.04 percent in 2011. With improvements in the health infrastructure, India has been able to successfully control a number of life threatening diseases such as small pox, cholera, polio, TB etc. As a result, there has been a fall in the death rate from 27.4 per thousand persons in 1950-51 to 7.3 per thousand persons in 2016. The life expectancy has increased from about 32.1 years in 1951 to 68.01 years in 2014. The infant mortality rate has declined from 149 per thousand in 1966 to 37.42 per thousand in 2015.

7. **Growth of Service Sector** : Service sector is the key contributor to the economic growth of India. The service sector contributed to about 53.2 percent of the gross value added growth in 2015-16. The contribution of the IT sector to India's GDP increased from about 1.2 percent in 1998 to 9.5 percent in 2015. The service sector has recorded a growth rate of about 138.5 percent in the last decade. Financial services, insurance, real

estate and business services are some of the leading services that have been recording a robust growth in the past few years. The rapid growth of the service sector in India could be attributed to the inflow of huge amount of FDI in this sector. India's share of service exports in the world service exports has increased from 0.6 percent in 1990 to 3.3 percent in 2011.

8. **Savings and Investment** : Savings and Investments are major driving forces of economic growth. The gross domestic savings in India as a proportion of GDP has increased from 8.6 percent in 1950-51 to about 30 percent in 2012-13. The gross capital formation has increased from 8.4 percent in 1950-51 to 34.70 in 2012-13. Capital accumulation is the key to economic development. It helps in achieving rapid economic growth and has the ability to break the vicious circle of poverty.

9. **Science and Technology** : India is the third most preferred destination for technology investments. It is among the top most countries in scientific research and space exploration. India is also making rapid progress in nuclear technology. ISRO has made a record of launching 104 satellites in one go on a single rocket. India today has the third largest scientific manpower after U.S.A and Russia. The government has undertaken various measures such as setting up of new institutions for science education and research, launching the technology and innovation policy in 2013, strengthening the infrastructure for research and development in universities, and encouraging public-private partnership etc.

10. **Foreign Trade** : On the eve of independence, India's primary exports were agricultural commodities and UK and US were its major trading partners. India was largely dependent on other countries for various capital and consumer goods. However, with the development of heavy industries during the five-year plans, India has been able to reduce its dependence on other countries and was able to achieve self-reliance in a number of commodities. With the liberalisation of trade, India now exports about 7500 commodities to about 190 countries and it imports about 6000 commodities from about 140 countries. The exports of the country increased from ₹ 54.08 billion in 1977-78 to ₹ 17,144.24 billion in 2015-16. And imports have increased from ₹ 60.20 billion in 1977-78 to ₹ 24, 859.27 billion in 2015-16.

7.5. Shortcomings of Economic Planning in India

1. **Slow Growth** : The planning process in India has been able to achieve considerable increase in the national income and per capita income. Yet, the rate of increase has been slow as compared to developing countries like China, which have been able to achieve more than 10 percent growth rate consistently. India was able to achieve a growth rate of only about 4 to 5 percent during the pre-reform period. It was only during the post reform period that is after 1991, that the country could experience a growth rate of over 7 percent.

2. **Neglect of Agriculture** : The five-year plans failed to pay attention to the agricultural sector except for the first five-year plan. As a result, the agricultural growth rate declined from 3.62 percent in 1991-92 to 0.81 percent during 2009-10. And the share of agriculture in GDP declined from about 50 percent during 1950-51 to about 16 percent of the GDP in 2015.

3. **Unemployment** : The plans have failed to address the problem of unemployment which is a cause of many social evils. The unemployment rate has marginally reduced from 8.35 percent during 1972-73 to about 6.53 percent in 2009-10. It was about 4.19 percent in 2013. The growth rate of employment has recorded a decline from 2.61 percent in 1972-73 to 1.50 percent during 2009-10. The employment in primary sector recorded a negative growth rate of 0.13 percent in 2009-10.

4. **Widespread Poverty** : Failure to address the problem of unemployment has resulted in widespread poverty in the country. The first four plans failed to address the problem of poverty. It was only during the fifth five-year plan that measures were taken to tackle poverty directly by introducing various poverty alleviation programmes. These programmes, however, have achieved only limited success. The poverty rate in India declined from about 26.1 percent in 2000 to 21.9 percent in 2011.

5. **Inflation** : Poverty is aggravated under the situation of inflation. The five-year plans have not been able to stabilise the prices due to which there has been a steep rise in the general prices. The inflation rate was around 10 percent in 2012.

6. **Rising Inequality** : With rapid economic growth, the country has been witnessing a rise in the level of inequality. It has been estimated that the richest 1 percent own about 58 percent of the country's wealth. Poor performance of the agricultural sector and lack of investments in rural infrastructure are cited as the primary reason for such rising inequalities.

7. **Political Instability** : Political instability and inefficient administration are the major hurdles in successful implementation of the plans. Though the plans are formulated after complete analysis of the economic situation, most of the plans fail to achieve the targets due to inefficient administration, corruption, vested interests and red tapism.

The achievements and failures of the economic planning in India, thus, reveal the underlying gaps in the process of planning. It is an undeniable fact that the current level of growth and development that the country has achieved could not have been possible without planning. Yet, systematic and efficient implementation of the plans and strategic policies to tackle the problem of unemployment and poverty could take the country to greater heights. It is strongly believed that the NITI Aayog would address these gaps that existed in the planning process in India and would strive to build a vibrant economy over the years.

7.6. NITI Aayog

The Planning Commission which has a legacy of 65 years has been replaced by the NITI Aayog. NITI Aayog or The National Institution for Transforming India came into existence on the 1st January, 2015 by means of a cabinet resolution, replacing the erstwhile Planning Commission. Its aim is to promote co-operative federalism and foster a spirit of harmony among the Union and State governments.

Structure of NITI Aayog

The NITI Aayog was established by a resolution of the central government. It will be governed by the Governing Council and will have a team chaired by the Prime Minister.

Governing Council

Governing Council is the highest body of NITI Aayog. It consists of following members :

1. Prime Minister of India as the Chairperson.
2. A Vice-Chairperson and a CEO, nominated by the Prime Minister.
3. The Chief Ministers of all the states and Lieutenant Governors of Union Territories.
4. Members: Two (Full-time).
5. Part-time members: Maximum of two from leading universities research organizations and other relevant institutions in an ex-officio capacity. Part-time members will be on a rotational basis.
6. Ex Officio members: Maximum of four members of the Union Council of Ministers to be nominated by the Prime Minister.

7.6.1 Objectives of NITI Aayog

1. To evolve a shared vision of national development priorities, sectors and strategies with the active involvement of States.
2. To foster cooperative federalism through structured support initiatives and mechanisms with the States on a continuous basis, recognizing that strong States make a strong nation.
3. To develop mechanisms to formulate credible plans at the village level and aggregate these progressively at higher levels of government.
4. To ensure, on areas that are specifically referred to it, that the interests of national security are incorporated in economic strategy and policy.
5. To pay special attention to the sections of our society that may be at risk of not benefiting adequately from economic progress.
6. To design strategic and long term policy and programme frameworks and initiatives, and monitor their progress and their efficacy. The lessons learnt through monitoring and feedback will be used for making innovative improvements, including necessary mid-course corrections.
7. To provide advice and encourage partnerships between key stakeholders and national and international like-minded think tanks, as well as educational and policy research institutions.
8. To create a knowledge, innovation and entrepreneurial support system through a collaborative community of national and international experts, practitioners and other partners.
9. To offer a platform for resolution of inter-sectoral and inter- departmental issues in order to accelerate the implementation of the development agenda.

10. To maintain a state-of-the-art Resource Centre, be a repository of research on good governance and best practices in sustainable and equitable development as well as help their dissemination to stake-holders.
11. To actively monitor and evaluate the implementation of programmes and initiatives, including the identification of the needed resources so as to strengthen the probability of success and scope of delivery.
12. To focus on technology upgradation and capacity building for implementation of programmes and initiatives.
13. To undertake other activities as may be necessary in order to further the execution of the national development agenda, and the objectives mentioned above.

7.6.2 Roles of NITI Aayog

1. To enhance the involvement of States in decision making process by fostering cooperative federalism.
2. To promote innovation, knowledge and entrepreneurial support system through a collaborative community of national and international experts.
3. Incorporating National security in economic strategy and policy formulated.
4. To maintain state-of-the-art Resource Center for best practices in sustainable and equitable development and promote good governance.
5. Formulate the strategies at village level and integrate these at higher levels of government.
6. To work towards the technology up-gradation for implementation of policies.
7. The design framework for strategic and long-term policies and monitor their progress.
8. The Aayog, will work on assessing the effectiveness of the on-going schemes.

7.6.3 Challenges before NITI Aayog

India's growth rate has been hovering around 5% for the past three years. NITI Aayog has to focus on improving the growth rate of country. It must also focus on levelling regional disparities in growth.

Agriculture, which has been neglected by the successive governments at the Centre and states, is an area that requires immediate attention. This sector requires more investments and policy care.

To decrease dependence on agriculture sector, rural infrastructure shall be developed and skill development schemes shall be taken to the villages.

Power sector is another critical area. The NITI Aayog must focus on solving the problems of state electricity boards. Development of power sector energizes the development of industry, service and agriculture sectors.

Summary

1. **Planning**—Planning is a continuous process that involves decision making and choices about allocation of available resources with the objective of achieving effective and efficient utilisation and growth of these resources.
2. **Objectives of Planning**—
   (i) Economic growth and development
   (ii) Increase in employment
   (iii) Increase in investment
   (iv) Social justice and equity
   (v) Balanced regional development
   (vi) Modernisation
3. **Targets and Achievements of the five-year plans**–

Five year plan	Period	Target (in %)	Achievement (in %)
1	1951-56	2.1	3.6
2	1956-61	4.5	4.3
3	1961-66	5.6	2.8
Annual Plans	1966-69	—	—
4	1969-74	5.7	3.3
5	1974-79	4.4	4.8
Rolling Plan	1978-80	—	—
6	1980-85	5.2	5.7
7	1985-90	5.0	6.0
8	1992-97	5.6	6.8
9	1997-02	6.5	5.4
10	2002-07	8.0	7.6
11	2007-12	9.0	8.0
12	2012-17	8.0	—

4. **Achievements of Economic Planning in India :**
   (i) Economic growth
   (ii) Progress in agriculture
   (iii) Industrial growth
   (iv) Public sector
   (v) Infrastructure
   (vi) Education and health care
   (vii) Growth of service sector
   (viii) Savings and investments
   (x) Science and technology
   (x) Foreign trade

5. **Shortcomings of Economic Planning in India :**
   (i) Slow growth
   (ii) Neglect of agriculture
   (iii) Unemployment
   (iv) Widespread poverty
   (v) Inflation
   (vi) Rising inequality
   (vii) Political instability
6. NITI Aayog came into existence on 1ˢᵗ January, 2015 by means of cabinet resolution, replacing the planning commission. It is govern by Governing Council with Prime minister as its chairperson.
7. The main aim of NITI Aayog is to promote co-operative federalism and faster a sprit of harmony among the and state government.

Exercise

◆ Short Answer Questions (2 marks)

1. Define planning.
2. What was the role of Planning Commission in India ?
3. State the objectives of planning.
4. When was the first five-year plan initiated in India and what were its objectives ?
5. What were the causes of failure of the third five-year plan ?
6. State the main objectives of the fifth five-year plan.
7. What do you understand by the term "plan holiday" ?
8. What is a rolling plan ?
9. What were the challenges in implementing the eighth plan ?
10. What was the focus of the ninth five-year plan ?
11. State the objectives of the eleventh plan.
12. What is NITI Aayog ?
13. State any four shortcomings of economic planning in India.

◆ Long Answer Questions (3-6 marks)

1. Define planning and explain the macro-economic objectives of planning.
2. Explain the process of economic planning in India.
3. Discuss the objectives and achievements of the five-year plans in India.
4. Write a short note on the eleventh five-year plan.
5. Write a brief note on NITI Aayog.
6. What are the roles and objectives of NITI Aayog ?
7. Critically evaluate the achievements of the five-year plans in India.
8. Discuss the weaknesses of planning in India.

Structural Changes in the Indian Economy After Liberalisation

8.1. Introduction—Economic Reforms

Economic reforms in India refer to the structural adjustments that were initiated in 1991 with the aim of liberalising the economy and to accelerate its rate of economic growth. The Narsimha Rao Government, in 1991, introduced the economic reforms in order to restore internal and external confidence in the Indian economy. The reforms aimed at bringing in greater participation of the private sector in the growth process of the Indian economy. Policy changes were introduced with respect to industrial licensing, technology upgradation, removal of restrictions on the private sector, foreign investments and foreign trade. The reforms were aimed at attaining a high rate of economic growth, reducing the rate of inflation, reducing the current account deficit and overcoming the balance of payments crisis. The important features of the economic reforms were Liberalisation, Privatisation and Globalisation, popularly known as LPG.

8.2. Need for Economic Reforms

The economic reforms introduced by the Government of India in 1991 brought in a number of neo-liberal policies aimed at rapid economic growth. The reforms were targeted at various sectors such as the industrial sector, trade, public sector, financial sector, etc. The need for the introduction of the reforms was because of the following factors :

1. **Poor Performance of the Industrial Sector** : Before the introduction of economic reforms, the industrial sector suffered due to bureaucratic controls. The industries had to obtain several licenses and permissions for any undertaking activity such as setting up a new firm, starting a new product line, expansion of existing business, foreign investments and so on. Many public-sector enterprises were incurring huge losses due to poor productivity. The main objectives of the industrial policy introduced in 1991 were :

(i) To unshackle the Indian industrial sector from the cobwebs of unscrupulous bureaucratic controls;

(ii) To introduce liberalisation with the objective of integrating the Indian economy with the world economy;

(iii) To remove restrictions on foreign investments and relieve the entrepreneurs from the restrictions of the MRTP Act; and

(iv) To shed the load of public enterprises that were incurring heavy losses.

2. **Adverse Balance of Payments** : India faced a severe economic crisis during the end of 1980s. India was unable to meet its international debt obligations and was pushed to a situation of near bankruptcy. The foreign exchange reserves were insufficient to pay the import bills. The Balance of Payments deficit could not be financed beyond a certain point. Some of the factors responsible for the crisis were :

(i) Rising level of expenditure over revenue;
(ii) Heavy government borrowing;
(iii) Inefficient utilisation of resources;
(iv) Excessive protection to domestic industries;
(v) Inefficient management of public sector enterprises;
(vi) Lack of technological development and innovation; and
(vii) Lack of investments in research and development.

3. **Rise in Fiscal Deficit** : Amidst the political instability and balance of payment crisis, there was a rising fiscal deficit. This was mainly due to the increase in the non-developmental expenditure of the government. The government had to borrow huge sum of money to finance the deficit and to meet the interest obligations on these debts. The government was in a debt trap. Thus, there was a need to bring in reforms in order to reduce the non-developmental expenditure and to bring about a fiscal discipline.

4. **Inflation** : Due to continuous borrowing by the government in order to meet its mounting expenditure, there was a rapid increase in the money supply. The government resorted to deficit financing wherein the RBI financed the borrowings by the Government of India by printing currency notes. This lead to a rise in the money supply. When money supply increased, the demand for goods and services also rose, thereby increasing their prices and causing an inflationary situation.

5. **The Gulf War** : The Gulf war during 1990-91 had a significant impact on the supply of oil. As a result, the price of oil shot up, increasing India's foreign currency outlays. The Gulf crisis also affected the flow of foreign currency into India. The NRI deposits were moving out of India and remittances from Indians employed abroad were also affected during the war. This further depleted the foreign currency reserves with the RBI. India, thus, had no other option but to look towards IMF for financial assistance.

Amidst the political instability, high inflation, rising fiscal deficit, balance of payment crisis and immense pressure from the international organisations such as IMF and World Bank, India introduced the economic reforms in 1991. With the introduction of economic reforms, many restrictions on the industrial sector were removed. Reforms were made in the trade, industrial and financial sector. The fiscal reforms aimed at mobilising private investments to boost the infrastructure growth in India. Reforms in the monetary policy aimed at controlling the inflation rate and ensuring smooth flow of resources to the industrial sector. Foreign trade policy removed several trade restrictions. Therefore, India started heading towards becoming a market oriented economy.

8.3. Meaning and Features of the New Economic Reforms

Economic reforms in India were implemented with the objective of changing the pattern of economic activities in order to liberalise the Indian economy and to accelerate the rate of economic growth. These new economic reforms brought about a structural change in the share of different sectors in the national income. The new economic reform policies mainly focused on structural reforms in agricultural sector, industrial sector, financial sector and global trade. Such economic reforms were possible with the help of broad and comprehensive policies on liberalisation, privatisation and globalisation.

8.3.1. Liberalisation : Meaning and Features

The new economic policy introduced a number of liberalisation measures to remove the unnecessary controls and regulations on the industrial sector. *Liberalisation refers to the removal of restrictions on trade and industry.* The main objective of liberalisation was to unshackle the industrial sector from the cobwebs of unnecessary bureaucratic controls.

The main features of liberalisation policy were :

1. **Abolition of Industrial Licensing** : The new industrial policy of 1991 abolished the industrial licensing for all the industries except for a selected 18 industries due to security and strategic concerns. These included industries manufacturing hazardous chemicals and industries that could cause environmental pollution.

2. **Removal of Restrictions** : All industries, other than those 18, could set up and sell shares without any restrictions, they could expand their business and start a new product line without the need of obtaining any license.

3. **Relaxation of MRTP Restrictions** : The MRTP Act aimed at controlling monopoly practices to prevent concentration of economic power. It also aimed at preventing unfair and restrictive trade practices to protect consumer's interest. Prior to the introduction of reforms, a number of restrictions were imposed on industries with an investment of ₹ 100 crores or more under the Monopolies and Restrictive Trade Practices (MRTP) Act. They had to undergo a pre-entry review for any investment decision. These restrictions were eliminated through the liberalisation policy.

The MRTP Act has now been replaced by the Competition Act, 2002, which came into effect from 2009. The Competition Act checks all anti-competitive practices and prohibits abuse of dominance. In order to protect consumer interest at large, it aims at promoting and sustaining competition in the market.

4. **Foreign Investment** : The 1991 reforms reduced a number of procedural bottlenecks for foreign investments. Approval was given for foreign direct investment up to 51 percent of equity in high priority industries. The liberalisation measures enhanced the investment ceiling on small scale industries. Industries were also allowed to raise investments from abroad with simple procedures.

5. **Foreign Technology** : Automatic approval was provided to Indian industries with respect to foreign technology agreements, especially in the case of high priority industries. Permissions were not required for hiring foreign technicians and experts and for foreign testing of indigenously developed technologies.

All these measures improved the performance of the industrial sector and domestic industries were compelled to become efficient in order to face the competition from industries abroad.

8.3.2. Globalisation : Meaning and Features

Globalisation may be defined as the integration of the domestic economy with the world economy with the objective of facilitating free movement of goods, services, people, ideas, technology etc. It refers to the opening up of the economy to international competition.

The major features of globalisation measures as undertaken in 1991 were :

1. **Reduction of Trade Barriers** : Trade barriers restrict free flow of goods and services between countries. With the introduction of globalisation measures, these restrictions were reduced. Globalisation created an environment for smooth exchange of goods and services between India and other nations. It provided immense opportunities to Indian industries to expand their markets abroad. It also offered Indian consumers a wide variety of quality goods at competitive prices.

The export-import policy announced for the period 1992-97 removed all restrictions on external trade and enhanced the export capabilities of the Indian industries. All the non-tariff barriers were eliminated and the customs duty that was as high as 250 percent was reduced to about 40 percent. As a result, the exports rose from 5.8 percent of the GDP in 1990-91 to about 16 percent of the GDP during 2012-13 and the imports increased from 8.8 percent of the GDP to 27 percent of the GDP during the same period.

2. **Promotion of Foreign Direct Investment** : With the introduction of globalisation, many Indian industries were opened to foreign direct investment. India became a favourable investment destination for foreign investors due to the low cost of production and availability of cheap labour resources. The efficiency of the banking sector also improved because of the competition from foreign banks.

The government of India further initiated a series of measures to promote foreign technical collaborations in case of high priority industries and for import of foreign technology. Foreign Investment Promotion Board (FIPB) was set up to facilitate foreign direct investments in India. The Foreign Direct Investment increased from USD 97 million in 1990-91 to USD 26,953 million in 2012-13.

3. **To Encourage Efficiency** : Globalisation encouraged domestic industries to become more competitive and efficient to face competition at the global level. The domestic industries had to produce quality goods at low cost to compete with the cheaper and superior quality goods of the foreign producers.

4. **Diffusion of Technology** : Globalisation provided an opportunity to India to have an access to global technology. It made diffusion of knowledge faster. India could utilise the technologies of developed countries without much investments in research and development.

The globalisation measures introduced in India acted as an engine of growth enabling access to a wide range of opportunities. These measures paved the way for access to latest technologies. It enlarged employment opportunities and increased labour productivity enabling a large proportion of population to rise above the poverty line.

8.3.3. Privatisation : Meaning and Features

Privatisation refers to the introduction of private ownership in public sector enterprises. The privatisation measures introduced during the economic reforms reduced the number of industries reserved exclusively for public sector from 17 to 8. The government holding in public sector enterprises was sold to increase private participation.

Many public-sector units were incurring losses due to inefficiencies in management and lack of innovation and investments in research and development. Privatisation measures enabled the use of modern technology and improved the quality of service and led to efficient utilisation of resources.

Various privatisation measures introduced in India included :

1. Transfer of ownership of public sector units, either fully or partly, to private hands through denationalisation.

2. Transfer of control to the private sector through disinvestment policies.

3. Opening of areas that were exclusively reserved for public sector.

4. Transfer of management to the private sector through franchising, contracting, and leasing.

5. Limiting the scope of the public sector.

The privatisation wave in India, which was a part of the economic reforms of 1991, increased the role of private sector and restricted the public sector to priority areas which included :

1. Physical and social infrastructure

2. Mining and oil exploration

3. Manufacture of products that were of strategic importance and where security concerns were involved like in the case of manufacture of defence equipment, and

4. Investments in technologies that required huge outlay and where private sector investment was inadequate.

Privatisation measures were introduced in India as part of the economic reforms in 1991 for the following reasons :

1. **To Reduce the Burden of the Government** : The public sector companies created the base for industrial growth in India. However, a number of public sector companies were incurring continuous losses due to delay in completion of projects and rise in cost of production. Many public sector units were only functioning to protect the interests of the labourers. Privatisation offloaded this burden from the government and reduced the strain on resources.

2. **To Promote Efficiency** : Many public sector companies were also struggling due to inefficient management, lack of transparency and corruptive practices. Poor industrial relations and over staffing reduced the productivity, causing losses to these units. Privatisation measures got rid of these problems and enabled the public sector units to achieve optimum productivity.

3. **To Enhance Investment Opportunities** : Privatisation helped in reducing the inconsistencies in management and improved the economic status of many public sector units. This brought in good returns and attracted investments.

4. **To Facilitate Growth of Infrastructure** : Privatisation of industries led to the growth of industrial sector on modern lines. The private enterprises, to provide competitive products and services, initiated and facilitated improvement of the infrastructure.

5. **To Reduce Unnecessary Bureaucratic Interventions** : Privatisation reduced unnecessary government intervention in the management, thereby giving the private enterprises more autonomy in management and operations. This enhanced their efficiency and profitability. Elimination of restrictions effectively reduced corruption and improved productivity.

However, privatisation also had its drawbacks. Some of them are listed below :

1. **Loss of Social Welfare** : Private sector is driven by profit motive and is less oriented towards public welfare and social objectives. This brought about distortions in balanced growth of the economy.

2. **Corruption** : Private sector sometimes tries to bypass government rules and regulations by corruptive practices which reduces economy's welfare.

3. **Lobbying** : Lobbying issues are also commonly observed in private sector enterprises which can affect labour productivity.

4. **Malpractices** : Malpractices in production, supplying low quality goods, manipulation of accounts to evade taxes are common in private enterprises.

5. **High Prices** : Private players also charge high prices for their products, since government subsidies are not applicable to these products, which results in reduced consumer welfare.

Thus, privatisation improve or reduce welfare of the people depending on the actions of its stakeholders. Yet, it has played a significant role in India and has helped in getting rid of conventional bureaucratic policies.

8.4. Disinvestment : Meaning

This is one of the most important strategies adopted by the Government of India as a part of its privatisation measures. Disinvestment is an act by which the government sells its complete or a part of its holding in a public sector unit to the private sector.

The disinvestment policies of the government also enables it to raise huge revenue to finance its fiscal deficit. About ₹ 20,000 crores were raised through disinvestment in public sector units between 1991-92 to 2001-02.

The funds raised through disinvestment are also used :

1. To shut down the industries declared sick by the Board of Industrial and Financial Reconstruction (BIFR) and settle their claims.

2. To restructure and modernise the public sector enterprises.

3. To settle public debt.

The disinvestment policies of the government, by bringing in private participation, improve the efficiency of public sector units by lowering their costs of production. It enables access to modern technology, thus, improving the quality of products and services. Disinvestment can be carried out through public issue of equities to retail investors through Initial Public Offer (IPO).

The Government of India, in its 2017 budget, has set a target of raising ₹ 72,500 crore through disinvestment during the financial year 2017-18.

Summary

1. **Economic Reforms**—Economic reforms in India refer to the structural adjustments that were initiated in 1991 with the aim of liberalising the economy and to accelerate its rate of economic growth.
2. **Need for reforms**—
   (i) Poor performance of the industrial sector
   (ii) Adverse balance of payments
   (iii) Rise in fiscal deficit
   (iv) Inflation
   (v) The gulf war
3. **Causes for Balance of Payments crisis**—
   (i) Rising level of expenditure over revenue
   (ii) Heavy government borrowing
   (iii) Inefficient utilisation of resources
   (iv) Excessive protection to domestic industries
   (v) Inefficient management of public sector enterprises
   (vi) Lack of technological development and innovation
   (vii) Lack of investments in research and development.
4. **MRTP Act**—The MRTP Act was passed in 1969 to control monopoly practices and to prevent concentration of economic power. It also aimed to prevent unfair and restrictive trade practices to protect consumers' interest.
5. **Meaning and Features of the New Economic Reforms**—
   (i) **Liberalisation :** Liberalisation refers to the removal of restrictions on trade and industry.
   (ii) **Globalisation :** Globalisation may be defined as the integration of the domestic economy with the world economy with the objective of facilitating free movement of goods, services, people, ideas, technology etc.
   (iii) **Privatisation :** Privatisation refers to the introduction of private ownership in public sector enterprises.
6. **Liberalisation**—Features
   (i) Abolition of industrial licensing
   (ii) Removal of restrictions
   (iii) Relaxation of MRTP restrictions
   (iv) Foreign investment
   (v) Foreign technology
7. **Globalisation**—Features
   (i) Reduction of trade barriers
   (ii) Promotion of foreign direct investment
   (iii) To encourage efficiency
   (iv) Diffusion of technology

8. **Need for Privatisation—**
   (i) To reduce the burden of the government
   (ii) To promote efficiency
   (iii) To enhance investment opportunities
   (iv) To facilitate growth of infrastructure
   (v) To reduce unnecessary bureaucratic interventions
9. **Drawbacks of privatisation—**
   (i) Loss of social welfare
   (ii) Corruption
   (iii) Lobbying
   (iv) Malpractices
   (v) High prices
10. **Disinvestment—**Disinvestment is an act by which the government sells its complete or a part of its holding in a public sector unit to the private sector.

Exercise

◆ Short Answer Questions (2 marks)

1. What are economic reforms ?
2. When was the new economic policy introduced in India ?
3. Write a short note on the MRTP Act.
4. State any two reasons for introduction of the economic reforms in India.
5. What is liberalisation ?
6. What do you understand by the term globalisation ?
7. Write a brief note on privatisation.
8. Discuss the benefits of privatisation.
9. State any two disadvantages of privatisation.
10. What are the different ways in which a public sector unit be privatised ?
11. What do you understand by the term 'Disinvestment' ?

◆ Long Answer Questions (3-6 marks)

1. Discuss the meaning and features of the new economic reforms.
2. Examine the features of liberalisation.
3. Explain the need for privatisation.
4. Explain the major features of globalisation measures taken by the Indian government.
5. What were the causes that led to the introduction of the economic reforms in India ?
6. Explain the implications of the disinvestment policies of the Government of India.
7. Write a brief note on LPG as drivers of new economic policy.

9 Current Challenges Facing Indian Economy

9.1. Introduction

Indian economy has been one of the largest contributors to global growth over the last decade, accounting for about 10% of the world's increase in economic activity since 2005. Yet, this period has also witnessed a rise in inequality, which has mainly been driven by income gaps between Indian states and a growing urban-rural divide. India continues to have the largest number of poor in the world. With one of the largest and youngest populations in the world, India needs to create millions of jobs in the near future to solve the problems of poverty and unemployment and to ensure decent living conditions for its citizens. To increase employability and productivity of the growing population, India needs to focus on provision of skill based education and quality health care.

Indian agriculture is also plagued by several problems such as low productivity, lack of rural credit, lack of marketing facilities, small and fragmented land holdings, soil erosion etc. This points to the urgent need for the farmers to resort to agricultural diversification and organic farming and for the government to extend credit facilities to the rural areas and take measures to improve marketability of agricultural products.

This chapter provides an insight into a few of these kinds of challenges faced by the Indian economy, their causes and the steps taken by the government to resolve those challenges.

9.2. Poverty

One of the major problems faced by the developing countries of the world is the problem of poverty and India is no exception. Poverty is a phenomenon in which a section of the community is unable to fulfil its requirements to attain a decent standard of living. Poverty can be as extreme as lack of necessities such as food, clothing, and shelter that are essential to sustain life or it could be a situation in which a person's standard of living is lower than that of others in the community. Thus, economists distinguish between two types of poverty—absolute poverty and relative poverty.

9.2.1. Absolute and Relative Poverty

Absolute poverty is a situation in which a person is unable to fulfil her/his basic requirements of food, clothing, shelter, basic education and health. A person, to live a healthy life, must consume a certain quantity of food and must have a decent housing condition with access to drinking water, sanitation facilities and decent clothing that protects him in different weather conditions. When income acts as a constraint in having access to these necessities, the person is said to be absolutely poor.

Relative poverty is a measure of the extent of inequality prevalent in a country. It is expressed in terms of income and standard of living of others living in the same community at the same point of time. When a small section of the community gets a larger share of income, it leads to inequality in the distribution of income. People are said to be relatively poor when their income and standard of living is lesser than the average level of the society.

Poverty in any country is measured with the help of poverty line. Poverty line is the minimum level of income that is considered adequate for a person to sustain her/his living. The World Bank has set the international poverty line as USD 1.90 per day in October 2015, increasing it from USD 1.25 per day earlier. Thus, a person who lives on less than USD 1.90 per day is considered as poor. According to the report of the World Bank in 2013, 767 million people, which are about 10.7 percent of the world's population were estimated to be living in poverty. This poverty line is determined in terms of Purchasing Power Parity (PPP) which refers to the amount required in a country to buy the same quantity of goods as 1 USD can buy in the USA. PPP enables comparison of income and consumption across countries. It ensures that the same quantity of goods are priced uniformly across countries.

In India, the poverty line was defined based on nutritional requirements. The Indian Council of Medical Research has recommended a calorie intake of 2400 calories per person per day in rural areas and 2100 calories per person per day in urban areas. This requirement is converted to monetary terms to determine the poverty line. In India, the expert recommendations are taken from time to time to estimate the poverty line. An expert group under Professor Suresh D. Tendulkar computed the poverty line and submitted its report in 2009. The Tendulkar Committee prescribed the benchmark expenditure as ₹ 27 per person per day for rural areas and ₹ 33 per person per day in urban areas. Later, Rangarajan committee, set up in 2012, raised the poverty line to ₹ 32 per person per day for rural areas and ₹ 47 per person per day for urban areas. At present, a 14 member task force under Arvind Panagariya, the Vice Chairman of NITI Aayog, has been assigned the task of coming up with realistic poverty line estimates.

9.2.2. Vicious Circle of Poverty

India is at present, entangled in the vicious circle of pvoerty. Vicious circle of poverty means that the poverty is both the cause and the effect. This vicious circle of poverty in India starts with the poverty and ends at poverty. Due to the poverty, the standard of living of the people is low so people are not able to meet their basic needs as a result their efficiency become low. The low efficiency decreases the level of productivity and output as a result the low level of productivity brings the level of income down and because of low level of income the workers are not able to get appropriate wages which further increases the poverty in the country. Thus, it becomes a vicious cirle. This vicious circle is explained in Fig. 9.1

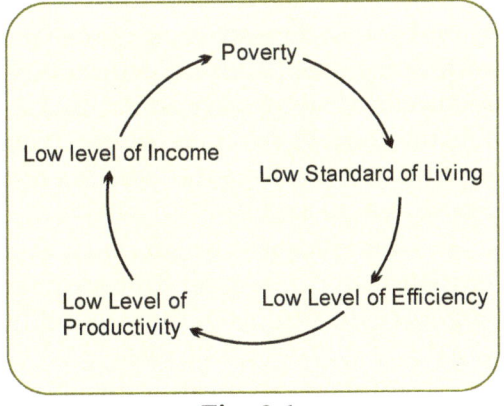

Fig. 9.1

9.2.3. Causes of Poverty

The causes of poverty are multi-dimensional. Poverty is one of the root cause of many evils in the society and is the biggest challenge facing India today. The major causes of poverty are as follows :

1. **Low Level of Income** : The income level of less developed countries like India is generally lower than that of the advanced countries. When the national income is low, the per capita income is also low. According to the estimates of the World Bank, the per capita income of US in 2015 was $ 56,166, whereas that of India was $ 6101. Low level of income restricts people's access to various resources and therefore, people with low income levels dwell in poor conditions.

2. **Inequality in the Distribution of Income** : Unequal distribution of income is another major cause of poverty. In India, there exists wide disparity in the distribution of income. When economic growth is not equally distributed, it results in rising inequality. One of the major causes of the unequal distribution of income is unequal distribution of assets. Large proportion of assets are concentrated in the hands of few rich people. In less developed countries, approximately 20 percent of the population own and control over 90 percent of the resources, whereas about 80 percent of the population own only 10 percent of the assets. As a result, the rich becomes richer and the poor becomes poorer.

3. **Rapid Rise in Population** : High growth of population brings down the per capita income. Higher the population, higher is the burden on the government to feed the growing population and ensure that they have access to necessities. Therefore, a large amount of productive resources gets diverted towards meeting the basic requirements of the people.

4. **Poor Agricultural Productivity** : In developing countries like India, a large proportion of the population is dependent on agriculture and when agricultural productivity is low, it results in poverty. Exploitation of the agricultural labourers by the rich landlords, lack of agricultural credit and crop insurance, poor irrigation facilities, lack of access to modern agricultural techniques etc., are some of the causes for low productivity in agriculture.

5. **Lack of Investments** : Investments are required for industrial expansion and for the development of infrastructure. When the income level of the people is low, the savings are also low. Savings are an important source of investments and when savings are low, investment does not take place. When investments are low, productivity is low and employment level is low. This, in turn, leads to low income and thereby the poor are caught in a vicious cycle of poverty.

6. **Unemployment** : This is another major cause of poverty. Due to rapid increase in population in developing countries like India, there exists chronic unemployment. When people are unemployed, they do not have the income to fulfil even their basic needs and they dwell in poor conditions.

7. **Illiteracy** : Education increases the earning capacity of the people. The literacy rates are generally low in developing countries. When people are illiterate, their employability is also low. Unemployment, in turn, leads to low income and lower standard of living.

8. **Poor Health Care** : Poverty is a situation where the basic needs of the people remain unfulfilled. People living in poverty do not have adequate nourishment to lead a healthy life. When health is affected, their productivity is also affected. And when productivity is affected, income is affected. The poor in developing countries live in inhumane housing conditions and lack access to sanitation facilities that are required for basic hygiene. This has a huge impact on their health conditions. The diseases and ailments make even the middle-income group vulnerable to poverty.

9. **Underutilisation of Resources** : Some of the African countries like Ghana, Uganda, Mozambique, etc., are rich in natural resources. But they are underdeveloped and a large proportion of the population in these countries live under extreme poverty. This is because they lack adequate investments to utilise their resources efficiently. Poor governance, corruption, colonial exploitation can also be cited as some of the reasons as to why many resource rich countries like India are poor.

10. **Social Factors** : Traditions, customs, caste system and dogmatic beliefs also hinder growth and intensify the problem of poverty. In India, for instance, children are considered as an asset and poor people tend to have more children as they are considered as an additional source of income. Early marriages also lead to a rapid rise in population. Further, women have been deprived of their rights for very long. As a result, the literacy rate is low among women and their income earning potential is also low.

11. **Political Factors** : Many less developed and developing countries were under the colonial rule for many years and were serving the interests of the advanced nations. For instance, India was under the colonial rule of the British for nearly two centuries. During their rule, the British exploited India's natural resources to meet their industrial requirements. This has been a major cause for poor industrial development in India. Political instability, corruptive practices, administrative inefficiency, poor planning, etc., have all aggravated the problem of poverty in India.

9.2.4. Poverty Alleviation Programmes

Poverty alleviation has been one of the most important objectives of the five-year plans. The Government of India through its five-year plans has announced several schemes and programmes to alleviate poverty. The most important among them are :

1. **Integrated Rural Development Programme (IRDP)** : IRDP was launched in India in 1978. It aimed at providing self-employment opportunities to rural poor through the acquisition of productive assets that could generate sufficient income. It is a centrally sponsored scheme and assistance is provided in the form of subsidies and bank credit. The programme provides 25 percent subsidy to small farmers, 33.3 percent subsidy to marginal farmers and 50 percent subsidy to families belonging to Scheduled Castes and Scheduled Tribes for acquiring capital assets. The IRDP has been successful in providing additional income to a number of poor families. Yet, the major constraint is the lack of productive investment opportunities and adequate marketing infrastructure for agricultural products. The programme has also been criticised with respect to the selection of families for assistance.

2. **Training of Rural Youth for Self-Employment (TRYSEM)** : This is another employment generation programme launched in 1979 that aims at providing technical

and entrepreneurial skills to the rural poor in the age group of 18 to 35 years to enable them to take up entrepreneurship. The programme provides specialised training through recognised ITIs and polytechnics. An evaluation of the programme revealed that there was a mismatch in the job skills in 53.3 percent of the districts studied. It was also observed that many of them who underwent training under the programme remained unemployed. Only a small proportion of beneficiaries took up self-employment. Lack of funds for investment and inadequate credit facilities could also be cited as reasons for failure of the programme.

3. **Development of Women and Children in Rural Areas (DWCRA)** : This programme was introduced as a component of IRDP in 1982-83. It aims at the betterment of the living conditions of the poor women and children in rural areas. It provides access to employment opportunities, skill acquisition, training and credit facilities to the poor women. It also aims at making them self-reliant by promoting the habit of thrift among rural women. The programme also provides child care facilities to the beneficiary women. The programme, however, suffered from several shortcomings such as lack of adequate funds, lack of productive investments, inadequate training and staffing etc.

4. **Jawahar Rozgar Yojana (JRY)** : JRY was launched on April 1, 1989 by merging National Rural Employment Programme (NREP) and Rural Landless Employment Guarantee Programme (RLEGP). The main objective of this programme was to provide gainful employment to the unemployed rural poor. Due to lack of adequate funds, however, the scheme could only generate very few jobs. JRY was re-launched in April 1999 as Jawahar Gram Samridhi Yojana (JGSY) with the objective of creating assets and infrastructure in the villages. It was again not successful due to inadequate funds and corruption. Later, from September 25, 2001, Jawahar Gram Samridhi Yojna was merged with Sampoorna Grameen Rozgar Yojana.

5. **Employment Assurance Scheme (EAS)** : EAS was launched on October 02, 1993 and was meant for the drought prone, desert, hilly and tribal areas of the country. It aimed at providing employment opportunities during the lean season. The National Food for Work Programme, which was started in 2004 as part of the EAS programme, provided wages in the form of food grains to the poor and unemployed. All these programmes were merged to form Sampoorna Gramin Rozgar Yojana (SGRY) in 2001. The programme aimed at creating community assets, establishing infrastructure and providing food security to the rural poor.

6. **Swaranajayanti Gram Swarozgar Yojana (SGSY)** : Due to various shortcomings, IRDP was replaced by SGSY in 1999. The million wells scheme and the DWCRA were merged into the SGSY scheme. The SGSY organised the poor into self-help groups and provided credit facilities to set up micro enterprises. The scheme also supported irrigation projects by way of subsidies.

7. **Pradhan Mantri Gramodaya Yojana (PMGY)** : PMGY launched in 2000-01, aimed at providing primary health care, education, drinking water and electricity in rural areas. Shelter being one of the basic requirements, PMGY provides housing with sanitation facilities to the rural poor.

8. **Rural Employment Generation Programme Opportunities (REGP)** : This was introduced in 1995 with the objective of creating self-employment opportunities in rural

areas. The Khadi and Village Industries Commission (KVIC) is involved in the implementation of this programme. Under this scheme, assistance is provided in the form of bank loans to set up village industries.

9. **Prime Minister's Rozgar Yojana (PMRY)** : This is another programme introduced in 1993 to provide self-employment opportunities to the educated unemployed youth whose family income is less than ₹ 40,000. Assistance is provided in the form of soft loans to educated youth to set up village industries.

10. **National Food for Work Programme (FWP)** : This programme was launched by the Central Government in 2004, as part of the EAS programme, in 150 most backward districts of India. It was a centrally sponsored scheme that provided unskilled labour work to the poor. The wages were paid in the form of food grains. The States had a major responsibility in implementing this scheme.

11. **Mahatma Gandhi National Rural Employment Guarantee Programme** : In 2004, the UPA Government, under Prime Minister Dr. Manmohan Singh, passed the National Rural Employment Guarantee Bill and National Rural Employment Guarantee Act (NREGA) was enacted in September 2005. The programme was renamed as Mahatma Gandhi National Rural Employment Guarantee Act (MGNREGA) on October 02, 2009. The act aims at enhancing the lives of the rural poor by providing them 100 days of guaranteed employment during a financial year. The programme considers employment as a right. The rural poor can, therefore, demand employment. The demand must be fulfilled within 15 days by the government officials. In the event of failure to provide employment, an unemployment allowance should be given. The programme aims at providing employment opportunities by building rural infrastructure through watershed development, tanks, canals, land development, prevention of soil erosion, construction of roads etc. MGNREGA has, however, been subjected to severe criticism for corrupt practices with respect to the payment of wages and creation of assets. It also restricts the employment to just 100 days which is insufficient to meet the requirements of the rural poor.

9.2.5. Causes for Poor Performance of the Poverty Alleviation Programmes (PAP)

It should be noted that several poverty alleviation programmes implemented to address the problem of poverty have been able to achieve only limited success. A number of causes could be cited for poor performance of these programmes. Some of them include :

1. **Poor Administration of the Programmes due to Inefficient Staffing** : The staffing is highly inadequate to administer the implementation of the various poverty alleviation programmes. Lack of adequate staff on the field leads to the problems of poor management, lack of accountability, poor monitoring of the work progress etc.

2. **Lack of Adequate Support in the Form of Credit and Marketing Facilities** : Some of the poverty alleviation programmes aim at imparting entrepreneurial skills to the unemployed poor. However, they do not ensure availability of credit and marketing facilities. Many poor farmers lack access to organised credit sources. Lack of access to credit and support for marketing results in exploitation of the poor by money lenders and other middlemen.

3. **Deficiencies in Planning and Implementation** : The programmes are centrally designed and planned by the officials belonging to the elite class who have no understanding of the problems at the grassroots. Planning is done without taking into consideration the size of the population and the incidence of poverty.

4. **Inadequate Investments** : The poverty alleviation programmes lack sustainability due to inadequate investments. Heavy investments in infrastructural support services such as electricity and water supply increases the operating cost. Due to lack of adequate funds, many facilities are abandoned and the work is also left unfinished. This has been the most prominent reason for closure of many programmes in the past.

5. **Corruptive Practices in Implementation** : Some of the poverty alleviation programmes are implemented merely for gaining victory in elections rather than for improving the welfare of the people. When poverty alleviation programmes are driven by self-interest, it results in corrupt practices in administration. There is a violation of material and labour norms and there are malpractices in choice of beneficiaries and in the record of works carried out under the programmes.

6. **Lack of Proper Mechanism for Identification of the Beneficiaries** : The identification of the beneficiaries in many cases is based on the Below Poverty Line (BPL) list maintained at the local offices. These lists are not updated and the poverty alleviation programmes sometimes benefit the non-poor due to wrong identification of beneficiaries.

7. **Lack of Community Participation** : Many poverty alleviation programmes are inappropriately designed due to the lack of involvement of beneficiaries in planning and implementation. When there is no community participation, people lack awareness about various poverty alleviation programmes.

8. **High Dependence on Subsidies** : Subsidies are highly inefficient as they do not always reach the intended beneficiaries. Subsidised products are generally misused as they are considered free by the recipients. Further, they also impose a heavy financial burden on the government.

9.3. Rural Development

Because of being an agrarian economy, a large proportion of India's population live in the rural areas. According to Census 2011, the rural population in India is about 68.84 percent. Yet, agriculture accounts for only 14 percent of India's GDP. Further, there also exists a wide disparity between rural and urban areas in terms of growth, infrastructure, and other socio-economic factors. Rural areas are always at a disadvantage when it comes to economic development. Therefore, economic policies in India attach a high priority to rural development.

The term 'Rural Development' refers to improving the lives of the rural people. It includes land reforms, provision of infrastructural facilities, creation of employment opportunities, credit facilities, education and health care facilities, drinking water, sanitation, electricity and so on. Most of the poverty alleviation programmes launched in India aim at improving the lives of the rural poor. They provide financial assistance to the rural poor in the form of subsidies and credit. The poor in rural areas do not have access to organised credit facilities and are, therefore, largely dependent on unscrupulous money lenders, who charge exorbitant rates of interest. Thus, the rural poor get caught in a debt trap from which they cannot escape.

9.3.1. Rural Credit

In agriculture, there is always a time gap between incurring an expenditure and in getting returns from farm produce. The need for implementing modern agricultural technology for efficient production also brings in the need for credit facilities. But there are a number of problems in extending credit facilities to the rural poor. Some of these challenges are listed below :

1. **High Risk** : Since the repayment and recovery rates are poor, there is a high risk involved in lending to the rural poor. Further, the rural communities are so poor that they do not own any assets that can be mortgaged for security purposes. This reduces their credibility and access to organised credit markets. As a result, they resort to borrowing from private money lenders who are willing to lend without any security but at exorbitant rates of interest.

2. **Illiteracy** : Many rural poor are illiterate and are, therefore, reluctant to go through complicated procedures of the banks and other organised lending institutions to obtain loans. Lack of administrative support forces them to seek help from money lenders at the local level.

3. **Insufficient Credit** : The amount of credit that currently flows from the organised institutions to rural areas is highly insufficient to meet their requirements due to the increase in the prices of various agricultural inputs.

4. **Unproductive Expenditure** : The credit provided to the rural poor is sometimes spent for unproductive expenditures. It is sometimes spent on occasions like wedding or for consumption. And over a period of time, the poor are unable to repay the borrowed sum.

5. **Lack of Adequate Banking Infrastructure** : Many rural areas are highly inaccessible due to the lack of adequate transportation infrastructure. Banks cannot be set up at these remote locations and thereby, these areas do not have access to the banking infrastructure. The number of banks located in rural areas is very minimal and they fail to cover the entire rural community. Some of these banks extend credit facilities to the rich farmers and ignore the needs of the poor and marginalised farmers.

6. **Red Tapism** : The cumbersome procedures involved in accessing organised credit facilities paves the way for corruptive practices. Therefore, the rural people are dependent on non-institutional sources of credit even though they are expensive.

It may, thus, be inferred that the rural poor do not have adequate access to organised credit markets due to complicated procedures and lack of security for borrowing. Thus, they resort to non-institutional sources of credit such as landlords and private money lenders. Later, they become subjects of exploitation by the money lenders. This necessitates expansion of institutional credit facilities to rural areas. Following are the institutions which are helping in extending the credit facilities to the rural areas :

1. **Co-operative Credit Institutions :** The cooperative credit institutions in rural areas enable pooling of resources and providing the same to their members for various productive purposes. The co-operative credit institutions provide long-term credit facilities for agriculture. Primary Agricultural Credit (PAC) Societies were set up at grass root level to provide short term credit facilities to agriculturists. PACs are generally dependent on the finances provided by the central cooperative banks. Commercial banks also finance these PACs. The cooperative credit institutions have played a significant role in :

(i) Providing credit facilities to peasants at low rates of interest and relieving them from the clutches of exploitative money lenders.

(ii) They have enabled the farmers to access improved agricultural technology such as the high yielding variety of seeds, manures, fertilizers and other farm equipments.

(iii) They have also played a major role in alleviating poverty in rural areas.

(iv) They train their members to make productive use of resources.

(v) They have also promoted a habit of thrift among peasants and discouraged them from spending recklessly on marriages and other ceremonies.

However, it has been observed that today, many of these PACs are merely serving as outlets for public distribution system. Their role has shrunk due to bureaucratic controls and accumulated losses due to poor recovery.

2. **Regional Rural Banks :** Regional Rural Banks were established under the Regional Rural Banks Act, 1976. They provide loans to small and marginal farmers, agricultural labourers and artisans. The main objective of setting up RRBs is to provide financial facilities for development of agriculture and other productive activities in rural areas. The performance of the RRBs, however, has not been quite satisfactory due to poor recovery rates. Many sponsoring banks had their own branches in rural areas and the revenue earning capacity of the RRBs was very poor due to various restrictions placed on them. The government, therefore, initiated a reform process of the RRBs in 2004, as a result of which the performance of the RRBs improved after 2010.

3. **National Bank for Agriculture and Rural Development (NABARD) :** NABARD was set up on July 12, 1982, to cater to the need for institutional credit in rural areas. With the NABARD coming into existence, the agricultural credit functions of the RBI were transferred to NABARD. The NABARD has been set up as an apex development bank for agricultural credit and it aims at financial empowerment of the rural poor. It was set up with an initial corpus fund of ₹ 100 crores. NABARD plays a very important role in rural development in the following ways :

(i) It provides financial assistance to cottage, small scale and village industries in rural areas.

(ii) It aims at integrated rural development.

(iii) It finances development projects in rural areas.

(iv) It monitors and evaluates development projects.

(v) It refinances financial institutions involved in rural credit.

(vi) It facilitates training of institutions involved in rural development and in provision of rural credit.

(vii) It also regulates cooperative banks and the regional rural banks. That means, it acts as a regulator of institutions associated with rural credit.

(viii) It provides short term, medium term and long term credit facilities to state co-operative banks and RRBs.

(ix) It provides long term loans to State Governments to finance the share capital of co-operative credit societies.

(x) It coordinates the functions of Central and State Governments in the development of small scale industries, village industries and cottage industries.

(xi) NABARD also promotes research in agriculture and rural development.

4. **Land Development Banks :** These banks provide long term loans to farmers for a period of 15 to 20 years, against the mortgage of their lands. The interest rates are generally very low and are beneficial to farmers, especially when huge investments are to be made in the farm. These banks provide loans only against the mortgage of land and hence, rich farmers holding large acres of land get benefitted more than the poor farmers. Therefore, the role of these banks has become quite insignificant and many people in rural areas are unaware of their existence.

5. **Commercial Banks :** Commercial banks extend credit facilities in rural areas by setting up their branches in these areas. They also have a responsibility to lend to the agricultural sector apart from catering to the urban financial needs. However, they are not actively involved in rural credit due to the high risk involved in lending to this sector. Many commercial banks at present are suffering losses due to the waiver of agricultural loans by the government.

9.3.2. Agricultural Marketing

Access to marketing infrastructure has been one of the major challenges faced by the Indian agricultural sector. In India, the farmers are unable to wait for a long period to sell their crops after the harvest as they must honour their debt obligations and lack of adequate storage facilities also makes it difficult to store the produce for a longer period. These factors force them to sell their produce at unremunerative prices. Many farmers sell their produce to the moneylenders and landlords at very low prices to settle their debts. The middlemen also exploit the poor farmers by taking a large share of the revenue earned from the sell of the produce. It is, therefore, essential to develop the physical infrastructure for marketing of agricultural produce. Setting up of regulated markets which eliminate middlemen and provision of warehousing facilities for storage are essential components of agricultural marketing infrastructure.

In India, the Commission for Agricultural Costs and Prices, Food Corporation of India, and specialised marketing bodies set up for cotton, jute, tea, coffee, tobacco, spices, etc., facilitate marketing of agricultural commodities. Grading and standardisation enhance the marketability of the agricultural products. Access to better transportation facilities enables movement of goods at low cost. Financial assistance for marketing also help the poor peasants in finding suitable markets for their produce.

9.3.3. Cooperative Marketing

Cooperative marketing is an arrangement by which the individual farmers organise themselves into cooperative societies for marketing their commodities. They pool the entire produce and sell it together and the sale proceeds are shared by the individual members in proportion to their contribution to the total produce. Cooperatives protect the farmers from selling the produce at unremunerative prices to landlords and money lenders. It also increases the bargaining capacity of the farmers and helps in stabilisation of prices. The National Agricultural Cooperative Marketing Federation of India Ltd. (NAFED) acts as an apex institution in India for marketing of agricultural produce. It was set up on October 02, 1958 and now acts as the largest procurement and marketing agency for agricultural products. It has established the National Spot Exchange and Commodities Exchange to promote trading in agricultural commodities.

The cooperative marketing system in India, at present, faces a number of challenges. Many marketing societies are not actively engaged in agricultural marketing. Farmers are still dependent on middlemen at many places for marketing their produce. The cooperative marketing societies, thus, have to be strengthened and equipped to play an active role in agricultural marketing. Research and development should also be encouraged to bring in innovative facilities that support agricultural marketing.

9.3.4. Agricultural Diversification

Agricultural diversification refers to the transformation from the traditional single crop cultivation to the production of a variety of crops to meet the current demand and to overcome the risks associated with agriculture. Agricultural diversification also refers to a shift from farm based activities to non-farm based activities. The increase in the production of fruits and vegetables and organic cereals, development of horticulture, sericulture, poultry farming and fisheries would help in agricultural diversification. The benefits that could be achieved through agricultural diversification are as follows :

1. Food security
2. Increase in the income of rural people
3. Generation of employment opportunities
4. Increase in agricultural productivity
5. Promotion of agricultural exports
6. Increased contribution of agriculture to India's GDP
7. Sustainability of agriculture

9.3.5. Organic Farming

Organic farming refers to the production of food commodities without the use of chemicals such as pesticides, fungicides, chemical fertilizers, etc. The green revolution, introduced in India in 1960s, recommended the use of these manufactured chemicals for increasing agricultural productivity. But, India has now realized the fact that such technologies are not sustainable in the long run as these technologies pose a threat to environment and life. This has necessitated a shift to organic farming which is considered appropriate for ecological stability. Organic farming method uses organic wastes such as crop, animal and agricultural wastes that would retain soil health. It combines modern technology with traditional farming practices. India holds a unique position among all the countries in organic farming. Indian organic exports have also been growing rapidly. However, lack of organic products across all food categories is a matter of concern. There is an immediate need to create awareness among farmers about organic farming and its prospects. This would conserve biodiversity and make agriculture sustainable.

9.4. Human Resources

Human beings are considered as both the means and an end to development. This is because the production of various goods and services is undertaken to fulfil the consumption needs of human beings. At the same time, these goods and services cannot be produced without human beings. The economic development of any country is also determined by the quality of its human resources. Economic growth requires both, physical capital and human capital. While physical capital refers to land, machinery, investments, etc., human capital refers to the knowledge, skills and health condition of human beings. Health and education are generally considered as human capital. Unlike physical capital, human capital never gets exhausted with use. It is priceless and difficult to quantify.

9.4.1. Role of Human Capital in Economic Development

Human capital plays a significant role in economic growth and development. Human capital contributes to economic development in the following ways :

1. Education and skills contribute to increased productivity, thereby, increasing the output.

2. Human capital enhances the quality of goods and services produced in an economy.

3. It increases the employability of people, thereby, increasing the income earning capacity of the individuals.

4. When a country's human resources are healthy, it reduces the financial burden on the country.

5. Better health also contributes to increased productivity.

6. Adoption of new technologies becomes easier when people are educated and skilled.

7. Educated people behave with civic sense, adopt small family norms and practice hygiene. They also recognise the importance of savings, which is essential for investment in the country.

9.5. Education Sector in India

Education is one of the most important components of human capital. The advanced countries of the world have achieved much progress due to their educated population.

Both public and the private sector play a major role in providing education in India. According to Census 2011, literacy rate in India was 74.4 percent with Kerala having the highest literacy rate of 94.65 percent. There has been a tremendous increase in the literacy rate from 64.84 percent during Census 2001 and 52.21 percent during Census 1991. India has more than 1.4 million schools and 36000 higher education institutions. The gross enrolment ratio for class 1 to 12 has increased from 55.8 percent in 2001 to 84.5 percent in 2011-12. The government expenditure on school education as a percentage of GDP has increased from 2.2 percent in 2006 to 2.68 percent in 2013. This is meager in comparison to 6 percent of GDP spent by advanced countries.

Several initiatives have been taken by the government to improve the literacy rates in India. The most prominent among them are :

1. **Sarva Siksha Abhiyan (SSA)** : This programme aims at universalisation of elementary education and is in operation since 2000–2001. It aims at providing free and compulsory education to children between 6 to 14 years of age. This programme plays a significant role in opening of new schools and provision of alternate schooling facilities, construction of schools and additional classrooms, construction of toilets, provision of drinking water, provision of free text books and uniforms, provisioning for teachers and so on.

2. **Mid-day Meal Scheme** : National Programme of Nutritional Support to Primary Education (NP-NSPE), popularly known as the 'mid-day meal', was launched on August 15, 1995 with the objective of increasing the enrolment rates in schools and for reducing the number of school drop outs. Under the mid-day meal scheme, the students enrolled in the primary government schools and government aided primary schools are provided cooked mid-day meals with a minimum content of 300 calories of energy and 8 to 12 grams of proteins per day for atleast 200 days. In October 2007, it was extended to cover children in upper primary classes and the scheme was renamed as 'National Programme of Mid-Day Meal in Schools'.

3. **Rashtriya Madhyamik Shiksha Abhiyan (RMSA)** : This scheme was launched in March 2009 to enhance the access to secondary education and to improve the quality of education at secondary level. The programme also aims at eliminating gender disparity and other socio economic barriers, ensuring universal access to secondary education by 2017 and at achieving universal retention by 2020. The scheme makes provision for construction of additional class rooms, laboratories, libraries, art and craft rooms, toilets, drinking water facilities and hostels for teachers in remote areas.

4. **National Programme for Education of Girls at Elementary Level (NPEGEL)** : This programme is targeted at the girls who are not enrolled in schools. The programme was launched in 2003 and it supports investment in girls' education. It also provides for setting up of model schools and supervision of girls enrolment. Development of gender sensitive learning materials, provision of need based incentives such as sports, stationery, uniforms, etc., are other highlights of the programme.

5. **Kasturba Gandhi Balika Vidhyalaya (KGBV)** : This scheme, introduced in August 2004, aimed at providing education to girls belonging to Scheduled Castes, Scheduled Tribes, backward classes, and minorities. KGBV aims at providing quality education and at making it accessible to girls belonging to the underprivileged sections

of the society. It also makes provision for setting up residential schools at the elementary level with boarding facilities.

6. **Rashtriya Uchchatar Shiksha Abhiyan (RUSA)** : This is a centrally sponsored scheme launched in 2013. It aims at improving the quality of the institutions functioning in the states and at ensuring that they conform to the norms and standards prescribed and also adopt accreditation process. It also undertakes initiatives to bring about reforms in the higher education system to promote the autonomy of the state universities and to improve the governance in the institutions. Upgradation of existing autonomous colleges to universities, infrastructure grants to universities, setting up of new model colleges, research development and quality improvement, faculty recruitment support, vocationalisation of higher education, institutional restructuring and reforms, capacity building etc., are some of the important features of RUSA.

While the formal education is a class room based education provided by trained teachers, informal education is also being provided in India. Informal education takes place outside the class rooms with the support of community-based organisations. Education is provided to people of various age groups through informal education system. Mass media plays a significant role in informal education system. Some of the recent initiatives in the education sector include introduction of Information and Communication Technologies, digitisation of books and materials, usage of multimedia in private schools and colleges, introduction of virtual classrooms wherein lectures are delivered through pre-recorded and live videos. The major focus of all these initiatives is to improve the quality of education in the country and to ensure that education facilities are accessible to all. While the economy is transforming from being a resource based economy to a knowledge based economy, the biggest challenge lies in restructuring the education system to meet the requirements of the global environment.

9.6. Unemployment

Unemployment refers to a situation in which a person who is willing to work and has the capability to work is unable to find a productive job. It is a situation which leads to the wastage of the productive manpower, poverty, poor health, low self-esteem and depression among the unemployed. Increased crime in the society is also a repercussion of widespread unemployment. Unemployment can be classified into various categories :

1. **Voluntary Unemployment** : This is a situation in which a person is unwilling to work at the prevailing wage rate despite the availability of jobs.

2. **Structural Unemployment** : This occurs when the economy is undergoing a structural change. Due to economic progress, when the demand for products change, some industries may shut down leading to unemployment of workers in that industry. For instance, many employees of blackberry became unemployed due to lower demand for blackberry phones after the introduction of smartphones.

3. **Frictional Unemployment** : This is a phenomenon in which a person remains unemployed for a short period of time in the course of switching from one job to another. This could happen due to lack of information about the availability of jobs, lack of mobility, etc.

4. **Seasonal Unemployment** : As the name suggests, this is a kind of unemployment in which a person remains unemployed for a particular season. This is more prevalent in the agricultural sector where many farmers remain unemployed during the lean season.

5. **Cyclical Unemployment** : This is the unemployment that arises due to business cycles. When the economy is prosperous, there is generally a rise in the employment opportunities whereas when there is a recession or depression, employment rate falls.

6. **Disguised Unemployment** : This refers to a situation in which the productivity of the worker is zero or negative. When the number of workers engaged in a job is more than the actual numbers required, it results in disguised unemployment. For instance, in case of family agriculture, the entire family may be engaged in agricultural activity and if one or two members leave, the output will not get affected.

9.6.1. Causes of Unemployment

Unemployment is caused due to the following reasons :

1. **Slow Rate of Economic Growth** : When the economic growth is slow, the output increases at a very slow rate and so does the employment opportunities. Slow growth rate, therefore, cannot generate adequate employment opportunities.

2. **Seasonal Nature of Agriculture** : In case of agricultural sector, many farmers remain unemployed during the lean season.

3. **Population Growth** : Rapid growth in population also leads to unemployment. Employment growth rate may become inadequate to provide jobs to the growing population.

4. **Low Levels of Savings and Investment** : To create employment opportunities, investments have to be made in productive activities. Many industries have to be set up and investments have to be made in agricultural and allied activities. However, investments become difficult when the rate of savings is low. Poor countries are generally trapped in vicious cycle of poverty where low levels of savings leads to low investments, low capital formation, low productivity and low income which, in turn, leads to low savings.

5. **Loss of Cottage and Small Scale Industries** : With the introduction of economic reforms in 1991, many cottage and small scale industries faced stiff competition from the foreign producers. Many such industries were forced to shut down after continued losses due to lack of demand.

6. **Rural-Urban Migration** : People in rural areas migrate to urban areas looking for better education and employment opportunities. Poor performance of agriculture also force many farmers to migrate to urban areas looking for casual work. When people migrate in large numbers to the urban areas, it leads to the problem of unemployment.

7. **Poor Quality of Human Capital** : Generally, poor people do not have access to education and proper health facilities due to lack of resources. Deficiency in health and education acts as a hindrance in finding productive employment opportunities. Further, the present education system fails to impart skill based education, which again affects the employability of a person.

9.6.2. Policy Measures to Address Unemployment

Indian Government has been initiating several programmes *(discussed already under poverty alleviation programmes)* from time to time to address the problem of unemployment. Yet, the average rate of unemployment has been around 7 percent. It reached a record low of 4.9% in 2013. Some of the strategies that could be adopted to address the problem of unemployment are :

1. **Development of Rural Infrastructure** : The problem of unemployment in rural areas could be addressed by investment in rural infrastructure. Laying of roads, assistance for setting up of cottage and small scale industries, investments in agriculture for modernisation of the sector, waste land management, diversification of agricultural activities can boost the employment opportunities in rural areas.

2. **Expansion of Agricultural Allied Sectors** : This includes development of dairy farming, poultry, horticulture, sericulture, fisheries, and other non-farm activities to generate productive employment opportunities in rural areas.

3. **Control of Population** : Population growth is one of the major causes for prevalence of unemployment. There is a need to create awareness about family planning measures and benefits of a small family through family welfare programmes to control population growth.

4. **Industrial Development** : Investments should be made to modernise the industrial sector in urban areas. New industries that have a high potential of creating large scale employment should be set up.

5. **Encouragement to Self-employment** : The government should also encourage individuals through financial assistance and technical training, to set up their own enterprises. This would help in creating large employment opportunities apart from the individuals becoming self-reliant.

6. **Development of Small Scale Industries** : Small scale industries should be supported and provided with necessary financial assistance to compete at the global level.

7. **Reforms in the Education Sector** : The current education system should be reformed and skill based education should be introduced to enhance employability of people.

8. **Revamping of Existing Programmes** : The existing poverty alleviation and employment generation programmes should be revamped and made more efficient. Corruptive practices should be eliminated by carrying out social audit periodically. This would also address the problem of wastage of resources.

9. **Efficient planning** : At present, there exists a large gap between the availability of jobs and the number of people trained for these jobs. This could be eliminated by efficient manpower planning where a forecast is made on the future requirements of various skills and enrolment of students in different fields of education should be based on such predictions.

It may, thus, be noted that the challenges faced India are multifaceted with one leading to the other. A proper planning mechanism that could bring about balanced development of all sectors is essential to overcome these challenges. While the planners earlier believed that economic growth will slowly trickle down to those at the bottom level of income, they have been disproved by the problems that the Indian economy face today. Thus, alternative strategies need to be developed and adopted to overcome these challenges efficiently.

Summary

1. **Poverty**—Poverty is a phenomenon in which a section of the community is unable to fulfil its requirements to attain a decent standard of living.
2. **Absolute Poverty**—Absolute poverty is a situation in which a person is unable to fulfil her/his basic requirements of food, clothing, shelter, basic education and health.
3. **Relative Poverty**—Relative poverty is a situation in which a person's standard of living is lower than that of others in the community.
4. **Causes of Poverty**—
    (i) Low level of income
    (ii) Inequality in distribution of income
    (iii) Rapid rise in population
    (iv) Poor agricultural productivity
    (v) Lack of investments
    (vi) Unemployment
    (vii) Illiteracy
    (viii) Poor health care
    (ix) Underutilisation of resources
    (x) Social factors
    (xi) Political factors
5. **Poverty Alleviation Programmes**—
    (i) Integrated Rural Development Programme (IRDP)
    (ii) Training of Rural Youth for Self-Employment (TRYSEM)
    (iii) Development of Women and Children in Rural Areas (DWCRA)
    (iv) Jawahar Rozgar Yojana (JRY)
    (v) Employment Assurance Scheme (EAS)
    (vi) Swaranjayanti Gram Swarozgar Yojana (SGSY)
    (vii) Pradhan Mantri Gramodaya Yojana (PMGY)
    (viii) Rural Employment Generation Programme (REGP)
    (ix) Prime Minister's Rozgar Yojana (PMRY)
    (x) National Food for Work Programme (FWP)
    (xi) Mahatma Gandhi National Rural Employment Guarantee Programme
6. **Causes for Poor Performance of the Poverty Alleviation Programmes**—
    (i) Poor administration of the programmes due to inefficient staffing
    (ii) Lack of adequate support in the form of credit and marketing facilities
    (iii) Deficiencies in planning and implementation

Current Challenges Facing Indian Economy | 143

    (iv) Inadequate investments
    (v) Corruptive practices in implementation
    (vi) Lack of a proper mechanism for identification of the beneficiaries
    (vii) Lack of community participation
    (viii) High dependence on subsidies

7. **Rural Development**—Rural development refers to improving the lives of the rural people. It includes land reforms, provision of infrastructural facilities, creation of employment opportunities etc.

8. **Problems of Rural Credit**—
   (i) High Risk
   (ii) Illiteracy
   (iii) Insufficient credit
   (iv) Unproductive expenditure
   (v) Lack of adequate banking infrastructure
   (vi) Red tapism

9. **Co-operative Credit Institutions**—Cooperative credit institutions in rural areas enable pooling of resources and providing the same to their members for various productive purposes. The co-operative credit structure provides long-term credit facilities for agriculture.

10. **Regional Rural Banks**—Regional Rural Banks were established under the Regional Rural Banks Act, 1976. They provide loans to small and marginal farmers, agricultural labourers and artisans.

11. **National Bank for Agriculture and Rural Development (NABARD)**—NABARD has been set up as an apex development bank for agricultural credit.

12. **Land Development Banks**—These banks provide long term loans to farmers for a period of 15 to 20 years, against the mortgage of their lands.

13. **Commercial Banks**—Commercial banks extend credit facilities in rural areas by setting up their branches in these areas. They also have a responsibility to lend to the agricultural sector apart from catering to the urban financial needs.

14. **Cooperative Marketing**—Cooperative marketing is an arrangement by which the individual farmers organise themselves into cooperative societies for marketing their commodities.

15. **Agricultural Diversification**—Agricultural diversification refers to the transformation from the traditional single crop cultivation to production of a variety of crops to meet the current demand and to overcome the risks associated with agriculture. Agricultural diversification also refers to a shift from farm based activities to non-farm based activities.

16. **Organic Farming**—Organic farming refers to the production of food commodities without the use of chemicals such as pesticides, fungicides, chemical fertilizers etc.

17. **Initiatives to Improve the Literacy Rates in India**—
    (i) The Sarva Siksha Abhiyan (SSA)
    (ii) Mid-day meal scheme

(iii) Rashtriya Madhyamik Shiksha Abhiyan (RMSA)
(iv) National Programme for Education of Girls at Elementary Level (NPEGEL),
(v) Kasturba Gandhi Balika Vidhyalaya (KGBV),
(vi) Rashtriya Uchchatar Shiksha Abhiyan (RUSA)

18. **Unemployment**—Unemployment refers to a situation in which a person who is willing to work and has the capability to work is unable to find a productive job.

19. **Types of Unemployment**—
    (i) Voluntary unemployment
    (ii) Structural unemployment
    (iii) Frictional unemployment
    (iv) Seasonal unemployment
    (v) Cyclical unemployment
    (vi) Disguised unemployment

20. **Causes of Unemployment**—
    (i) Slow rate of economic growth
    (ii) Seasonal nature of agriculture
    (iii) Population growth
    (iv) Low levels of savings and investment
    (v) Loss of cottage and small scale industries
    (vi) Rural-urban migration
    (vii) Poor quality of human capital

21. **Policy Measures to Address Unemployment**—
    (i) Development of rural infrastructure
    (ii) Expansion of agricultural allied sectors
    (iii) Control of population
    (iv) Industrial development
    (v) Encouragement to self-employment
    (vi) Development of small scale industries
    (vii) Reforms in the education sector
    (viii) Revamping of existing programmes
    (ix) Efficient planning

Exercise

◆ Short Answer Questions (2 marks)

1. Define Poverty.
2. Distinguish between absolute and relative poverty.
3. What is a poverty line ?

4. State any four programmes implemented in India for alleviation of poverty.
5. What is TRYSEM ?
6. What is IRDP ?
7. What is DWCRA ?
8. Write a note on JRY.
9. What is EAS ?
10. What is National food for work programme ?
11. Write a note on PMRY.
12. State the reasons for poor performance of the poverty alleviation programmes in India.
13. What is rural development ?
14. Explain the role played by NABARD in rural development.
15. What is cooperative marketing ?
16. State the importance of agricultural diversification.
17. What are the benefits of organic farming ?
18. 'Human beings are both the means and an end to development'—Justify.
19. What is human capital ?
20. What is SSA ?
21. What is unemployment ?
22. State any four types of unemployment.
23. Differentiate between seasonal and cyclical unemployment.
24. What is disguised unemployment ?

◆ Long Answer Questions (3-6 marks)

1. Write about poverty in India.
2. Explain the reasons for poverty in India.
3. Evaluate the various poverty alleviation programmes implemented in India.
4. Explain the role of MGNREGA in poverty alleviation in India.
5. Examine the role of cooperative credit institutions in rural development.
6. Analyse the role of regional rural banks and NABARD in rural credit.
7. What are the challenges involved in rural credit ?
8. Explain the role of human resources in economic development.
9. Analyse the growth of education sector in India.
10. Write a note on the initiatives taken by the Indian Government in the education sector to improve the literacy rates.
11. What are the causes for unemployment in India ?
12. What measures do you suggest to address the problem of unemployment in India ?
13. Explain the concept of vicious circle of poverty.

10. Economic Growth and Development

10.1. Economic Growth versus Economic Development

The terms economic growth and economic development are generally used like synonyms and are often considered as two sides of the same coin. Though they are used interchangeably, there is a conceptual difference between the two. Growth, in simple terms, is an increase in the size and magnitude of output in the economy. An increase in the size of the economic variables like the national income, per capita income, agricultural output, number of industries, volume of savings, investments, etc., is referred to as economic growth. However, development goes beyond a mere increase in size. Development is not only an increase in the size and magnitude of output, but it is also an improvement in the living conditions of the people. Economic development focuses on those factors that improve the standard of living of the people like health, education, access to drinking water, electricity and other basic infrastructure etc.

According to Prof. Schumpeter, "Development is a discontinuous and spontaneous change in the stationary state which for ever alters and displaces the equilibrium state previously existing while growth is a gradual and steady change in the long run which comes about by general increase in rate of saving and population." Prof. Ursula Hicks has stated that "Development should relate to backward countries, where there is possibility of developing and using hitherto unused resources. The term growth is applicable to economically advanced countries, where most of the resources are already known and developed." It may thus be stated that economic development is the problem in underdeveloped countries, while economic growth is the problem of developed countries. While underdeveloped countries are working towards achieving development to relieve the people from the clutches of poverty, illiteracy and other infrastructural inadequacies, the developed nations of the world are striving to achieve further growth in their national income as they have already provided better living conditions for their people.

Kindleberger distinguished between economic growth and economic development as "Economic growth means more output, while economic development implies both more output and changes in the technical and institutional arrangement by which it is produced and distributed. Growth may well involve not only more output derived from greater amounts of inputs but also greater efficiency *i.e.*, an increase in output per unit of input. Development goes beyond this to imply changes in the composition of output and in the allocation of inputs by sectors."

Growth is thus a quantitative aspect whereas development is both quantitative and qualitative. An increase in the income may not necessarily improve welfare, even though income is an important factor that influences welfare. If increased income could provide improved living conditions to the people then development takes place. The natural and human resources of a country, savings and investment, human capital, economic and political stability, population, planning, technological advancement, investments in research and development, freedom from colonial rule are some of the most important factors contributing to economic development of a country. An economy may grow by a high rate of increase in national income. But, if population grows at a faster rate than the national income, it may not bring about an economic development. An economy cannot develop if there exists chronic poverty, inequalities, unemployment, scarcity of resources, scarcity of savings and investments and lack of technical progress. Development cannot take place without economic growth, but economic growth may occur even without economic development.

China with a population of 1.3 billion and GDP of about $11 trillion is the second largest economy in the world after US. China was among the poorest countries in the world in 1970s. But today, it has become successful in lifting half of its population out of poverty. It has been witnessing a strong growth over the past two decades. It is also the world's manufacturing hub with its labour-intensive and export-oriented production. Chinese goods have found their place in every market with their low prices. This was made possible by China's shift from being a centrally planned economy to a market based economy. China initiated its reform process in 1978 and since then, it has been experiencing rapid economic and social development. Yet, China continues to be among the developing countries as its reform process has not been very effective in alleviating rural poverty. Further, China is now under demographic pressure with its aging population. It is struggling to make its development sustainable as its high growth rates have caused imbalance in the environment.

10.1.1 Difference between Economic Growth and Economic Development

Basis of Comparison	Economic Growth	Economic Development
Definition	Increase in the real output of a nation in a particular period of time.	It refers to the overall development of the quality of life in a nation which includes economic growth.
Span of Concept	It is a narrower concept than economic development.	It is a broader concept than economic growth.
Scope	It is a uni-dimensional approach which deals with the economic growth of the nation such as GDP, per capita income etc	It is a multi-dimensional approach that looks into the income as well as the quality of life of the nation such as life expectancy, mortality rate, poverty rate etc.
Term	It is a short-term process.	It is a long-term process.
Measurements	Upward movement in national income.	Upward movement in real national income.
Applicable to	Developed Economies.	Developing Economies.
Government Support	It is an automatic process that may or may not require intervention from the government.	It requires intervention from the government as all the developmental policies are formed by the government.
Kind of changes expected	Quantitative changes.	Quantitative as well as qualitative changes.

10.2. A Comparative Study of Indian and Chinese Economies

It is interesting to study the economic growth and development of the Indian economy in comparison with the Chinese economy because both are considered as emerging economies with very high rates of economic growth. Yet there is a huge difference in terms of the level of economic growth and development achieved by the two countries over the past decades. While India adopted the strategy of planned economic development on the eve of independence in 1947 and introduced the first five-year plan in 1951, China adopted the new economic development path in 1950. India adopted a mixed economic model where public and private sectors co-exist while China resorted to a socialistic form of economic system with state's control over maximum resources.

10.2.1. Comparison of GDP, GDP per capita, GDP PPP, Poverty, Unemployment, FDI and Inflation of Indian and Chinese Economies

The reform process in India was crisis driven whereas it was a planned one in China. But in the last 25 years, since the introduction of economic reforms in India in 1991, China's per capita income trebled while that of India's only doubled. According to the report of the International Monetary Fund, India takes the 9th place and China takes the 2nd place in terms of the nominal GDP. Whereas, in terms of the Purchasing Power Parity (PPP), China and India are at the 1st and 3rd place respectively as of 2014. The GDP of China is about 5.06 times more than that of India in nominal terms and 2.39 times more in terms of PPP.

The nominal GDP is the GDP valued at current prices. The value of the finished goods and services in the country are valued at the current market prices to calculate the GDP in nominal terms. However, to facilitate international comparison, the GDP of all the countries are converted to a standard unit or uniform currency which is US dollars at present. The PPP refers to the amount of a country's currency that is required to buy the same amount of goods that 1 USD can buy in US.

GDP per capita is a measure of a country's economic output that accounts for population. That means, it divides the country's gross domestic product by its total population.

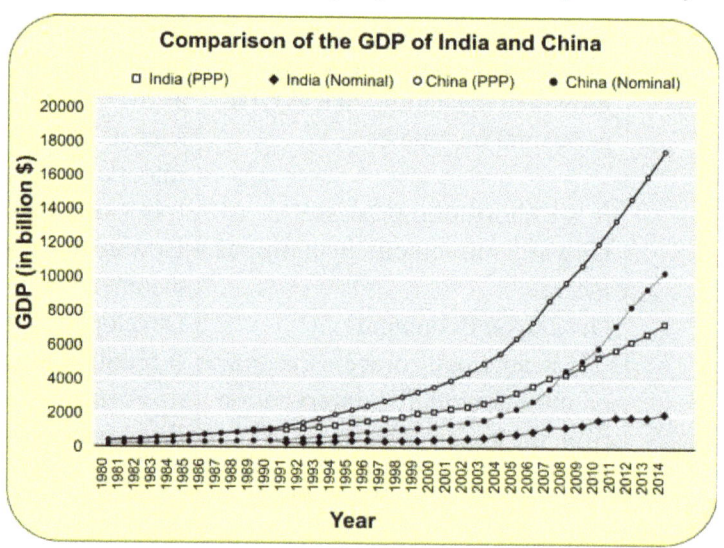

Fig. 10.1

The average GDP growth of China between 1980 to 2014 was around 9.8 percent whereas that of India during the same period was only about 6.2 percent. With the demonetisation announced by the Prime Minister Narendra Modi on November 08, 2016, the IMF has further slashed India's growth estimate for the current fiscal year to 6.6 percent from 7.6 percent while raising China's growth estimate to 6.7 percent from 6.5 percent. Thus, there has been a widening gap between India and China in terms of growth rate in the recent years.

The GDP per capita of China in nominal terms has increased from USD 313 in 1980 to USD 6958 in 2013. The GDP per capita of India has only increased from USD 265 to USD 1508 during the same period. This also indicates the widening gap in per capita income between the two countries.

Poverty : The rapid expansion of both Indian and Chinese economies has resulted in a massive reduction of poverty in both the countries. Yet, China has recorded an impressive rate of reduction in poverty as compared to India. China has a significant record in reducing the proportion of population which is extremely poor and deprived. According to the World Bank estimates, the proportion of population living at less than the international poverty line of USD 1.90 per capita per day in terms of PPP was 7.9 percent in China and 21.2 percent in India. During the early 2000s, both India and China had more than 30 percent of their population living below poverty line. China has been successful in reducing its poverty figures due to its rapid economic growth and massive investments in physical and social infrastructure including health and education. Active role of the state in bringing about an inclusive growth has enabled China to reduce its proportion of population living below the poverty line.

Unemployment : Lack of adequate employment opportunities is the ultimate cause of poverty in many countries. Both China and India face the problem of unemployment. They also have a huge number of migratory population. People living in rural areas who are unable to find productive employment move to urban areas and take up various unskilled jobs. They are not entitled to any social security schemes as enjoyed by the workers of the organised sector. The rapid urbanisation process of the Chinese economy has forced people to move from rural to urban areas. The unemployment rate in China has averaged at around 4 percent in last decade whereas it has been around 7 percent in India. As per the World Development Indicators Report published by World Bank in 2014, the unemployment rate in India was around 3.6 percent while that of China was 4.6 percent. However, the unemployment rates are expected to increase marginally in both the countries due to the labour market conditions prevailing in developed countries.

Foreign Direct Investment (FDI) : Because of the liberalisation of trade, both the countries have seen a substantial increase in foreign direct investments. Prior to 1991, Indian economy was highly regulated. The reforms, however, paved the way for an increased role of the private sector. Regulations related to FDI were liberalised and even 100 percent foreign equity was allowed in priority sectors like infrastructure, hospitals, shipping, power, hotels etc. The FDI in India brought with it various technological innovations for rapid expansion of the industrial sector. In 2015, India, for the first time, became the leading country in FDI with an inflow of USD 63 billion. It is strongly believed that this boost in FDI was the result of the 'Make in India' initiative launched by the

Indian Government on September 04, 2014, through which the government encouraged multinational companies to manufacture their products in India.

In case of China, the state has played a major role as it had adopted a socialistic model. After the country passed certain laws liberalising foreign investments, FDI started flowing in from 1992. China had no FDI inflow in 1970s whereas it was more than USD 100 billion during 2008. India's FDI was lesser than USD 0.2 billion in 1980s. It was about USD 48 billion in 2008. FDI has enabled China to modernise its industrial sector and to enhance its export potential. Thus, FDI has been playing a predominant role in the development of both Indian and Chinese economies.

Inflation : Rising level of prices has always been a challenge to developing countries. Inflation reduces the real income of the people and absorbs their purchasing power. It redistributes income in favour of the rich. The interest rates are often high during inflation and when the cost of borrowing is high, it curtails the consumption expenditure, thereby affecting economic growth. The average rate of inflation has been around 7.7 percent in India from 2011 to 2016, whereas in China, it has been around 2.7 percent during the same period. However, the inflation rate in China has been highly fluctuating, reaching an all-time high of 28 percent in February 1989 and an all-time low of – 2.2 percent in April 1999. In case of India, the highest inflation rate of 12 percent was experienced in November 2013 and the lowest has been around 3 percent in January 2017. This indicates that the price level in India is more stable as compared to China.

Despite the remarkable progress that has been achieved by both the countries so far, they are still considered as emerging economies. This is due to the various developmental challenges faced by both the countries. China exports more and consumes less while India needs to increase its exports and raise investments in sectors like agriculture, industry, health and education etc. India must strive towards bringing down its unemployment and poverty rates. And to achieve this, it should invest in sectors that are labour intensive. India has the advantage of having a higher proportion of younger population while China has an aging population due to its one child norm. This could be utilised as an opportunity to achieve rapid economic development by investing in human capital which could take India ahead of China.

Summary

1. **Economic Growth**—Growth, in simple terms, is an increase in the size and magnitude of output. An increase in the size of the economic variables like the national income, per capita income, agricultural output, number of industries, volume of savings, investments, etc., is referred to as economic growth.
2. **Economic Development**—Development is not only an increase in the size and magnitude of output, but it is also an improvement in the living conditions of the people.
3. **Purchasing Power Parity**—The PPP refers to the amount of a country's currency that is required to buy the same amount of goods that 1 USD can buy in US.
4. A comparative study of India and China shows that in most of the development parameters, China has performed better than India.

Exercise

◆ Short Answer Questions (2 marks)

1. Define economic growth.
2. How would you distinguish economic development from economic growth ?
3. What is GDP per capita ?
4. What do you understand by the term PPP ?
5. Write a brief note on poverty in India.
6. State any two effects of inflation.

◆ Long Answer Questions (3-6 marks)

1. Growth is quantitative while development is qualitative. Do you agree ? Substantiate your views.
2. What is the difference between economic growth and economic development ?
3. Compare the economic growth of India with that of China.
4. To what extent has India and China been successful in eliminating poverty ?
5. Write a note on unemployment in India and China.
6. Do you think that inflation rates in India are more stable than that in China ? Discuss.
7. Write a short note on the Foreign Direct Investment in India and China.
8. Write a note on the recent initiatives taken by the government of India to encourage FDI.

11 Sustainable Development

11.1. Economic Development and Environment

Advancements in technology have made the lives of people much easier and comfortable today. Technology has evolved and progressed consistently and has drastically changed the way we live, the way we purchase products, the way we travel, the way we learn and so on. Technological advancements in agriculture have changed the way in which farmers cultivate crops and this has resulted in increased productivity and abundant food supply.

Technological advancement has simplified the way we do things which helps in saving time and it has also simplified communication. It has improved health care and it has also improved our educational environment. The commodities that were once considered as luxury have now become a necessity. Air conditioners, refrigerators, laptops, smart phones, cars etc., are being used by people across different sections of the community.

The increase in the consumption of various goods and services has paved the way for better standard of living. Increase in the consumption has also led to an increase in the demand for various resources required for the production of these commodities. The green revolution in 1960s introduced technology in the field of agriculture and the industrial revolution introduced technology in the industrial sector. Technology has enabled production in large scale at lesser cost. However, the resources that are available to produce these goods and services are limited and exhaustible.

Large scale production has a drastic impact on the environment that sustains various forms of life. Increase in consumption of electricity has resulted in the use of higher amount of coal leading to increased pollution levels. Use of high yielding variety of seeds requires greater amount of water. Borewells and water pumps have reduced the level of ground water. Chemical fertilizers and pesticides have degraded the soil and have polluted the underground water.

In the urban areas, increased demand for private transport has resulted in congestion on the city roads and has also degraded the air quality. Increased usage of refrigerators and air conditioners has resulted in the release of greater amounts of chlorofluorocarbons, hydrofluorocarbons and hydrochlorofluorocarbons in the environment which has become the major cause of ozone hole depletion. The water that people once consumed from the nearby wells, pumps and rivers is not safe for consumption anymore as it has been polluted by the industrial waste. Even those living in high rise apartments in the metropolitan cities are facing scarcity of water. There is an increase in the demand for packaged water and inappropriate disposal of these water cans and lack of an efficient recycling mechanism has resulted in the accumulation of non-biodegradable plastic waste. Even though rapid economic development has led to improved standards of living and increased welfare of the people, it has also deteriorated the quality of the environment resulting in loss of biodiversity, increased levels of air, water and soil pollution, increased incidences of natural disasters and the lingering threat of global warming.

11.2. Sustainable Development—Meaning

The concept of sustainable development came into light in 1983 at the meeting of World Commission on Environment and Development. It is popularly known as the Brundtland Commission as the commission was chaired by Gro Harlem Brundtland, the former Prime Minister of Norway and former Secretary General of the United Nations. In 1987, the Brundtland Commission published its report, 'Our Common Future', in an effort to link the issue of economic development with environmental stability. The Brundtland report defined sustainable development as the "development that meets the needs of the present without compromising the ability of future generations to meet their own needs".

The concept of sustainable development formed the basis of the United Nations Conference on Environment and Development held in Rio de Janeiro in 1992. The summit marked the first international attempt to draw up action plans and strategies for moving towards a more sustainable pattern of development. On the 20th anniversary of the United Nations Conference held at Rio in 1992, in 2012, the Rio +20 Summit (the short name for the United Nations Conference on Sustainable Development) reviewed the progress made since 1992 and concluded that sustainable development is the only viable path for development of nations.

11.2.1. Principles of Sustainable Development

The main principles of sustainable development are given below :

1. **Principle of Intra-generational and Inter-generational Solidarity** : The main focus of sustainable development is on people. The developmental and environmental needs of the present generations must be addressed without compromising the ability of the future generations to meet their own needs.

2. **Principle of Social Justice** : The right to adequate conditions for living must be recognised and must be guaranteed to all. Every individual should have equal opportunities for acquiring knowledge and skills, required to become a worthy member of a society.

3. **Principle of Sustainable Management of Resources** : Resources should be managed in a sustainable manner keeping in mind the limitations of the carrying capacity of the environment. By using natural resources in a prudent and thrifty way, we can preserve the same for future development. Biodiversity is also a natural resource and we should attach high priority to its conservation.

4. **Principle of Integration** : In the course of elaborating, evaluating, and implementing sectoral policies, plans, and programmes, economic, social, and environmental considerations and their relationships must also be taken into account to ensure that they mutually reinforce each other and so that environmental degradation resulting from the implementation of those policies and programmes is minimised. Local, regional and national activities must also be coordinated.

5. **Principle of Utilising Local Resources** : Efforts should be made to fulfil the needs of local communities from local resources themselves. Local features and diversity should also be preserved.

6. **Principle of Public Participation** : People's knowledge about sustainable development, its social, economic and environmental implications, and about sustainable

solutions and approaches must be made use of while formulating environmental policies. Public participation in decision making should also be encouraged.

7. **Principle of Social Responsibility** : To enable sustainable development and to make possible a higher quality of life, unsustainable patterns of production and consumption must be changed. Businesses' social responsibilities must be strengthened, along with co-operation between the private and the public sector.

8. **Polluter Pays Principle** : One of the core principles of sustainable development is the "Polluter Pays" principle which recognises that the polluter must pay for any damage caused to the environment or to humans because of his activities. The importance of this principle is that the damage to the environment must be remedied which is the pre-requisite for sustainable development.

11.2.2. Need for Sustainable Development

Today every nation has a responsibility to adopt sustainable development measures to overcome the diverse environmental problems confronting them. Sustainable development has become a necessity due to the following reasons :

1. **To Improve the Quality of the Environment** : The stage of economic development, the production strategies and techniques and composition of output determines the intensity of environmental problems faced by a country. Developed countries of the world today are degrading the environment at a faster rate than the underdeveloped countries. The development policies of these countries lead to over-exploitation and depletion of natural resources. Further, production technologies employed are not eco-friendly and deteriorate the quality of the environment. Sustainable development helps us to conserve and enhance our resource base by gradually changing the methods in which we develop and use technologies.

2. **To Improve the Quality of Life** : The greed of the developed countries and the need of the developing countries has a huge impact on the environment and the quality of life of the people. To bring about an improvement in the quality of life, it is necessary to make development sustainable. Sustainable development aims at improving the lives of the people without deteriorating the quality of the environment. When quality of environment improves, it improves the health condition of the people and enables them to live long and healthy lives.

3. **To Address the Problem of Poverty** : In developing countries, due to the prevalence of mass poverty and unemployment, a large proportion of the population is dependent on nature for their livelihood. Sustainable development policies would enable the poor to have access to these natural resources and also to clean drinking water and air. When people are healthy, they are more productive. Higher the productivity, higher is their income earning capacity which would help them to escape the vicious cycle of poverty.

4. **To Ensure Food Security** : Due to the commercialisation of agriculture, farmers have adopted a number of unsustainable practices such as increased use of chemical fertilisers and pesticides, over exploitation of the underground water resources, etc. These practices deplete the health of the soil and pollute the underground water. Over-exploitation of ground water reduces the underground water level. The land becomes barren over time due to loss of soil fertility and unavailability of water which, in turn, affects agricultural output. Countries are then forced to import food grains at a very

high price. Sustainable agricultural practices are, therefore, essential to overcome such problems and to ensure food security.

    5. **To Prevent Loss of Biodiversity** : Habitat destruction is a major cause for biodiversity loss. Habitat loss is caused by deforestation, over-population, rapid urbanisation and industrialisation. Species which are physically large and those living in forests or oceans are more affected by habitat reduction. Water pollution and disasters like oil spills affects marine life and leads to loss of marine bio-diversity.

    6. **To Mitigate the Impact of Natural and Man-made Disasters** : Bhopal gas tragedy of 1984, the forest fires in Indonesia in 1997, the Great London smog in 1952, Fukushima nuclear accident in July 2012 in Japan are all examples of natural and man-made disasters. While man-made disasters can be averted by appropriate precautionary measures and technologies, natural disasters are beyond human control. However, the intensity of destruction due to natural disasters could be controlled if environment friendly development strategies are adopted. The destruction caused by floods could be controlled by afforestation, acid rain could be prevented by reducing the emissions and so on. This necessitates the need for sustainable development measures which can prevent the quality of air, water and soil from deteriorating.

11.2.3. Measures to Achieve Sustainable Development

    Development depends on the use of natural resources. Without protecting and conserving these natural resources, long term development cannot be achieved. Some of the measures that could be adopted for attaining sustainable development are as follows :

    1. **Adopting Eco-friendly Technologies** : Developing countries are expanding their industrial base rapidly. While the developed countries can afford to invest in pollution control technologies, the developing countries lack adequate resources to make such huge investments. Industries producing paper, chemicals, iron and steel are largely concentrated in developing countries and are responsible for high levels of air pollution. It is, therefore, necessary to encourage polluting industries to adopt eco-friendly technologies. Financial support should be provided to those industries that adopt pollution abatement techniques. Sustainable agricultural practices like organic farming should also be encouraged.

    2. **Development of Infrastructure** : Lack of adequate transport infrastructure and poor maintenance of roads leads to heavy congestion in big cities which ultimately leads to high levels of vehicular emissions. Further, due to lack of adequate sanitation and drainage facilities, sewage and industrial wastes flow into nearby canals, rivers and lakes, polluting these water bodies. Because of poor sanitation coverage in developing countries, there is a prevalence of open defecation which affects the quality of the environment. It is, thus, necessary to develop physical and social infrastructure to protect environmental quality. Transport infrastructure should be developed and maintained to reduce emissions. People should be educated on the health benefits of adopting toilets. Measures should also be taken to treat industrial waste before it is disposed off and to incentivise industries to adopt pollution abatement technologies.

    3. **Creating Awareness** : Environmental education should be included as a part of the curriculum at every level of school and higher education. People should be educated

about the need for sustainable development. They should recognise that the carrying capacity of the earth is limited and consequently, there is a need to adopt environment friendly practices. Government should actively participate in spreading such awareness among people.

4. **Measures to Address Poverty** : Poor people are largely dependent on the nature to fulfil their day to day requirements. When a large proportion of people in a country are poor, this results in overuse of natural resources. It is, therefore, the responsibility of the government to take measures for alleviation of extreme poverty. Achieving social equity is essential to make development sustainable.

5. **Measures that could be Adopted at Individual Level** : Each one of us has the responsibility to make efforts to conserve resources and to leave behind a resource rich world for the generations to come. We can mitigate the environmental impact of our activities by adopting few sustainable practices like :

(i) Purchasing five star electrical appliances which would help in energy conservation.

(ii) Turning off appliances when not in use.

(iii) Reducing consumption, reusing what can be reused and recycling products effectively.

(iv) Disposing the waste in an environment friendly manner. Food waste can be dumped in a pit in the back yard and simple composting techniques could be followed so that soil can be made fertile. Using compost as a fertilizer is the best alternative to using chemical fertilizers.

(v) Planting trees around the house and on the road sides.

(vi) Using environment friendly bicycles for short distances and car pooling wherever possible.

(vii) Using energy efficient solar appliances can reduce the amount of coal used for generating electricity.

(viii) Minimising the use of chemical fertilisers and replacing them by biocomposting.

(ix) Using CNG in the vehicles instead of diesel to reduce pollution levels.

11.3. Global Warming

The energy from the sun warms up the earth's surface through a natural process called the greenhouse effect. When the sun's energy reaches the earth's atmosphere, some of it is reflected back to space and the rest is absorbed by the land and the oceans, heating the earth. Some of the heat radiating from the earth towards the space is trapped by greenhouse gases in the atmosphere, keeping the earth warm enough to sustain life. This is a natural balancing mechanism by which the temperature of the earth is maintained within a range in which life can sustain. In the absence of greenhouse effect, the earth would be very cold and uninhabitable. The greenhouse gases that naturally occur pose no harm to life. The primary greenhouse gases in Earth's atmosphere are water vapour, carbon dioxide, methane, nitrous oxide, and ozone. When the greenhouse effect is intensified due to human activities such as burning of fossil fuels, increase in population, increase in industrial waste and landfills, it poses a threat to life on earth and leads to global warming.

Global warming is the increase in the average temperature of the earth's surface due to the emission of greenhouse gases such as carbon dioxide, methane, nitrous oxide, ozone etc. Burning of coal and deforestation are considered as the main causes of global warming. Methane is released into the air by burning of fossil fuels and by landfills. A landfill is a site where garbage is dumped or buried. Nitrous oxide is released when chemical fertilizers are used. Further, use of refrigerators, air conditioners and other cooling systems release fluorinated gases which are also a cause of global warming.

The temperature of the earth has risen rapidly over the past 50 years and is rising every year. The rising temperature is causing heat waves, floods, hurricanes, drought, heavy rainfall and so on. These events are considered as effects of global warming.

11.3.1. Causes of Global Warming

Global warming, which is a biggest challenge that the economies of the world are currently facing, is caused due to various reasons. Some of them are discussed below :

1. **Burning of Fossil Fuels** : A large proportion of the electricity is generated from coal. Burning of coal to generate electricity, burning of petrol to power up vehicles, burning of firewood for cooking and burning of other fossil fuels like oil or wood releases huge amounts of carbon dioxide into the air. Presence of huge amounts of carbon dioxide in the atmosphere increases the surface temperature of the earth causing global warming.

2. **Deforestation** : Forests have the ability to absorb carbon dioxide and release oxygen that is required for survival of human beings and animals. When forests are destroyed for various purposes, the concentration of carbon dioxide increases in the atmosphere, leading to a rise in surface temperature. Burning of forests to clear them for settlements also releases huge amounts of carbon dioxide into the atmosphere.

3. **Decomposition** : In the process of decomposition of organic matter, the bacteria produces methane which slowly escapes into the earth's atmosphere. Accumulation of solid waste in landfills, untreated sewage waste and animal wastes also release methane in the environment. Thus, proper solid waste management practices such as setting up of landfill gas operations and installation of bio-digesters are necessary to harness methane and mitigate the effects of global warming.

4. **Natural Gas Extraction** : Natural gas is extracted through a process called hydraulic fracturing during which large amounts of methane escapes into the earth's atmosphere. Methane is a stronger green house gas when compared to carbon-dioxide.

5. **Use of Chemical Fertilizers** : Chemical fertilizers used in agriculture release nitrous oxide into the atmosphere. Nitrogen based fertilizers stimulate the microbes in the soil which converts nitrogen into nitrous rapidly.

(vi) **Release of Chlorofluorocarbons** : Chlorofluorocarbons are said to have destructive impact on the ozone layer. They do not occur naturally but are released into the atmosphere by the use of aerosols, foaming agents and cooling systems such as refrigerators and air conditioners.

11.3.2. Effects of Global Warming

The effects of global warming are diverse in nature and are very severe. Some life threatening effects of global warming are as follows :

1. **Rise in the Sea Levels** : When the average temperature of earth rises, the glaciers start melting. This leads to a rise in sea level, thereby, flooding the low lying areas and islands and threatening human life and destroying biodiversity. The melting of ice is also a threat to wild life inhabiting these cold and glaciatic regions.

2. **Desertification** : Rising temperature make arid and semi-arid areas drier. Due to shortage of water, vegetation is affected and land is degraded. Deforestation can further reduce rainfall and drylands, over time, can turn into deserts. It is said that in Iran, of the 18 to 21 million hectares of forests only 12 million survive now. It is also believed that ancient Iraq was a green land with rich plant life. The arid climate that exists now is due to massive hunting and deforestation.

3. **Hurricanes and Cyclones** : Global warming also makes oceans warmer. When water gets heated, it expands and therefore, the sea level rises. Higher ocean temperatures result in stronger hurricanes and storms. When warmer surface water evaporates as water vapour, even smaller ocean storms can become more powerful and cause widespread devastation. Warming up of oceans and seas kills sea lions, sea otters, sea urchins and is a big threat to fish population.

4. **Heat Waves and Wild Fires** : Heat waves are often reported in newspapers during summers. Greenhouse gases cause unexpected heat waves which can cause a hot weather. People living in poor housing conditions face a real threat during hot summers. Number of deaths are reported due to heat waves. Hot weather can also cause forest fires which again reduce the oxygen content and releases huge amount of carbon dioxide into the atmosphere.

Apart from these effects specified above, global warming also causes acid rain, loss of plankton life, bleaching of coral reefs, changes in pattern of rainfall, reduction in agricultural productivity, extreme events like floods and cyclones, spread of diseases etc.

11.3.3. Steps Taken on International Level for Achieving Sustainable Development and for Mitigating the Effects of Global Warming

To ensure sustainable development and to prevent global warming, a number of initiatives have been taken at the global level. Some of these are as follows :

1. United Nations Environment Programme (UNEP) creates awareness on environment protection across the world through the celebration of World Environment Day on the 5th of June every year.

2. At the United Nations Summit held on September 25th, 2015, the countries adopted a set of Sustainable Development Goals (SDGs), officially known as Transforming our world : the 2030 Agenda for Sustainable Development. It is a set of 17 'Global Goals' with 169 targets in them. The targets of each of these goals are to be achieved over the next 15 years. These goals are aimed at ending poverty, ending hunger and achieving food security, ensuring inclusive and equitable quality education, ensuring healthy lives and promoting well-being, achieving gender equality, ensuring access to affordable, reliable, sustainable and modern energy, making cities and human settlements inclusive, safe, resilient and sustainable, taking urgent action to combat climate change and its impacts by regulating emissions and promoting developments in renewable energy, etc. Though these goals are not legally binding on the nations, they are expected to take ownership and establish a framework for the achievement of the said goals.

3. The Paris Agreement, which is the world's first comprehensive agreement on climate change, came into force on November 4th, 2016, after it was adopted by the countries at the 21st conference of the parties of UNFCCC (United Nations Framework Convention on Climate Change) in Paris on December 12, 2015. The agreement aims at strengthening the global response to the threat of climate change by :

(i) Holding the increase in the global average temperature to well below 2 °C above pre-industrial levels and to pursue efforts to limit the temperature increase to 1.5 °C above pre-industrial levels, recognizing that this would significantly reduce the risks and impacts of climate change;

(ii) Increasing the ability to adapt to the adverse impacts of climate change and foster climate resilience and lower greenhouse gas emissions, in a manner that does not threaten food production;

(iii) Making finance flows consistent with a pathway towards low greenhouse gas emissions and climate-resilient development.

Successful implementation of the Paris agreement can make achievement of sustainable development goals possible and address the impact of climate change effectively.

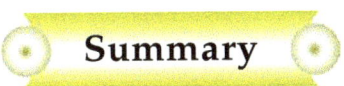

Summary

1. **Sustainable Development**—Sustainable development refers to the development that meets the needs of the present generations without compromising the ability of the future generations to meet their own needs.
2. **Principles of Sustainable Development**—
    (i) Principle of intra-generational and inter-generational solidarity
    (ii) Principle of social justice
    (iii) Principle of sustainable management of resources
    (iv) Principle of integration
    (v) Principle of utilising local resources
    (vi) Principle of public participation
    (vii) Principle of social responsibility
    (viii) Polluter pays principle
3. **Need for Sustainable Development**—
    (i) To improve the quality of the environment
    (ii) To improve the quality of life
    (iii) To address the problem of poverty
    (iv) To ensure food security
    (v) To prevent loss of biodiversity
    (vi) To mitigate the impact of natural and man-made disasters
4. **Measures to Achieve Sustainable Development**—
    (i) Adopting eco-friendly technologies
    (ii) Development of infrastructure
    (iii) Creating awareness
    (iv) Measures to address poverty
    (v) Measures that could be adopted at individual level
5. **Global Warming**—Global warming is the increase in the average temperature of the earth's surface due to the emission of greenhouse gases such as carbon dioxide,

methane, nitrous oxide, ozone etc. Burning of coal and deforestation are considered as the main causes of global warming.

6. **Causes of Global Warming—**
   (i) Burning of fossil fuels
   (ii) Deforestation
   (iii) Decomposition
   (iv) Natural gas extraction
   (v) Use of chemical fertilizers
   (vi) Release of chlorofluorocarbons

7. **Effects of Global Warming—**
   (i) Rise in sea levels
   (ii) Desertification
   (iii) Hurricanes and cyclones
   (iv) Heat waves and wild fires

Exercise

◆ Short Answer Questions (2 marks)

1. What do you mean by sustainable development ?
2. Differentiate between development and sustainable development.
3. Define global warming.
4. State any two effects of global warming.
5. Name two greenhouse gases.
6. Give any two causes of global warming.
7. State any two things which we can do at our home to ensure sustainable development.
8. When do we celebrate 'World Environment Day' ?
9. Write a brief note on 'earth summit'.

◆ Long Answer Questions (3-6 marks)

1. What do you mean by global warming ? Discuss its causes and effects.
2. Discuss the need for sustainable development and steps required to achieve sustainable development.
3. Explain the steps which can be taken at individual level to achieve sustainable development.
4. Explain long term adverse effects of global warming on the environment.
5. What are the steps taken at the international level to achieve sustainable development ?
6. What are SDGs and when were they adopted ?

12. Introduction to Statistics

12.1. Meaning and Definition

The term 'statistics' is derived from the Latin word 'status' which refers to a group of numbers or figures that represents some information. In India, statistical tools were applied by Chanakya which becomes evident when one reads the Arthashastra. Today, statistical tools are widely used in data analysis in every field.

Webstar defines statistics as "The classified facts representing the condition of the people in a state—especially those facts which can be stated in numbers or in tables of numbers or in any tabular or classified arrangement."

In the words of A.L. Bowley, "Statistics are numerical statements of facts in any department of enquiry placed in relation to each other."

According to Croxton and Cowden, "Statistics may be defined as the collection, presentation, analysis and interpretation of numerical data."

From the definitions above, we can infer the following features of statistics:

1. **Statistics refers to a Collection of Facts**: Single or isolated figures cannot be considered as statistics because such figures are unrelated and are incomparable. Statistics as a collection of facts do not just give information about one particular person or an object but it gives information about a group of people and many objects.

2. **Statistics is Expressed Numerically**: The data collected is usually expressed in numbers. It proves facts with numbers.

3. **Statistics is Collected in a Systematic Manner**: The data that is collected has to be accurate, therefore, it is collected in a systematic manner and all possible precautions are adopted to avoid errors.

4. **Statistics Classifies Facts and Enables Data Interpretation**: The data collected is organised in a systematic manner to facilitate analysis. In addition to facilitating data analysis using appropriate statistical techniques, statistics also provides guidelines for interpretation of the numbers.

12.2. Steps Involved in Statistical Analysis

Statistics involves collection, organisation, presentation, analysis and interpretation of data. These steps have been described below:

1. **Collection**: Collection of data is the primary step in any statistical analysis. It is essential to ensure that data is always taken from authentic sources. The investigator can collect the data from the field or can use published data or data from authorised sources for the purpose of analysis.

2. **Organisation**: Organisation of the data collected is the next step in statistical analysis. Data has to be organised in order to make it meaningful. Incomplete information has to be eliminated or completed before considering the same for analysis.

3. **Presentation :** After the data has been organised in a meaningful manner, it can then be presented using simple tools such as diagrams, graphs and tables for easy understanding and analysis.

4. **Analysis :** Once the data has been presented in a simple form, it can then be analysed further using sophisticated statistical techniques for better understanding of the data and to achieve the intended objective.

5. **Interpretation of Data :** Once the data is analysed, the result or the output is then interpreted appropriately to prove the facts. Interpretation of the data enables one to come out with concrete findings.

12.3. Scope of Statistics

Statistics has a wide scope of application in diverse fields. Statistics has proved to be vital in the following fields :

1. **Business :** Statistics is useful in production, marketing, financing, accounting, etc., in a business. Especially in the field of marketing, it helps in studying the consumer's tastes and preferences for a product so that the production can be planned accordingly. It assists in decision making as to what to produce, how to produce and for whom to produce.

2. **Planning :** Statistics helps policy makers in economic planning and decision making. It helps in the allocation of scarce resources. Statistics also helps the government in accelerating the economic development by providing it with essential facts and figures.

3. **Finance :** Statistics also helps in making strategic decisions on investment planning for businesses as well as for state. It helps in identifying the sectors that require investments and can provide highest returns.

4. **Management :** Statistics provides essential information to the management on the performance of the company, its departments and its various assets. This would help the top management to have a better track over the resources of the company and to have a control over different departments so as to make wise decisions.

5. **Science :** Statistics also helps in identifying the causes of various scientific problems and happenings, whether in physical or chemical or medical areas and helps in developing remedies for those problems.

6. **Economics :** Statistics is extremely useful in addressing various economic problems. It helps in studying changes in productivity, inflation, business cycles, market competition, population changes and other economic problems such as poverty, unemployment, inequality, illiteracy, etc. It helps in analysing the demand and supply conditions and thereby, facilitates price determination. It analyses historic data and helps in making vital predictions for the future. It enables understanding of the cause and effect relationship between economic variables. For instance, it helps in understanding the relationship between price and supply, price and demand etc. It helps in optimal allocation of resources. It analyses trends in unemployment, illiteracy, population growth, poverty and other economic problems and helps in formulating policies to tackle these issues. It helps in making decisions on public finance and taxation. It may, thus, be stated that statistics is of immense use in economics in making vital decisions related to production, consumption and distribution.

12.4. Limitations of Statistics

1. **Statistical Tools are Limited for Qualitative Data :** Statistics majorly deals with quantitative data. The tools available for qualitative analysis are limited. It is difficult to analyse qualitative aspects such as honesty, integrity, happiness, welfare, etc.

2. **Individual Items are Not Given Importance :** As the definition of statistics states that statistics deals with aggregates, it ignores the individual aspects of a person or an object.

3. **It Does Not Provide the True Picture :** Statistical analysis may be useful in making predictions and provide numerical output for an analysis, but it may not be able to explain the reasons for the results. One may have to study the empirical data and then apply one's mind to understand and explain certain results. The analysis is generally based on a number of assumptions and certain facts may be ignored if they are proved insignificant by the results, even when they are critical in influencing one's behaviour.

4. **Misleading Results :** Statistical results may sometimes be misused. If the average marks of a class in economics examination are 80, it does not mean that everyone in the class has secured 80 marks. Due to this limitation, statistics can sometimes be misused to one's advantage. It may also lead to some faulty conclusions. For example, results of a statistical analysis may show relationship between calories consumed and obesity. But it may not be true. Because it is not just the calories consumed that causes obesity, lack of regular exercise can also make one obese. The results of the analysis may be misleading when some factors are ignored.

5. **Liable to Manipulation :** Statistical results may also be manipulated to make a product or service attractive to people. Results of a study may say that 2000 people prefer a product in City A and 1000 people prefer a product in City B. This does not mean that the product is more popular in City A. It could be due to the fact that the population of City B is much lesser than City A.

Despite its limitations, statistical analysis and its results are highly relied upon in decision making at various levels. It is essential to ensure that data used for the analysis is adequate and accurate. This would help in solving many problems that arises with respect to the reliability of the data. External factors should also be considered in data analysis. The reliability of statistical analysis also depends upon the knowledge and ability of the investigator to use the various statistical techniques appropriately.

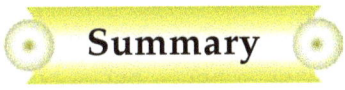

Summary

1. **Definition of Statistics**—According to Croxton and Cowden, "Statistics may be defined as the collection, presentation, analysis, and interpretation of numerical data."
2. **Steps Involved in Statistical Analysis**—Statistics involves
    (i) Collection
    (ii) Organisation
    (iii) Presentation
    (iv) Analysis, and
    (v) Interpretation of data.

3. **Scope of Statistics**—Statistics is widely used in
   (i) Business
   (ii) Planning
   (iii) Finance
   (iv) Management
   (v) Science
   (vi) Economics
4. **Limitations of Statistics**—
   (i) Statistical tools are limited for qualitative data
   (ii) Individual items are not given importance
   (iii) It does not provide the true picture
   (iv) Misleading results
   (v) Liable to manipulation

Exercise

◆ Short Answer Questions (2 marks)

1. Define statistics.
2. What are the steps involved in statistical analysis ?
3. State any two fields in which statistics is applied.
4. Statistical results can be misleading. Do you agree ?
5. Highlight any two limitations of statistics.

◆ Long Answer Questions (3-6 marks)

1. Define statistics and explain the scope of statistics.
2. Discuss the importance of statistics in various fields.
3. Examine the limitations of statistics.

13. Data Collection and Presentation

13.1. Introduction

Data is a collection of facts and figures. It can be a collection of numbers, set of measurements, observation or description of objects. Statistical tools are applied on a data to obtain meaningful results. Data collection is an important component in any research. Data can be collected either from primary sources or secondary sources.

13.2. Types of Data

Generally, we can gather data from two sources, namely, primary sources and secondary sources. Primary sources of data collection include direct personal interviews, questionnaires, surveys, etc., while, secondary sources of data collection include magazines, books, documents, journals, reports, web etc.

On the basis of the source of collection, data may be categorised as :

1. Primary data (collected from primary sources) and,
2. Secondary data (collected from secondary sources)

Primary data is the data that is collected for the first time specifically for the purpose of the study. So, this data is collected directly from the field. For example, if a researcher is interested in finding out the demand for a commodity in a local market, then the researcher has to collect data from all the households in that particular market regarding their preference for that commodity. The data that is collected by the researcher is a primary data. Other examples of primary data include the data collected during the Census, market surveys for a product etc.

Secondary data is the data that is obtained from some other source. It could be a data that has already been published or it may not have been published for various reasons and might have been kept only as a record. Data published by the Reserve Bank of India on various economic indicators pertaining to India, data published by the World Bank on the performance of countries on social indicators and the data taken from the Census of India are all examples of secondary data. There are several sources from which secondary data could be obtained. These are :

1. Reports of international organisations such as World Bank, International Monetary Fund, United Nations etc.
2. Data published on the websites of various ministries like Ministry of finance, labour, education, health etc.
3. Reports of expert committees.
4. Reports of the Planning Commission.
5. Publications of local bodies like municipal corporations.
6. Publications of private institutions.
7. Publication by researchers.

8. Journals
9. Newspapers and magazines.
10. Books
11. Annual reports of organisations etc.

13.3. Methods of Collecting Primary Data

There are various methods that can be applied for collecting primary data. The most popular methods have been explained below :

1. **Direct Personal Interviews** : In a personal interview, the researcher personally collects data from the field. The researcher may be prepared with a set of questions that have to be asked. The information collected through this method is more accurate as the researcher is personally involved in data collection. Chances of bias are limited. However, this method may be very expensive and time consuming, if the data has to be collected from a large number of people. The researcher should also possess excellent communication skills.

2. **Indirect Oral Interview** : In this method, the necessary information is collected from the third parties. For example, in case of theft, the police may conduct an enquiry in the neighbourhood. They may be asked to provide witness and so on. Similarly, if a retailer in a locality is suspected to be selling substandard products, an enquiry may be conducted in the neighbourhood to ascertain the facts. In such sensitive cases, approaching the retailer directly may be futile as he may not disclose the true facts.

3. **Questionnaires** : This is another popular method of data collection. A structured questionnaire is prepared and is mailed to the respondents, requesting them to complete the questionnaire and mail it back to the address provided. The questionnaire would contain several questions essential for the study. Questionnaires could also be e-mailed which would reduce postage cost. Today, questionnaires could also be prepared using various web based applications where the questionnaires are mailed to the respondents in the form of a hyperlink. Google forms are widely used for surveys these days. They help in developing structured questionnaires and the data collected is neatly organised automatically and can be downloaded as required. Basic analysis on the data is also provided by these web based applications.

4. **Schedules** : Schedules are also similar to questionnaires. However, the questionnaires are generally filled by the respondents but, in schedules, the enumerators fill in the information. The response rate may be low in questionnaires since the respondents may or may not mail back the questionnaire. In case of schedules, the enumerators meet the respondents, explain to them the purpose of the study and fill in the responses given by the interviewees. Thus, the response rate is higher in case of schedules. Sometimes, the schedules may also be handed over to the respondents and the enumerators guide them in filling in the questionnaire. This again is an expensive method like direct personal interviews.

5. **Observation** : In an observation method, the investigator directly observes what happens and does not ask any questions to the respondents. The observer may observe the situation and record the information by being part of the situation or the observer may also be detached from the situation and record the observation. The former is called

as the participant observation and the latter is called as the non-participant observation. The information collected through observation method is often limited and sometimes external factors can act as a hindrance in this method of data collection. Data can only be collected about the present situation and historical facts are not available under this method.

13.4. Organisation of Data

Organisation of data is defined as the method of classifying or grouping the data based on certain characteristics. Organising data systematically helps in simplifying complex data and facilitates understanding. It is also easy to compare and analyse data when it is properly organised.

13.4.1. Types of Variables

All research studies analyse some kind of variable or variables. A variable is defined as a number, characteristic or some quantity that increases or decreases over time. It takes different values at different points of time and in different situations. Variables are broadly classified into two categories—dependent variable and independent variable.

A dependent variable is one whose value depends upon the independent variable. An independent variable, also known as the predictor variable, is a variable whose value is not dependent on the other variable. For example, if one wishes to study the performance of students in a test then the dependent variable here could be taken as the marks obtained by students in that test, the independent variables could be those factors that influences the marks of the students such as time spent in studying, student's intelligence, time spent in watching television and so on. These are all independent variables. Similarly, if one wants to study the demand for a commodity, the quantity demanded is taken as the dependent variable and the factors influencing the demand such as price of the commodity, income of the consumer, prices of substitute products are all independent variables that influence demand for a commodity and the quantity demanded of a commodity is dependent on all these variables.

Other Common Types of Variables

1. **Categorical Variables** : Categorical variables are those variables that could be classified into different categories. Classification by gender (male and female), by income (high, middle and lower income) are examples of categorical variables.

2. **Continuous Variables** : These are the variables that can take any value between their minimum and maximum limit. For instance, if the height of students in a class range between 4 to 4.5 feet, the variable height can take any value such as 4.2 feet, 4.25 feet, 4.255 feet, 4.2555 feet and so on.

3. **Discrete Variable** : A discrete variable is one that can take only finite number of values. For instance, if the number of vehicles passing through a toll in a day is between 80 to 100, then the variable can only take values such as 82, 83, 84, 90, 98 and so on. It is not possible for 85.5 vehicles to cross the toll. Thus, the variable can only take a finite number of values.

13.4.2. Classification of Data

Classification of data refers to the grouping of data into various classes or homogeneous groups. For example, data on consumers demanding a certain product can be classified based on their geographical location, age, gender, income, etc. Classification helps in condensing huge amount of data on the basis of common features. It facilitates comparison and enables easy understanding.

Types of Classification

The following are the common types of data classification :

1. **Geographical Classification** : The data is classified by area, city, districts, states, countries etc. This type of classification is based on the geographical location. For example, the data on literacy rates in India can be classified state wise or district wise.

Rank	State	Literacy	Male	Female
1.	Kerala	94.00	96.11	92.07
2.	Lakshadweep	91.85	95.56	87.95
3.	Mizoram	91.33	93.35	89.27
4.	Goa	88.70	92.65	84.66
5.	Tripura	87.22	91.53	82.73
6.	Daman and Diu	87.10	91.54	79.55
7.	Andaman and Nicobar islands	86.63	90.27	82.43
8.	Delhi	86.21	90.94	80.76
9.	Chandigarh	86.05	89.99	81.19
10.	Puducherry	85.85	91.26	80.67

2. **Chronological Classification** : This type of classification is adopted when the data over a period of time is observed. For example, production of rice in India from 1950-51 to 2012-13 can be classified in a chronological order as follows :

Year	Production (in million tons)
1950-51	20,576
1960-61	34,574
1970-71	42,225
1980-81	53,631
1990-91	74,291
2000-01	84,980
2010-11	95,900
2011-12	105,310
2012-13	105,240

3. Qualitative Classification : Under qualitative classification, data is classified based on qualitative characteristics of the population such as gender, literacy, religion, etc. For example, to study the distribution of population between rural and urban areas, the population can be classified into number of people living in villages and number of people living in urban areas. This can further be classified by gender to understand the proportion of male and female population in rural and urban areas.

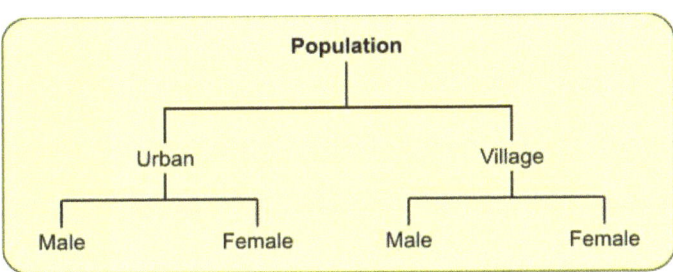

4. Quantitative Classification : This refers to the classification of data on the basis of a quantitative measure such as height, weight, profits, marks etc.

Marks	Number of Students
0 – 10	5
10 – 20	10
20 – 30	4
30 – 40	6
40 – 50	7
50 – 60	3
60 – 70	2
70 – 80	2
80 – 90	3
90 – 100	9
Total	**51**

13.5. Presentation of Data

Presentation of data is the process of organising and arranging the data in an orderly manner and displaying it in a manner that is convenient to read, understand and interpret. Data can be presented in various forms depending on the nature of data collected, size of the data and the amount of information available. Generally, there are three ways of presenting a data :

1. Textual Presentation of Data : When the data is presented in the form of a paragraph, it is called textual representation of data. This style of representation is appropriate in academic reports as well as in scientific journals. Example of textual representation of data is as follows :

"Of the 60 teachers, 22 or 36.67 percent have earned a degree in Masters of Arts, 26 or 43.33 percent have earned a degree in Masters of Science and 12 or 20 percent have earned a degree in Masters of Commerce. According to the government regulations, all the teachers are qualified to teach in the high school."

2. Tabular Presentation of Data : When data is presented in the form of a table in rows and columns, it is called the tabular presentation of data. Given below is an example of tabular presentation of data.

Year	Population	Male	Female
2001	16312	8211	8101
2002	16317	8227	8090
2003	16315	8193	8122
2004	16340	8201	8139
2005	16561	8311	8250
2006	16740	8396	8344
2007	16805	8420	8385
2008	16952	8490	8462
2009	17113	8572	8541
2010	17216	8620	8596

The table, given above, shows the population of a village from 2001 to 2010. The years are taken in the rows. The total population, number of males and females are presented in separate columns. Each row gives the total population and the number of males and females for the specified year.

Other commonly used forms of tabular presentation of data are as follows :

(i) **Frequency Distribution Table :** Frequency distribution table given below is also an example of tabular presentation of data. A frequency distribution table is a table that shows how often each value occurs. It helps in summarising categorical or numerical values. For example, data on the marks obtained by 100 students in a class in a statistics test can be presented in the form of a frequency distribution as follows :

Marks	Number of Students
0 – 10	2
11 – 20	6
21 – 30	4
31 – 40	12
41 – 50	15
51 – 60	12
61 – 70	20
71 – 80	13
81 – 90	5
91 – 100	11
Total	**100**

If the marks are in between 10 and 11, they can be rounded to the nearest whole number and included in the appropriate category. For example, 10.5 can be considered as 11 and 10.4 can be considered as 10.

The process of preparing this frequency distribution is quite simple. In order to find out the number of times a particular value appears, a column of tallies is prepared. Every time a particular value is repeated, a vertical bar is drawn against the corresponding class or that particular value. The number of bars is then counted to obtain the frequencies. For example, in the table given below, the items in the class interval 15-18 occur 7 times every four items are represented by four vertical bars and every fifth item is represented by a diagonal bar across the previous four bars binding them together.

Class Interval (Age)	Tally Marks	No. of Students Frequency
6 – 9	|||||	5
9 – 12	||||	4
12 – 15	||||	4
15 – 18	||||| ||	7
18 – 21	|||	3
21 – 24	||||| ||	7
	Total	30

(ii) Cumulative Frequency Distribution Table : Cumulative frequency is calculated by adding a class frequency and all class frequencies before it, in a frequency distribution. It can be used to determine the number of items that have values below or above a particular level. Example of a cumulative frequency distribution table is given below :

The following table gives the frequency distribution and cumulative frequency distribution of marks obtained by 30 students in a particular test.

Marks	Number of Students	Cumulative Frequency
50	5	5
60	9	5+9=14
70	10	14+10=24
80	6	24+6=30
Total	30	

3. **Diagrammatic Presentation of Data** : It refers to the use of diagrams and graphs for the presentation of data. Graphical presentation of data, that is, presentation of data using graphs, is also a form of diagrammatic presentation of data. Diagrams are attractive and they make complex data, simple. They help the observers to remember the facts and have a long-lasting impression on them. However, they consume time and exact measurements may not be possible sometimes. They are also liable to be misinterpreted. Some popular diagrammatic forms of data presentation are :

(i) **Bar Diagram** : A bar diagram presents the data using rectangle bars. The bars can either be drawn horizontally or vertically. The data on population in the previous example is presented below using a bar diagram :

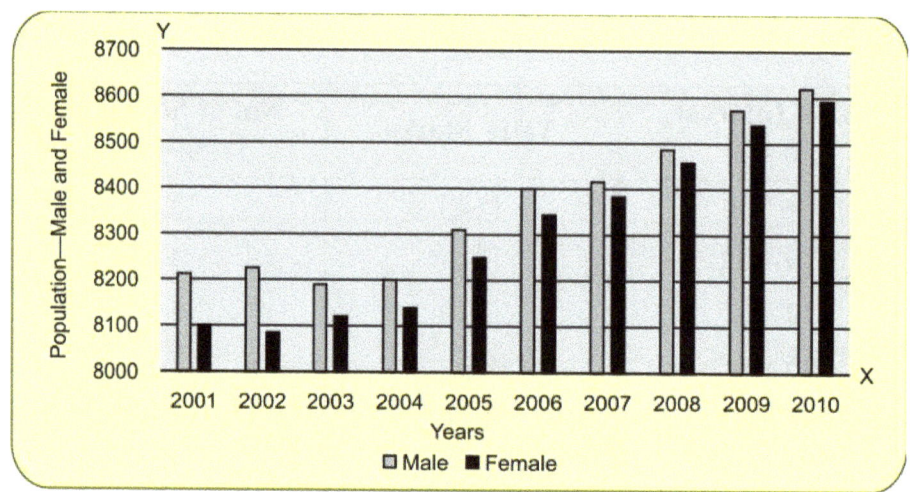

(ii) **Pie Diagram** : A pie diagram is used to present categorical data. It is a circle that is divided into slices, also called as wedges, in proportion to each category in the data. The total value of the pie is 100 percent. Each category is first expressed in percentage and then is multiplied by 360, since a full circle has 360 degrees. For example, out of 20 people who viewed a movie, 10 of them have rated it as excellent, 6 of them have given the rating as good and the remaining 4 have rated the movie as poor. The following calculations are carried out before drawing the pie diagram.

Rating	No. of people	Percentage	Central Angle
Excellent	9	$\frac{9}{20} \times 100 = 45$	$\frac{45}{100} \times 360° = 162°$
Good	7	$\frac{7}{20} \times 100 = 35$	$\frac{35}{100} \times 360° = 126°$
Poor	4	$\frac{4}{20} \times 100 = 20$	$\frac{20}{100} \times 360° = 72°$
Total	20	100	360°

A protractor is then used to measure degree of each category and divide the circle accordingly.

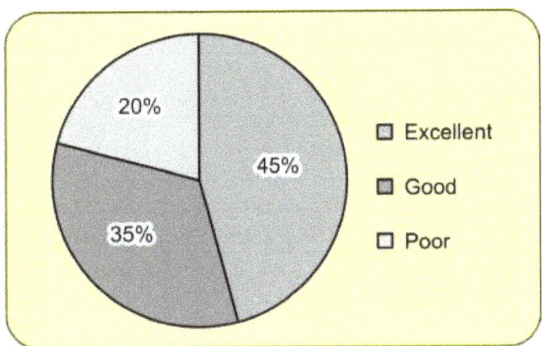

(iii) **Line Graph :** A line graph is useful in depicting data in the form of a trend. The timeline is taken on the X-axis, while the variable values are taken on the Y-axis. A line graph on the population data used in the earlier example is presented below :

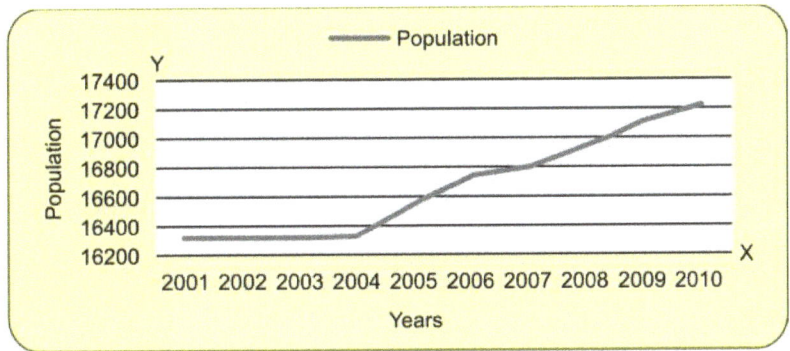

(iv) **Histogram :** A histogram presents the data in an interval scale. The area of each rectangle is proportional to frequency of the corresponding variable. And the width of the rectangle is equal to the class interval. A data on the marks of students is presented in the form of a histogram below :

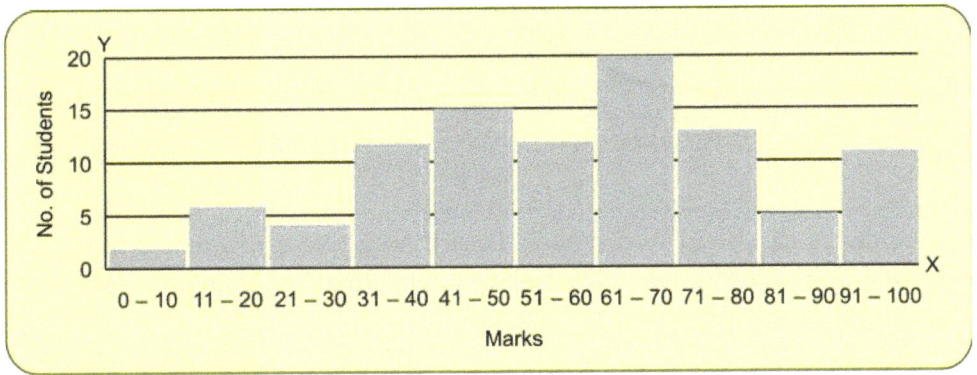

(v) **Frequency Polygon :** A frequency polygon is obtained when a line is drawn connecting the mid-points of top of all the rectangles of a histogram.

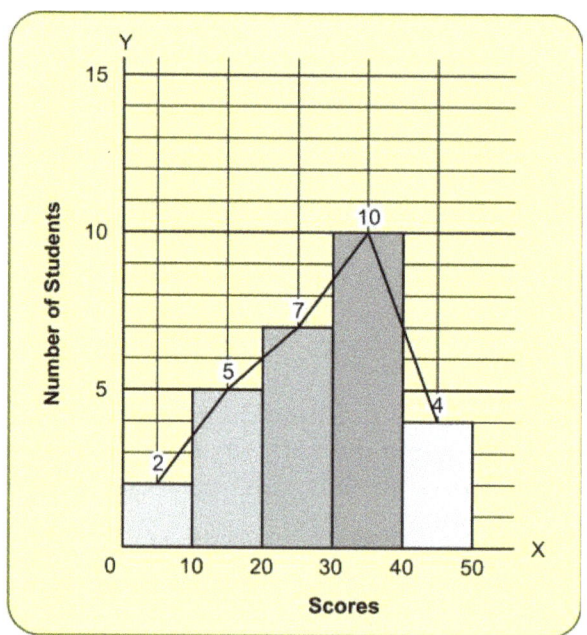

(vi) **Ogive :** An ogive is a cumulative frequency graph. It plots the cumulative frequencies on the Y-axis and the class intervals on the X-axis. An ogive curve for the data on the marks of the students used in the earlier example is presented below :

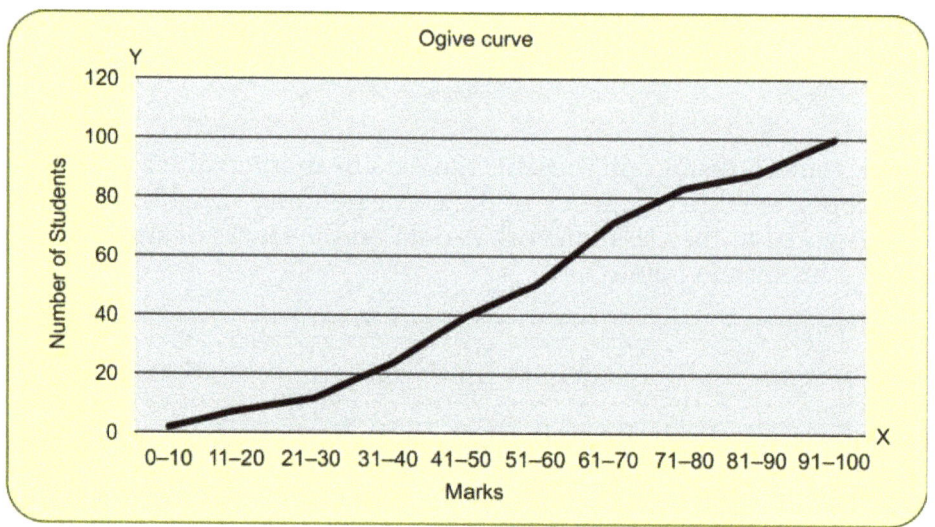

An ogive curve can be of two types—Less than ogive and greater than ogive.

The ogive graph given above is a 'less than ogive'. In a 'less than ogive', the cumulative frequencies are in ascending order as given below :

Marks	Number of Students	Cumulative Frequency
0 – 10	2	2
11 – 20	6	2 + 6 = 8

Marks	Number of Students	Cumulative Frequency
21 – 30	4	8 + 4 = 12
31 – 40	12	12 + 12 = 24
41 – 50	15	24 + 15 = 39
51 – 60	12	39 + 12 = 51
61 – 70	20	51 + 20 = 71
71 – 80	13	71 + 13 = 84
81 – 90	5	84 + 5 = 89
91 – 100	11	89 + 11 = 100
Total	100	

In a 'greater than ogive', the cumulative frequencies are in descending order as shown below.

Marks	Number of Students	Cumulative Frequency
0 – 10	2	100
11 – 20	6	100 – 2 = 98
21 – 30	4	98 – 6 = 92
31 – 40	12	92 – 4 = 88
41 – 50	15	88 – 12 = 76
51 – 60	12	76 – 15 = 61
61 – 70	20	61 – 12 = 49
71 – 80	13	49 – 20 = 29
81 – 90	5	29 – 13 = 16
91 – 100	11	16 – 5 = 11
Total	100	0

The ogive curve in a 'greater than ogive' appears as shown below :

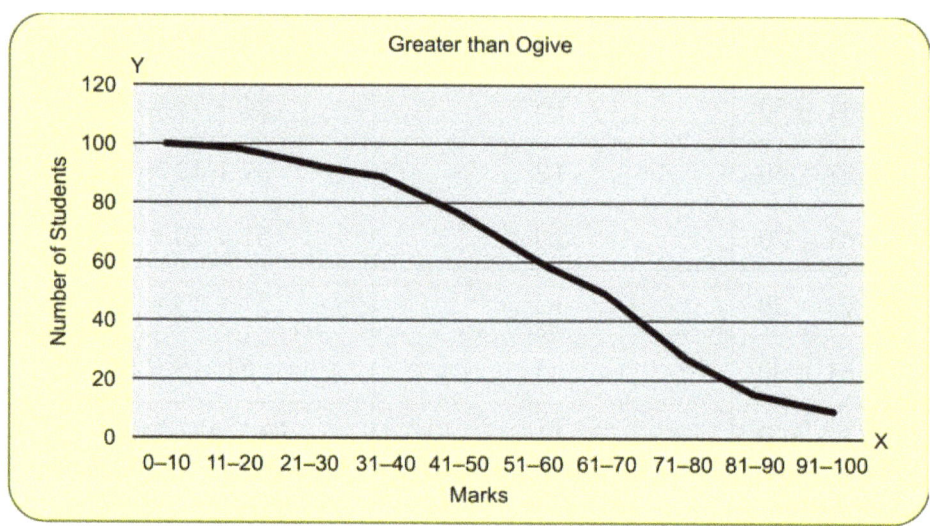

Data classification and tabulation is an important step before analysis of the data. Data collected cannot be effectively analysed and interpreted unless it is neatly arranged. Various types of classification and tabulation of data enables easy understanding of the data and facilitates further analysis. When data is appropriately classified, the significant features of the data can be spotted at a glance. Classification and tabulation of data also helps in eliminating unnecessary information. Relationship between different variables can be studied easily when the data is organised and classified. Classification and tabulation of data also facilitates further statistical treatment.

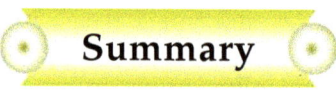

Summary

1. **Data**—Data is a collection of numbers, set of measurements, observation or description of objects.
2. **Primary Data**—Data that is collected for the first time specifically for the purpose of the study is a primary data.
3. **Secondary Data**—Secondary data is the data that is obtained from some other source.
4. **Methods of Collecting Primary Data**—
    (i) Direct personal interviews
    (ii) Indirect oral interview
    (iii) Questionnaires
    (iv) Schedules
    (v) Observation
5. **Organisation of Data**—Organisation of data is defined as the method of classifying or grouping the data based on certain characteristics.

6. **Types of Variables**—
   (i) **Dependent Variable :** A dependent variable is one whose value depends upon the independent variable.
   (ii) **Independent Variable :** An independent variable, also known as the predictor variable, is a variable whose value is not dependent on the other variable.
   (iii) **Categorical Variable :** Variables that could be classified into different categories.
   (iv) **Continuous Variable :** Variables that can take any value between their minimum and maximum limit.
   (v) **Discrete Variable :** A discrete variable is the one that can take only finite number of values.
7. **Classification of Data**—It refers to the grouping of data into various classes or homogenous groups.
8. **Types of Classification**—
   (i) Geographical classification
   (ii) Chronological classification
   (iii) Qualitative classification
   (iv) Quantitative classification
9. **Presentation of Data**—The process of organising and arranging the data in an orderly manner and displaying it in a manner that is convenient to read, understand and interpret.
10. **Textual Presentation of Data**—When the data is presented in the form of a paragraph, it is called textual representation of data.
11. **Tabular Presentation of Data**—When data is presented in the form of a table in rows and columns, it is called the tabular presentation of data.
12. **Diagrammatic Presentation of Data**—It refers to the use of diagrams and graphs for presentation of data. Graphical presentation of data, that is, presentation of data using graphs, is also a form of diagrammatic presentation of data.
13. **Bar Diagram**—A bar diagram presents the data using rectangle bars. The bars can either be drawn horizontally or vertically.
14. **Pie Diagram**—A pie diagram is used to present categorical data. It is a circle that is divided into slices, also called as wedges, in proportion to each category in the data. The total value of the pie is 100 percent.
15. **Line Graph**—A line graph is useful in depicting data in the form of a trend. The timeline is taken on the X-axis, while the variable values are taken on the Y-axis.
16. **Histogram**—A histogram presents the data in an interval scale. The area of each rectangle is proportional to frequency of the corresponding variable.
17. **Frequency Polygon**—A frequency polygon is obtained when a line is drawn connecting the mid-points of top of all the rectangles of a histogram.
18. **Ogive**—An ogive is a cumulative frequency graph. It plots the cumulative frequencies on the Y-axis and the class intervals on the X-axis.

◆ Short Answer Questions (2 marks)

1. Define data.
2. Differentiate between primary and secondary data.
3. State any two sources of secondary data.
4. State any two methods of collecting primary data.
5. What is meant by organising a data ?
6. Name the different types of variables.
7. Differentiate between dependent and independent variables.
8. What are the different tools you can use to present your data ?
9. What are tally bars ?
10. Differentiate between quantitative and qualitative classification.
11. Is a histogram different from a bar diagram ?
12. What is an ogive ?
13. When would you use a line graph ?

◆ Long Answer Questions (3-6 marks)

1. Explain the different sources of data.
2. What is a primary data ? Discuss the methods of collecting primary data.
3. What is a secondary data and what are the various sources of secondary data ?
4. How do you organise data ?
5. Explain the different types of data classification.
6. Explain the diagrammatic methods of data presentation.

14   Measures of Central Value

14.1. Meaning

A measure of central value is a value that represents the entire data. It is the value around which most of the other values congregate. Average is one of the most popular and commonly used measures of central value. There are two major objectives of the measures of central value. They are :

1. **To provide a single value that describes the entire data** : Measures of central value condenses the data to one single measure and helps in understanding certain characteristics of the data. For example, the average marks of a class in a test is an indicator of the performance of the class as a whole.
2. **To facilitate comparison of different data sets** : The central value computed for different data sets can be compared which enables one to understand the basic differences between data sets. For instance, the average income, which is a measure of central value, can be compared for different countries to understand the differences in the standard of living across countries. The average marks of different batches of students can be compared to understand which batch performed relatively better.

According to Croxton and Cowden, "An average is a single value within the range of the data that is used to represent all the values in the series. Since an average is somewhere within the range of the data, it is sometimes called a measure of central value." The most important measures of central value applied in statistics are as follows :

1. Arithmetic mean
2. Median
3. Mode
4. Geometric mean, and
5. Harmonic mean

14.2. Arithmetic Mean (AM)

It is a commonly used average to represent a data. It is obtained by simply adding all the values and dividing them by the number of items. Arithmetic mean can be a simple arithmetic mean or weighted arithmetic mean.

1. **Simple Arithmetic Mean** : Simple arithmetic mean is calculated differently for different sets of data, that is, the calculation of arithmetic mean differs for individual observations, for discrete series and for continuous series. Let us have a look at each of them :

(i) Individual Observations

(a) Direct Method : In simple arithmetic mean, there are no frequencies. To calculate simple arithmetic mean under direct method all the observations are added and divided by the total number of items.

When a variable X takes the values $x_1, x_2, x_3, x_4, ...x_n$, the average value of X is given by the formula,

$$\bar{X} = \frac{x_1 + x_2 + x_3 ... + x_n}{N}$$

Where, $\bar{X}$ is the mean, and
N is the number of values.

The formula can also be written as

$$\bar{X} = \frac{\Sigma x}{N}$$

Illustration 1 : The following table gives the wages earned by a worker for five months. Calculate the average wages.

Month	Wages (in ₹)
January	1000
February	1200
March	900
April	800
May	1100

Solution :

$$\bar{X} = \frac{\Sigma x}{N}$$

$\Sigma x = 1000 + 1200 + 900 + 800 + 1100 = 5000$
$N = 5$

$$\bar{X} = \frac{\Sigma x}{N}$$

$$= \frac{5000}{5} = 1000$$

The average wage of the worker is ₹ 1000.

(b) Short-cut Method : In short-cut method, an arbitrary origin is taken and deviations are calculated from this arbitrary origin. Then, the mean is calculated using the following formula :

$$\bar{X} = A + \frac{\Sigma d}{N}$$

Where, A is the assumed mean, and
d is the deviation of the values from the assumed mean.

Measures of Central Value | 181

Illustration 2 : Calculate arithmetic mean by taking 900 as the assumed mean.

Month	Wages (X) (in ₹)	d = X – 900
January	1000	100
February	1200	300
March	900	0
April	800	– 100
May	1100	200
		Σd = 500

$$\bar{X} = A + \frac{\Sigma d}{N}$$

$$\bar{X} = 900 + \frac{500}{5}$$

$$= 900 + 100$$

$$= 1000$$

(ii) Discrete Series

In discrete series, the arithmetic mean is calculated by the following methods :

(a) **Direct Method :** In direct method, the arithmetic mean is calculated by the following formula :

$$\bar{X} = \frac{\Sigma fx}{\Sigma f}$$

Where, $\bar{X}$ = Arithmetic mean,
f = Frequency,
X = Variable, and
Σf = Sum of the frequencies

The above formula shows that the sum of product of frequencies with their respective variables (Σfx) is to be divided by the sum of the frequencies (Σf) to derive arithmetic mean.

Illustration 3 : Calculate the arithmetic mean by direct method :

Price per Share (X)	No. of Shares (f)	fX
5	10	50
3	15	45
6	20	120
4	5	20
	Σf = 50	Σfx = 235

$$\bar{X} = \frac{\Sigma fx}{\Sigma f}$$

$$= \frac{235}{50} = 4.7$$

(b) **Short-cut Method :** The following formula is used to calculate the mean by this method.

$$\bar{X} = A + \frac{\Sigma fd}{\Sigma f}$$

Where, A = Assumed mean,

$d = X - A$,

Σf = Sum of the frequencies, and

f = Individual frequency.

Under this method, the AM is calculated by multiplying respective frequencies (f) with the deviations (d) of the variables from the assumed mean. Then, this total of the product of deviation and respective frequencies (Σfd) is divided by the sum of the frequencies (Σf) and added to assumed mean (A).

Illustration 4 : Calculate the arithmetic mean by short-cut method :

Price per share (X)	No. of Shares (f)	d = X – 6	fd
5	10	– 1	– 10
3	15	– 3	– 45
6	20	0	0
4	5	– 2	– 10
	Σf = 50		Σfd = – 65

$$\bar{X} = A + \frac{\Sigma fd}{\Sigma f}$$

$$\bar{X} = 6 - \frac{65}{50}$$

$$= 6 - 1.3$$

$$= 4.7$$

(iii) **Continuous Series**

When the data is very large, it may be difficult to add every item and divide it by the number of values to obtain the arithmetic mean, therefore, the data has to be grouped. For instance, if there are 50 students in a class, rather than adding the marks of all the 50 students they can be grouped into different classes such as the number of students who have scored between 0 to 10, 10 to 20, 20 to 30, 30 to 40, 40 to 50 and so on. Here, the upper limit of one class is the lower limit of the next class. A student who has scored exactly 10 marks can be included in the 10 to 20 class interval. This method is known as exclusive method. In an inclusive method, the class interval may be taken as 0 to 10, 11 to 20, 21 to 30 and so on. Mean is, then, calculated by taking the middle value of each class and applying the formula used in discrete series.

(a) **Direct Method :**

Illustration 5 : Calculate the arithmetic mean from the following data :

Price (in ₹)	15-18	18-21	21-24	24-27	27-30	30-33	33-36
Quantity Demanded	28	23	17	18	8	4	2

Solution :

Here, the mid-point for each class is calculated by adding the lower limit and the upper limit and dividing it by 2. For the first class 15-18, it is calculated as (15+18)/2 = 16.5. Then, the midpoints (*m*) are multiplied by frequencies of the respective classes and the product is divided by sum of frequencies (Σf) to derive AM.

Price (in ₹)	Mid-point (*m*)	Frequency (*f*)	*fm*
15 – 18	16.5	28	462
18 – 21	19.5	23	448.5
21 – 24	22.5	17	382.5
24 – 27	25.5	18	459
27 – 30	28.5	8	228
30 – 33	31.5	4	126
33 – 36	34.5	2	69
		Σf = 100	Σfm = 2175

$$\bar{X} = \frac{\Sigma fm}{\Sigma f}$$

$$\bar{X} = \frac{2175}{100}$$

= ₹ 21.75

(b) **Short-cut Method or Step Deviation Method :** The average can also be calculated by assuming one of the values from the given figures as the assumed mean. The mean is then calculated using the following formula :

$$\bar{X} = A + \frac{\Sigma fd}{\Sigma f}$$

Where, A is the assumed mean,

f is the frequency of each class,

d = deviations from the mid-point $(m - A)$, and

Σf is the total frequency.

The method of calculating the mean taking deviations from the assumed mean is also called as the step deviation method.

Illustration 6: Calculate the arithmetic mean of the following data using the step deviation method.

Price (in ₹)	0 - 10	10 - 20	20 - 30	30 - 40	40 - 50
Quantity Supplied	2	4	6	8	10

The assumed mean (A) is taken as 25.

Solution:

Price (in ₹)	Quantity Supplied (f)	Mid-point (m)	d = m − A	fd
0 – 10	2	5	− 20	− 40
10 – 20	4	15	− 10	− 40
20 – 30	6	25	0	0
30 – 40	8	35	10	80
40 – 50	10	45	20	200
	Σf = 30			Σfd = 200

$$\bar{X} = A + \frac{\Sigma fd}{\Sigma f}$$

$$= 25 + \frac{200}{30}$$

$$= 25 + 6.7$$

$$= ₹ \ 31.7$$

Calculation of Arithmetic Mean in Open-end Class Intervals

Open-end classes are those that do not have a lower or an upper boundary. For example, in a data on income distribution, when the last income class is written as 30 lakhs and above, it is an open end class. And, when the lowest income class is written as less than one lakh, it is also an open-end class. In such cases, an assumption has to be made about the upper or lower limits. The lower limit could be assumed as zero for the income 'less than one lakh' and the upper class limit for the income class '30 lakhs and above', could be assumed based on the other class intervals.

For example, observe the following data :

Marks	No. of students
Below 20	5
20 – 40	6
40 – 60	10
60 – 80	5
Above 80	4

In this example, the appropriate assumption for first class would be 0 – 20 and since the class interval is 20, the appropriate assumption for the last class would be 80 – 100.

Illustration 7 : Calculate the arithmetic mean for the following data :

Wages	No. of workers
Below 100	10
100 – 200	5
200 – 300	14
300 – 400	12
400 and above	9

Solution :

The assumed mean (A) has been taken as 250.

Wages (X)	No. of workers (*f*)	Mid-point (*m*)	d = m – A	fd
0 – 100	10	50	– 200	– 2000
100 – 200	5	150	– 100	– 500
200 – 300	14	250	0	0
300 – 400	12	350	100	1200
400 – 500	9	450	200	1800
				Σfd = 500

$$\bar{X} = A + \frac{\Sigma fd}{\Sigma f}$$

$$\bar{X} = 250 + \frac{500}{50}$$

$$= 250 + 10$$

$$= 260$$

2. Weighted Arithmetic Mean

Simple arithmetic mean gives equal importance to each item in the series. But in practice, the importance of each item in the series may be different. This factor is taken into consideration by weighted arithmetic mean which takes into account the weights (importance) assigned to each and every value. The weights represent the relative importance of each item.

When weights are provided, the arithmetic mean is calculated using the following formula :

$$\bar{X}_w = \frac{\Sigma wX}{\Sigma w}$$

Illustration 8 : A student secures following marks in the subjects of class X. But the weight attached to each subject is different. Calculate weighted arithmetic mean :

Subject	Marks (X)	Weight (w)
Maths	60	1
Hindi	70	2
English	50	1
History	75	3
Geography	65	3

Solution : The weighted arithmetic mean is calculated in the following manner :

Subject	Marks (X)	Weight (w)	wX
Maths	60	1	60
Hindi	70	2	140
English	50	1	50
History	75	3	225
Geography	65	3	195
		$\Sigma w = 10$	$\Sigma wX = 670$

$$\bar{X}_w = \frac{\Sigma wX}{\Sigma w}$$

$$= \frac{670}{10} = 67$$

14.2.1. Merits of Arithmetic Mean

Arithmetic mean is a widely used measure of central value due to the following advantages :

1. It is easy to understand.

2. It is simple to compute.
3. It takes each and every item into consideration.
4. It is a reliable measure as the value does not change when computed at different points of time.

14.2.2. Demerits of Arithmetic Mean

1. It is affected by extreme values.
2. It is not an appropriate measure when the distribution is skewed.
3. It is not accurate when items are missing.
4. It cannot be applied when the data is qualitative in nature like honesty, level of satisfaction etc.
5. Assumptions regarding class intervals in case of open end classes may be inaccurate.

14.3. Median

Median is the middle value in a distribution. It is a positional average. Median divides the data into equal halves, wherein 50 percent of the values lie below the median and 50 percent of the values lie above the median. Before determining the middle value, the observations have to be arranged in an ascending or descending order. Once the data is arranged in ascending or descending order, the middle most value is the median value. It is the size of $\frac{N+1}{2}$ th item, where N is the number of items in the data.

1. Individual Observations

Illustration 9. Calculate the median of 10, 5, 11, 8, 22, 15, 18, 17, 13.

Solution :

Arrange the values in an ascending order.

5, 8, 10, 11, 13, 15, 17, 18, 22.

There are 9 values here.

Median = Size of $\frac{(9+1)}{2}$ th item

= $\frac{10}{2}$ = 5th item

The 5th item in the series is 13.

Median = 13

Illustration 10. Calculate the median of 9, 10, 5, 11, 8, 22, 15, 18, 17, 13.

Solution :

Arrange the values in an ascending order.

5, 8, 9, 10, 11, 13, 15, 17, 18, 22.

There are 10 values here.

Median = $\frac{N+1}{2}$ th item.

$$= \frac{(10+1)}{2} = \frac{11}{2} = 5.5^{\text{th}} \text{ item}$$

i.e., $\frac{(5^{\text{th}} \text{ item} + 6^{\text{th}} \text{ item})}{2}$

$$= \frac{(11+13)}{2} = \frac{24}{2} = 12$$

Median = 12

2. Discrete Series

When the data is in the form of a frequency distribution, the median is calculated following the steps given below :

(i) Arrange the data in ascending order or descending order.
(ii) Calculate the cumulative frequencies.
(iii) Apply the formula for calculating the median. Median = Size of $\frac{N+1}{2}$ th item, where N is the total of frequencies.
(iv) In the cumulative frequency column, look for the cumulative frequency that is equal to $\frac{N+1}{2}$ or cumulative frequency that is just higher than this.
(v) The corresponding value of the variable is the value of the median.

Illustration 11. Calculate the median from the data given below.

Wages per day (in ₹)	150	155	160	180	185	170
No. of labourers	24	23	19	21	5	29

Solution :

Wages per day (X) (in ₹)	No. of labourers (f)	Cumulative frequency (c.f.)
150	24	24
155	23	24 + 23 = 47
160	19	47 + 19 = 66
170	29	66 + 29 = 95
180	21	95 + 21 = 116
185	5	116 + 5 = 121

$$\text{Median} = \text{Size of } \frac{N+1}{2} \text{th item}$$

$$= \frac{(121+1)}{2} = \frac{122}{2} = 61$$

The number 61 is not there in the cumulative frequency column. Therefore, the cumulative frequency that is just above 61 is taken. And its corresponding value of the variable is the median. The cumulative frequency, therefore, is 66 and the median is ₹ 160.

3. Continuous Series

When the variable is in the form of a continuous series, the series corresponding to size $\frac{N}{2}$ should be noted. This is the class in which the median lies. The median is then calculated using the following formula :

$$M = L_1 + \frac{\frac{N}{2} - cf}{f} \times C$$

Where, M = Median
N = Number of observations
L_1 = Lower limit of the median class
cf = Cumulative frequency of the class preceding the median class
f = Frequency of the median class
C = Class interval

Illustration 12. Calculate the median for the data given below :

Wages per day (in ₹)	150-155	155-160	160-165	165-170	170-175	175-180
No. of labourers	24	23	19	29	21	5

Solution :

Wages per day (X) (in ₹)	No. of labourers (f)	Cumulative frequency (c.f.)
150 – 155	24	24
155 – 160	23	24 + 23 = 47
160 – 165	19	47 + 19 = 66
165 – 170	29	66 + 29 = 95
170 – 175	21	95 + 21 = 116
175 – 180	5	116 + 5 = 121

$$\frac{N}{2} = \frac{121}{2} = 60.5$$

The number 60.5 is not there in the cumulative frequency column. Therefore, the class corresponding to the cumulative frequency of 66 is taken as the median class (*Note :* 66 is considered because it is just above 60.5).

The median class is 160 – 165, where 160 is lower limit and 165 is the upper limit of the class.

$$M = L_1 + \frac{\frac{N}{2} - cf}{f} \times C$$

$$M = 160 + \frac{\frac{121}{2} - 47}{19} \times 5$$

$$= 160 + \frac{60.5 - 47}{19} \times 5$$

$$= 160 + 3.55$$

$$= 163.55$$

14.3.1. Merits of Median

1. It is easy to compute.
2. It is easy to understand.
3. It can be computed accurately even in case of open end classes.
4. It is unaffected by extreme values.
5. It can be used when data is qualitative in nature and is ranked or arranged in order.
6. It can be calculated by mere observation.

14.3.2. Demerits of Median

1. The data has to be arranged in an ascending or descending order.
2. It is not based on all the values.
3. It could be affected by errors in sampling.
4. It is not an appropriate measure when the data is small.

14.4. Mode

Mode is the value that occurs with the greatest number of frequency. For example, if the given set of values are 2, 3, 2, 4, 5, 2, 3, 1, 6 , the mode here would be 2 which appears thrice. However, when there are 2 or more values appearing with same frequencies then the mode is said to be ill-defined. Such series is called as bi-modal or multi-modal. Mode is an appropriate measure than average and median under certain circumstances. For instance, while studying the income earned by the workers in a company, mode reflects the wages earned by a large number of workers. Average income of the workers, on the other hand, may be much higher just because few employees in higher positions are earning a very high level of income. Majority votes are considered in decision making where mode is applied to see the choice preferred by a large number of people.

Measures of Central Value | 191

1. **Individual Observations**

   Illustration 13. Calculate the mode from the data given below showing the marks obtained by 10 students.
   75, 80, 82, 76, 82, 74, 75, 79, 82, 70
   Solution :
   The mode here is 82 as it appears with the highest frequency.

2. **Discrete Series**

   Illustration 14. Calculate the mode for the data pertaining to the size of shoes.

Size of shoes	4	5	6	7	8
No. of persons	25	32	45	42	38

   Solution :
   The mode here is 6 as it has the highest frequency.

3. **Continuous Series**

   Mode for a data in the form of a continuous series is calculated using the formula

   $$M_o = L + \frac{f_1 - f_0}{2f_1 - f_0 - f_2} \times i$$

   Where, M_o = Mode

   L = Lower limit of the modal class
   f_1 = Frequency of the modal class
   f_0 = Frequency of the class preceding modal class
   f_2 = Frequency of the class succeeding modal class
   i = Class interval

   Illustration 15. Calculate the mode from the data given below pertaining to the marks obtained by the students in a test.

Marks	No. of students
0 – 10	2
10 – 20	3
20 – 30	5
30 – 40	4
40 – 50	19
50 – 60	17
60 – 70	18
70 – 80	12
80 – 90	15
90 – 100	5

Solution :

By observation, it is known that the modal class is 40 – 50 as this class has the highest frequency.

$$M_o = L + \frac{f_1 - f_0}{2f_1 - f_0 - f_2} \times i$$

$$M_o = 40 + \frac{19 - 4}{2(19) - 4 - 17} \times 10$$

$$M_o = 40 + \frac{15}{17} \times 10$$

$$M_o = 40 + 8.82$$

$$\text{Mode} = 48.82$$

14.4.1. Calculation of Mode - Grouping Method

Ascertaining the mode by mere observation can be erroneous when there is a very low frequency preceding or succeeding the highest frequency. In such cases, a grouping table and an analysis table is prepared to ascertain the modal class. A grouping table consists of six columns. The maximum frequency is marked in the first column. The frequencies are grouped in two's in the second column. In the third column, the first frequency is left out and the remaining frequencies are grouped in two's. In the fourth column, the frequencies are grouped in three's. In the fifth column, the first frequency is left out and the remaining frequencies are grouped in three's. In the sixth column, the first two frequencies are left out and the remaining frequencies are grouped in three's. In each of these columns the maximum value is observed.

The analysis table is prepared taking the column numbers on the left and the probable values of mode on the right. The probable values of mode are those values against which the frequencies are the highest in the grouping table. The values are entered by means of a bar in the analysis table. The column total is then taken and the one which has the maximum value is the modal value.

Illustration 16. Calculate the value of mode for the following data.

Wages (X) (per day)	10	15	20	25	30	35	40
No. of workers (f)	9	12	39	34	28	19	9

Solution :

Grouping Table

X	f (1)	2	3	4	5	6
10	9					
		9+12=21				
15	12		12+39=51			
				9+12+39=60		
20	**39**				12+39+34=**85**	

		39+34=**73**				
25	34					39+34+28=**101**
			34+28=**62**			
30	28			34+28+19=**81**		
		28+19=47				
35	19				28+19+9=56	
			19+9=28			
40	9					

Analysis Table

Column No.	20	25	30
1	/		
2	/	/	
3		/	/
4		/	/
5	/	/	
6	/	/	/
Total bars	4 bars	5 bars	3 bars

The modal value is 25 as it has the maximum total of 5 bars.

14.4.2. Merits of Mode

1. It can be easily observed from the data.
2. It is easy to compute.
3. It is unaffected by extreme values.
4. Mode can be determined even if the distribution has open end class.
5. It can also be determined easily by graphic method.
6. It is easy to understand.

14.4.3. Demerits of Mode

1. Mode is ill-defined when there are distributions with two modes.
2. It is not based on all the values.
3. It cannot be accurate when there are sampling fluctuations.
4. When mode is computed through different methods, the value may differ in each of the methods.

14.5. Relationship between Mean, Median and Mode

Distribution of statistical data shows how often the values in the data set occur. A distribution is said to be symmetrical when the values of mean, median and mode are equal. That is, there are equal number of values on both sides of the mean which means the values occur at regular frequencies. In a histogram that is constructed for a data that is normally distributed, the columns would form a symmetrical bell shape, as shown below in Figure 14.1.

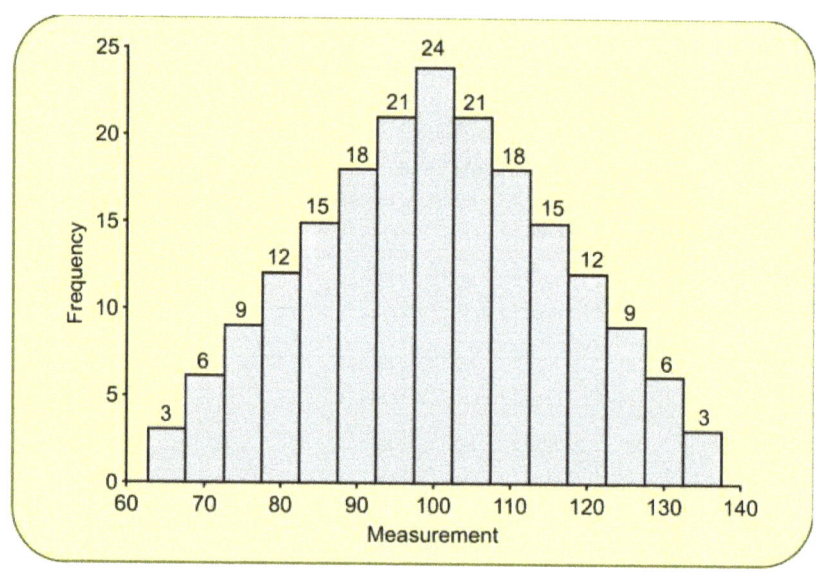

Fig. 14.1

The graph drawn on such a data is known as a 'normal curve' or a 'bell curve' and appears as shown below in Figure 14.2.

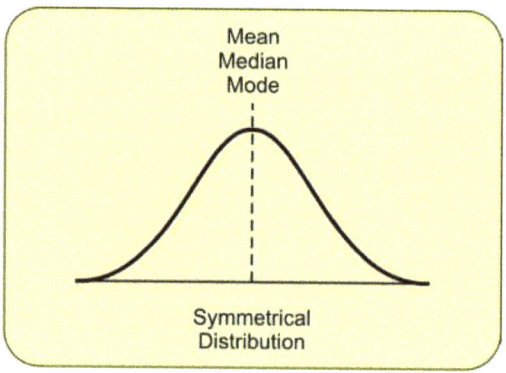

Fig. 14.2

When the values of mean, median and mode are not equal, then the distribution is said to be asymmetrical or skewed. A skewed distribution can either be positively skewed or negatively skewed. Histograms in case of skewed distribution would be as shown below in Figure 14.3.

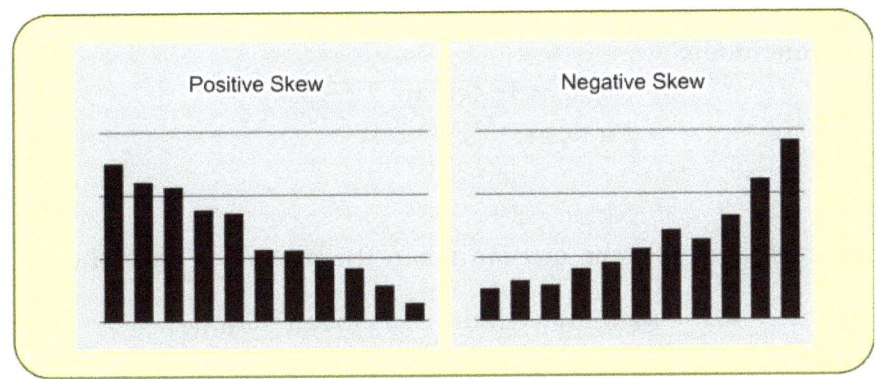

Fig. 14.3

In a positively skewed distribution, the median and mode would be to the left of the mean. That means that the mean is greater than the median and the median is greater than the mode (Mean > Median > Mode) (Fig. 14.4). Whereas, in a negatively skewed distribution, the median and the mode would be to the right of the mean. That means that the mean is less than the median and the median is less than the mode (Mean < Median < Mode) (Fig. 14.5).

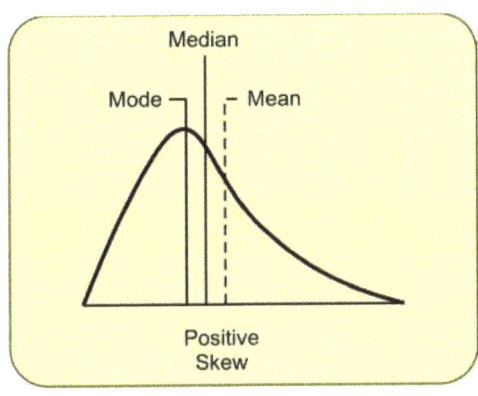

Fig. 14.4

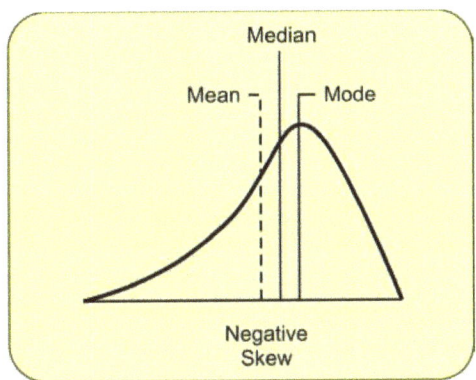

Fig. 14.5

Empirical studies have proved that in a distribution that is moderately skewed, a very important relationship exists between the mean, median and the mode. The distance between the mean and the median is about one-third the distance between the mean and the mode. This relationship has been expressed by Karl Pearson in the following formula :

$$\text{Mean} - \text{Median} = \frac{1}{3}(\text{Mean} - \text{Mode})$$

3 (Mean − Median) = Mean − Mode

Mode = Mean − 3 (Mean − Median)

Mode = 3Median − 2Mean

Or 3 Median = Mode + 2 Mean

$$\text{Or Median} = \text{Mode} + \frac{2}{3}(\text{Mean} - \text{Mode})$$

Illustration 17 : In a moderately skewed distribution, the mean is 17 and the median is 21. Calculate the mode.

Solution :

Mode = 3 Median − 2 Mean
Mode = 3 (21) − 2(17)
= 63 − 34
Mode = 29

Illustration 18. Calculate the median when the mode is 32 and the mean is 35.

Solution :

$$\text{Median} = \text{Mode} + \frac{2}{3}(\text{Mean} - \text{Mode})$$

$$\text{Median} = 32 + \frac{2}{3}(35 - 32)$$

$$= 32 + \frac{2}{3}(3)$$

Median = 34

Alternatively, Mode = 3 Median − 2 Mean
32 = 3 × Median − 2 × 35
32 = 3 × Median − 70
32 + 70 = 3 × Median
3 Median = 102

$$\text{Median} = \frac{102}{3} = 34.$$

14.6. Geometric Mean (GM)

Geometric mean is a special type of average. The geometric mean is the *n*th root of the product of *n* values and is symbolically expressed as follows :

$$GM = \sqrt[n]{(X_1)(X_2)(X_3)\ldots(X_n)}$$

Geometric mean is generally used to compare things with different properties. It is a better measure than the arithmetic mean for describing proportional growth or exponential growth. It is applied in the calculation of the Human Development Index (HDI) which is based on three dimensions, namely, life expectancy, education and income. Usage of geometric mean in the calculation of HDI decreases the level of substitutability between dimensions. Geometric mean is also applied in computing financial indices as it is more reliable and a better measure than arithmetic mean.

14.7. Harmonic Mean (HM)

Harmonic mean is calculated as the average of the reciprocals of the values given. It is symbolically expressed as follows :

$$HM = \frac{n}{\frac{1}{x_1} + \frac{1}{x_2} + \ldots + \frac{1}{x_n}} = \frac{n}{\sum_{i=1}^{n} \frac{1}{x_i}}$$

Harmonic mean is an appropriate measure when average of rates or ratios has to be computed. It is widely applied in physics in calculating quantities such as speed.

14.7.1. Relationship between Arithmetic Mean, Geometric Mean and Harmonic Mean

Relationship between arithmetic mean (AM), geometric mean (GM) and harmonic mean (HM) can be expressed as :

$$AM \times HM = GM^2$$

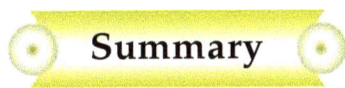

Summary

1. **Measure of Central Value**—A measure of central value is a value that represents the entire data. It is the value around which most of the other values congregate. The most important measures of central tendency applied in statistics are :
   (i) Arithmetic mean
   (ii) Median
   (iii) Mode
   (iv) Geometric mean, and
   (v) Harmonic mean

2. **Arithmetic Mean**—It is a simple average obtained by adding all the values and dividing them by the number of items. Arithmetic mean can be a simple arithmetic mean or weighted arithmetic mean.

3. **Median**—Median is the middle value in a distribution. Median divides the data into equal halves, wherein 50 percent of the values lie below the median and 50 percent of the values lie above the median.

4. **Mode**—Mode is the value that occurs with the greatest number of frequency.

5. **Relationship between Mean, Median and Mode**—The relationship between mean, median and mode can be expressed as :

   Mode = 3 Median – 2 Mean

6. **Symmetrical or Normal Distribution**—A distribution is said to be symmetrical when the values of mean, median and mode are equal.

7. **Skewed Distribution**—When values of mean, median and mode are not equal, then the distribution is said to be asymmetrical or skewed :
   (i) **Positive Skew :** In a positively skewed distribution, the median and mode would be to the left of the mean. The mean is greater than the median and the median is greater than the mode.
   (ii) **Negative Skew :** In a negatively skewed distribution, the median and the mode would be to the right of the mean. The mean is less than the median and the median is less than the mode.

8. **Geometric Mean**—The geometric mean is the *n*th root of the product of *n* values.
9. **Harmonic Mean**—Harmonic mean is calculated as the average of the reciprocals of the values.
10. Relationship between arithmetic mean (AM), geometric mean (GM) and harmonic mean (HM) can be expressed as :

$$AM \times HM = GM^2$$

Exercise

◆ **Short Answer Questions (2 marks)**

1. Define average.
2. What is a measure of central value?
3. Differentiate between mean and median.
4. What is a mode?
5. Calculate the arithmetic mean of 55, 82, 34, 28, 45, 50, 63.
6. Calculate the median of 5, 7, 3, 2, 4, 12, 8, 10, 9.
7. Calculate the mode of 5, 4, 8, 3, 2, 4, 8, 9, 8, 3.
8. State the relationship between mean, median and the mode.
9. What is a skewed distribution?

◆ **Long Answer Questions (3-6 marks)**

1. Calculate the arithmetic mean, median and mode for the following data

Marks in Statistics	15	20	25	28	32	40	48	49
No. of Students	5	4	6	11	18	3	2	1

2. Calculate the arithmetic mean, median and mode from the following data

Income	1000 – 2000	2000 – 3000	3000 – 4000	4000 – 5000
No. of persons	18	25	35	22

3. Differentiate between a normal and a skewed distribution.
4. State the relationship between the mean, median and mode in a skewed distribution.
5. Calculate the arithmetic mean, median and mode from the following data

Marks	10 – 20	20 – 30	30 – 40	40 – 50
No. of Students	5	15	22	28

6. Calculate the arithmetic mean, median and mode from the following data

Marks in Economics	0-25	25 – 50	50 – 75	75 – 100	100-125
No. of Students	10	17	27	14	22

7. Calculate the arithmetic mean, median and mode from the following data

Wages	0 – 20	20 – 40	40 – 50	50 – 60	60-70
No. of Workers	4	8	15	13	10

8. Calculate the arithmetic mean, median and mode from the following data

Income	500 – 1000	1000 – 1500	1500 – 2000	2000 – 2500
No. of persons	25	15	40	20

9. In a moderately skewed distribution, the mean is 32 and the median is 48. Calculate the mode.

10. From the following information, calculate the average wages earned by the workers.

Wages (in ₹)	No. of workers
Below 100	50
100 – 200	75
200 – 300	60
300 – 400	70
Above 400	45

11. Calculate the mode from the following observations using grouping method.

Age	15	25	35	45	55	65	75	85
No. of persons	4	10	12	22	25	10	8	3

12. Calculate the mean from the following data using the step deviation method.

Income	No. of employees
0 – 1000	13
1000 – 2000	17
2000 – 3000	15
3000 – 4000	10
4000 – 5000	20
5000 – 6000	12
6000 – 7000	8
7000 – 8000	5

13. Calculate the mean from the following data using assumed mean method.

Marks of students	10	15	20	25	30	35	40	45	50
No. of students	5	12	3	15	20	6	19	16	4

15. Measures of Dispersion

15.1. Concept of Measures of Dispersion

An average, which is a measure of central value, is a simple representation of a set of observations. This single measure alone is inadequate to represent the entire data. For example, in a class of 10 students, 5 of them have scored 100 and 5 of them have scored 0, the average marks of the class is 50. In another class of 10 students, if all the students have scored 50, the average is still 50. By looking at the average marks of both the classes, it appears that there is no difference in the performance of the students in both the classes. However, the fact is that there are many poor performers as well as top performers in the former class while all of them are only average students in the latter class. Thus, it is necessary to measure the variability or the dispersion of the data.

In the words of A.L. Bowley, *"Dispersion is the measure of the variation of the items"*. In the example above, the marks are highly dispersed in the class where 50 percent of the students have scored 100 and 50 percent have scored 0. Whereas, there is no dispersion of values in the class where all of them have scored 50. Measures of dispersion helps us in understanding how the values are dispersed or deviated from the mean value.

15.1.1. Objectives of the Measures of Dispersion

1. To estimate the reliability of an average.
2. To control for the variability in the data.
3. To facilitate comparison of two or more variables with respect to their variability.
4. To enable the application of other statistical measures such as correlation, regression etc.

15.1.2. Types of Measures of Dispersion

Measures of dispersion can broadly be classified as absolute and relative measures of dispersion.

1. **Absolute Measures of Dispersion** : When the values are expressed in the same units as that of the original data, such as kilograms, watts, rupees etc., it is said to be an absolute measure of dispersion. When there are two sets of data which are expressed in same units, absolute measures of dispersion can be used to check and compare the variability in both the data sets. However when two sets of data are not in same units, for example, income may be expressed in rupees and electricity consumption may be expressed in kilowatts, in such cases, absolute measures of dispersion do not facilitate comparison. Therefore, relative measures of dispersion are used.

2. **Relative Measures of Dispersion** : A relative measure of dispersion is a number that is independent of any units. It is a coefficient of dispersion and a ratio of measure of absolute dispersion to an appropriate average.

15.1.3. Significance of the Measures of Dispersion

Measures of dispersion are of great significance in statistical analysis as they fulfil the following purposes :

1. Measures of dispersion determine the reliability of an average. An average is considered to be reliable only when the deviations are small. It becomes unreliable when there are large deviations. Measures of dispersion are therefore useful in understanding the reliability of the average.
2. Measures of dispersion help in analysing the cause of variation, thereby helping in controlling the variation.
3. They facilitate comparison of two or more sets of data and understanding the differences in their variability. When the variability differs in two sets of data, it shows the lack of uniformity between the data sets.
4. Measures of dispersion enable application of statistical measures such as correlation, regression, testing of hypothesis, analysis of variance and co-variance etc.

15.2. Methods of Studying Variation

The following are some of the most important measures of studying variation in the data :

1. Range
2. Quartile deviation
3. Mean deviation
4. Standard deviation
5. Coefficient of variation
6. Lorenz curve

15.2.1. Range

Range is the simplest measure of studying dispersion. It is the difference between the largest and smallest value in the distribution. It is given by the formula

$$Range = L - S$$

Where, L = Largest value
S = Smallest value

Calculation of Range

1. **Individual Observations :** Individual observations refer to a group of individual items or individual values. In such a group, the range is calculated by deducting the lowest value from the highest value in the group or series.

Illustration 1 : Following is the data of sales (in ₹) of a firm in different weeks. Calculate the range :

10000, 12000, 3000, 15000, 9000, 19000, 1000, 6500

Solution : Range = L – S
L = 19000, S = 1000

Hence, Range = 19000 – 1000 = 18000

2. **Discrete Series**: Data is said to be discrete when the variable takes only particular values, that is, only integer values. For example, number of students in a class, results of rolling two dice etc., cannot have values as fractions.

Illustration 2: The following data gives the number of customers who had visited a retail store from Monday to Sunday. Calculate the range.

Monday	50
Tuesday	45
Wednesday	55
Thursday	40
Friday	65
Saturday	70
Sunday	75

Solution:

$$\text{Range} = L - S$$
$$= 75 - 40 = 35$$

3. **Continuous Series**: Continuous series can take any values in a given range. For example, the height of a person can be any value within the minimum and maximum height of human beings and when time is a variable, it can take any value and can also be measured to fractions of a second.

Range for a continuous series can be calculated by subtracting the midpoint of the lowest class from the midpoint of the highest class.

Illustration 3: Calculate the range for the following data.

Marks	10-20	20-30	30-40	40-50	50-60	60-70	70-80
No. of students	5	4	11	25	15	28	12

Solution:

Midpoint of the lowest class (10-20) is 15 and the midpoint of the highest class (70-80) is 75.

$$\text{Range} = 75 - 15 = 60$$

Merits of Range

1. Range is the simplest measure of dispersion among all the methods.
2. It is easy to understand.
3. It can be computed easily and quickly.

Limitations of the Range

1. It is not based on each and every variable in the data.
2. It fluctuates from sample to sample.
3. It cannot describe the characteristics of a distribution as it is merely based on two extreme values.

15.2.2. Quartile Deviation

A quartile is a measure that divides the data into four quarters. The first quartile, denoted by Q_1, lies in the middle of the first half of the data set. It covers the first 25 percent of the data set. The second quartile, denoted by Q_2, divides the data such that 50 percent of the data lies below it and 50 percent of the data lies above it. This is called as the median. The third quartile, denoted by Q_3, lies in the middle of the second half of the data set. 75 percent of the data would lie below the third quartile and 25 percent of the data would be greater than the third quartile.

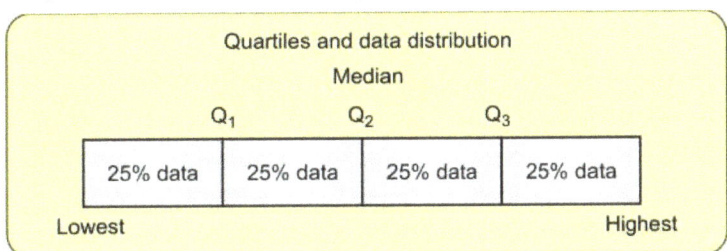

Fig. 15.1

The interquartile range is a measure of absolute dispersion. It is calculated based on the lower quartile and the upper quartile, that is, the first quartile and the third quartile respectively. The interquartile range is the difference between the third quartile and the first quartile.

$$\text{Interquartile range} = Q_3 - Q_1$$

Quartile deviation is a measure that reduces the interquartile range to semi-quartile range. Quartile deviation is obtained by dividing the interquartile range by 2.

$$\text{Quartile Deviation (Q.D.)} = \frac{Q_3 - Q_1}{2}$$

It gives the average value by which the two quartiles differ from the median value.

Computation of Quartile Deviations

1. **Individual Observations :** The important thing to be kept in mind while calculating first quartile and third quartile, in case of individual observations, is that the data set should first be arranged in an ascending or descending order.

The formula for first quartile (Q_1) is—

$$Q_1 = \text{Size of } \frac{N+1}{4} \text{th item}$$

The formula for the third quartile (Q_3) is—

$$Q_3 = \text{Size of } 3\left(\frac{(N+1)}{4}\right)^{\text{th}} \text{item}$$

Where, N is the number of observations in the data set.

Illustration 4 : Calculate the quartile deviation for the following data on the height (in cms.) of students.

120, 125, 122, 126, 128, 129, 130, 132, 131, 129, 127

Solution :

The values have to be first arranged in an ascending order.

120, 122, 125, 126, 127, 128, 129, 129, 130, 131, 132.

$$Q_1 = \text{Size of } \frac{N+1}{4}\text{th item}$$

$$= \frac{11+1}{4} = 3^{rd} \text{ item which is } 125$$

$$Q_3 = \text{Size of } 3\left(\frac{(N+1)}{4}\right)^{th} \text{ item}$$

$$= \frac{3(11+1)}{4} = 9^{th} \text{ item which is } 130$$

$$\text{Q.D.} = \frac{Q_3 - Q_1}{2}$$

$$= \frac{130 - 125}{2} = 2.5$$

2. **Discrete Series :** In case of a discrete series, we first calculate the cumulative frequency (*c.f.*). Cumulative frequency is calculated by adding a class frequency and all class frequencies before it, in a frequency distribution.

The formulae for calculating Q_1 and Q_3, in this case, remain the same as the ones used in the case of individual observations.

Illustration 5 : Calculate the quartile deviation from the following data pertaining to hours of work and the number of units produced.

Hours (X)	1	2	3	4	5	6	7	8	9
Output (*f*)	5	12	19	25	35	39	42	44	46

Solution :

X	f	c.f.
1	5	5
2	12	17
3	19	36
4	25	61
5	35	96
6	39	135
7	42	177
8	44	221
9	46	267

$$Q_1 = \text{Size of } \frac{N+1}{4}\text{th item, in this example } N = 267$$

$$= \frac{267+1}{4} = 67\text{th item which is } 5$$

$$Q_3 = \text{Size of } 3\left(\frac{(N+1)}{4}\right)^{th} \text{item}$$

$$= \frac{3(267+1)}{4} = 201\text{st item which is } 8$$

$$Q.D. = \frac{Q_3 - Q_1}{2}$$

$$= \frac{8-5}{2} = 1.5$$

3. **Continuous Series :** In case of continuous series, we first calculate cumulative frequency, as done in the case of discrete series. However, the formulae used for calculating Q_1 and Q_3, in this case are :

$$Q_1 = L + \frac{\frac{N}{4} - c.f.}{f} \times i$$

$$\text{and, } Q_3 = L + \frac{\frac{3N}{4} - c.f.}{f} \times i$$

Where, L = Lower limit of the quartile class
i = Class interval
c.f. = Cumulative frequency corresponding to the preceding class.
f = Frequency of the class in which Q_1 or Q_3 lies

Illustration 6 : Calculate the quartile deviation for the following data.

Income	1000–2000	2000–3000	3000–4000	4000–5000	5000–6000
No. of workers (f)	39	50	36	25	10

Solution :

Class	f	c.f.
1000–2000	39	39
2000–3000	50	89
3000–4000	36	125
4000–5000	25	150
5000–6000	10	160

$$Q_1 = L + \frac{\frac{N}{4} - c.f.}{f} \times i$$

Here, size of $\frac{N}{4}$th item = $\frac{160}{4}$ = 40th item

Therefore, Q_1 lies in the class 2000–3000

$$Q_1 = L + \frac{\frac{N}{4} - c.f.}{f} \times i$$

$$= 2000 + \frac{\frac{160}{4} - 39}{50} \times 1000$$

$$= 2020$$

and, $$Q_3 = L + \frac{\frac{3N}{4} - c.f.}{f} \times i$$

Here, size of $\frac{3N}{4}$th item = $\frac{3(160)}{4}$ = 120th item

Therefore, Q_3 lies in the class 3000–4000

$$Q_3 = 3000 + \frac{\frac{3(160)}{4} - 89}{36} \times 1000$$

$$= 3000 + 861$$

$$= 3861$$

$$Q.D. = \frac{3861 - 2020}{2} = 920.5$$

Merits of Quartile Deviation

1. It is considered to be superior to range.
2. It is extremely useful in open end distributions (when one or more classes do not have a boundary) or when the data is ranked and measured quantitatively.
3. In case of skewed distributions, quartile deviation is an appropriate measure of dispersion as it is least affected by the presence of extreme values.

Demerits of Quartile Deviation

1. It ignores 50 percent of the data as it considers only first 25 percent and last 25 percent of the data.
2. The value is not based on every item in the data.
3. It does not indicate how the values are dispersed around the average.
4. It does not facilitate further mathematical treatment.

15.2.3. Mean or Average Deviation

The mean deviation, also known as the average deviation, is the average difference between the values in the distribution and the mean or the median. This method shows the average scatteredness of the values in the distribution around the mean or the median. This means that the mean deviation can be calculated in the following two ways :

1. Mean Deviation (M.D.) about the mean value, and
2. Mean Deviation (M.D.) about the median value.

Computation of Mean Deviation

1. **Individual Observations :** In case of individual observations, mean deviation is calculated using the formula :

$$M.D. = \frac{1}{n}\Sigma|X - A|$$

or

$$M.D. = \frac{1}{n}\Sigma|D| \text{ where, } |X - A| = |D|$$

Where, n is the number of observations in a distribution.
X is a particular observation in the distribution, and
A is either the median value or the mean value.
$|X - A|$ or $|D|$ means that the deviation values are taken as absolute values.

Illustration 7 : Calculate the mean deviation for the following data:

Weight (in kgs) : 45, 40, 50, 52, 48, 54, 56

Solution :

Calculation of MD from median (A)—

To calculate M.D. from median, the data has to be organised in ascending or descending order :

40, 45, 48, 50, 52, 54, 56

$$\text{Median (A)} = \text{Size of } \frac{n+1}{2}\text{th item}$$

$$= \text{Size of } \frac{7+1}{2} = 4^{th} \text{ item}$$

$$= 50$$

X	|X – A| or |X – 50|
45	5
40	10
50	0
52	2
48	2
54	4
56	6
	$\Sigma|X - A| = 29$

$$M.D. = \frac{1}{n}\Sigma|X - A|$$

$$= \frac{1}{7}(29) = 4.14$$

Calculation of M.D. from Mean—

X	|X − A| or |X − 49.29|
45	4.29
40	9.29
50	.71
52	2.71
48	1.29
54	4.71
56	6.71
	Σ|X − A| = 29.71

$$\text{Mean (A)} = \frac{\Sigma X}{N}$$

$$= \frac{345}{7} = 49.29$$

$$\text{M.D.} = \frac{1}{n}\Sigma|X - A|$$

$$= \frac{1}{7}(29.71) = 4.24$$

2. **Discrete Series** : In case of a discrete series, we first calculate the cumulative frequency (c.f.). Cumulative frequency is calculated by adding a class frequency and all class frequencies before it, in a frequency distribution. The formula used for calculating mean deviation in this case is :

$$\text{M.D.} = \frac{1}{N}\Sigma f|X - A|$$

$$\text{or M.D.} = \frac{1}{N}\Sigma f|D|$$

Where, N is the total of all frequencies in a distribution,
f is the frequency of any given observation,
X is a particular observation in the distribution, and
A is either the median value or the mean value.
\|X − A\| or \|D\| means that the deviation values are taken as absolute values.
Illustration 8 : Calculate the mean deviation for the following data.

X	1	2	3	4	5	6	7	8
f	4	12	10	7	6	14	9	13

Solution :
Computation of M.D. from Median

X	f	c.f.	|D| or |X − A|	f|D| or f|X − A|
1	4	4	4	16
2	12	16	3	36
3	10	26	2	20
4	7	33	1	7
5	6	39	0	0
6	14	53	1	14
7	9	62	2	18
8	13	75	3	39
	N = 75			$\Sigma f\|D\|$ = 150

$$\text{Median (A)} = \text{size of } \frac{N+1}{2}\text{th item}$$

$$= \frac{75+1}{2} = \text{size of 38}^{\text{th}} \text{ item}$$

Median (A) = 5

Here, A is the median value and is equal to 5.

$$\text{M.D.} = \frac{1}{N}\Sigma f|X - A|$$

$$= \frac{150}{75} = 2$$

Computation of M.D. from Mean

X	f	fX	|D| or |X − A|	f|D| or f|X − A|
1	4	4	3.9	15.6
2	12	24	2.9	34.8
3	10	30	1.9	19
4	7	28	.9	6.3
5	6	30	.1	.6
6	14	84	1.1	15.4

7	9	63	2.1	18.9
8	13	104	3.1	40.3
	N = 75	Σ fX=367		Σ f|D| = 150.9

$$\text{Mean } (\bar{X}) = \frac{fX}{N} = \frac{367}{75} = 4.9$$

Here, A is the mean value and is equal to 4.9

$$\text{M.D.} = \frac{1}{N}\Sigma f|X - A|$$

$$= \frac{150.9}{75} = 2.012$$

3. **Continuous Series**: In case of a continuous series, the formula used for calculating mean deviation remains the same as stated in the case of discrete series with one important exception that now, the deviations are the difference between midpoints of various classes and the mean or the median value.

$$\text{M.D.} = \frac{1}{N}\Sigma f|m - A|$$

$$\text{or M.D.} = \frac{1}{N}\Sigma f|D|$$

Where, N is the total of all frequencies in a distribution,

f is the frequency of a class interval,

m is the mid-point of the class intervals, and

A is either the median or the mean value.

$|m - A|$ or $|D|$ means that the deviation values from mid-points of class intervals are taken as absolute values.

Illustration 9: Calculate the mean deviation for the following data.

Marks	0-20	20-40	40-60	60-80	80-100
No. of students (f)	5	18	21	30	26

Solution: Computation of M.D. from Median—

Marks	f	c.f.	Mid point (m)	|D| = |m − A| or |D| = |m − 64|	f|D|
0-20	5	5	10	54	270
20-40	18	23	30	34	612
40-60	21	44	50	14	294
60-80	30	74	70	6	180
80-100	26	100	90	26	676
	N = 100				Σf|D| 2032

Median = size of $\frac{N}{2}$th item = $\frac{100}{2}$ = 50th item

Therefore, the Median lies in the class 60-80

$$\text{Median} = L + \frac{\frac{N}{2} - c.f.}{f} \times i$$

$$= 60 + \frac{\frac{100}{2} - 44}{30} \times 20$$

$$= 60 + 4 = 64$$

Here, A is the median value and is equal to 64.

$$\text{M.D.} = \frac{1}{N} \Sigma f |D|$$

$$= \frac{1}{100}(2032) = 20.32$$

Computation of M.D. from Mean—

Marks	f	Mid point (m)	fm	$\|D\| = \|m - A\|$ or $\|D\| = \|m - 60.80\|$	f|D|
0-20	5	10	50	50.80	254
20-40	18	30	540	30.80	554.4
40-60	21	50	1050	10.80	226.8
60-80	30	70	2100	9.2	276
80-100	26	90	2340	29.2	759.2
	N = 100		Σfm = 6080		Σf|D| 2074.4

$$\text{Mean} = \frac{\Sigma fm}{N}$$

$$= \frac{6080}{100}$$

$$= 60.80$$

Here, A is the mean value and is equal to 60.80.

$$\text{M.D.} = \frac{1}{N} \Sigma f |D|$$

$$= \frac{1}{100}(2074.4) = 20.74$$

Merits of Mean Deviation

1. It is simple to understand.
2. It is easy to compute.

3. It is based on each and every value in the data set.
4. It is less affected by the presence of extreme values.
5. It facilitates comparison of two or more data sets.

Demerits of Mean Deviation

1. It ignores the algebraic signs, that is, the positive and the negative signs. This means that it takes only absolute deviations. Thus, it is not very accurate.
2. It does not support further algebraic treatment.

15.2.4. Standard Deviation

Standard deviation is the square root of the average of the squared deviations from the mean. It measures the absolute deviation of the values from the mean. Greater the value of standard deviation, greater is the deviation of the values from the mean.

Computation of Standard Deviation

1. Individual Observations :

(i) **Direct Method** : In case of individual observations, the formula used for calculating standard deviation using direct method is

$$S = \sqrt{\frac{\Sigma(X-\bar{X})^2}{N}}$$

Where, $\bar{X}$ = Mean of the values given in the data.
X = Any particular observation in the data
N = Number of observations in the data

Illustration 10 : The weight of 10 persons who were in a diet schedule is as follows. Calculate the standard deviation of weight.

42, 40, 38, 48, 50, 52, 49, 46, 45, 40

Solution :

X	X − $\bar{X}$	(X − $\bar{X}$)²
42	− 3	9
40	− 5	25
38	− 7	49
48	3	9
50	5	25
52	7	49
49	4	16
46	1	1
45	0	0
40	− 5	25
(ΣX) = 450		Σ(X − $\bar{X}$)² = 208

$$\bar{X} = \frac{\Sigma X}{N} = \frac{450}{10} = 45$$

$$S = \sqrt{\frac{\Sigma(X - \bar{X})^2}{N}}$$

$$S = \sqrt{\frac{208}{10}} = 4.56$$

(ii) **Assumed Mean Method** : Standard deviation can also be calculated by assumed mean method using the following formula

$$S = \sqrt{\frac{\Sigma d^2}{N} - \left(\frac{\Sigma d}{N}\right)^2}$$

Where, $d = X - A$ and it represents deviations from assumed mean.

A = assumed mean

X = any particular observation in the data.

N = number of observations in the data.

Illustration 11 : The weight of 10 persons who were in a diet schedule is as follows. Calculate the standard deviation of weight.

42, 40, 38, 48, 50, 52, 49, 46, 45, 40

Assumed mean has been taken as 50.

Solution :

X	d = X – 50	d^2
42	– 8	64
40	– 10	100
38	– 12	144
48	– 2	4
50	0	0
52	2	4
49	– 1	1
46	– 4	16
45	– 5	25
40	– 10	100
	$\Sigma d = -50$	$\Sigma d^2 = 458$

$$\text{S.D.} = \sqrt{\frac{\Sigma d^2}{N} - \left(\frac{\Sigma d}{N}\right)^2}$$

$$= \sqrt{\frac{458}{10} - \left(\frac{-50}{10}\right)^2}$$
$$= \sqrt{45.8 - 25}$$
$$= 4.56$$

2. **Discrete Series :**

(i) **Direct Method** : In case of a discrete series, standard deviation is calculated using the formula given below

$$S = \sqrt{\frac{\Sigma f(X - \bar{X})^2}{N}}$$

Where, f = Frequency of a given observation
X = Any particular observation in the data.
$\bar{X}$ = Mean of the values given in the data.
N = Number of observations in the data.

(ii) **Assumed Mean Method** : Using the method of assumed mean, the standard deviation can be calculated for a discrete series using the following formula :

$$S = \sqrt{\frac{\Sigma f d^2}{N} - \left(\frac{\Sigma f d}{N}\right)^2}$$

Where, f = Frequency of an observation.
$d = X - A$ and represents deviations from the assumed mean
A = Assumed mean, and
N = Sum of frequencies.

Illustration 12 : Calculate the standard deviation for the following data on size of the jeans and quantity demanded.

Size (X)	30	32	34	36	38	40
Demand (f)	25	22	28	30	27	18

Solution :
Assumed Mean (A) = 35

X	f	d = X – A	fd	fd²
30	25	– 5	– 125	625
32	22	– 3	– 66	198
34	28	– 1	– 28	28
36	30	1	30	30
38	27	3	81	243
40	18	5	90	450
	N = 150		Σfd = – 18	Σfd² = 1574

$$S = \sqrt{\frac{1574}{150} - \left(\frac{-18}{150}\right)^2} = \sqrt{10.49 - 0.0144}$$
$$= 3.24$$

3. **Continuous Series** : When the data is in the form of a continuous series then the midpoints of each class are taken as X and deviations of these mid points from assumed mean is calculated.

Step deviation method is the most commonly used method in case of a continuous data set. In a step deviation method, the mid-points are calculated and then the deviations of assumed mean from the mid-point is taken and divided by the width of the class interval. The standard deviation is then calculated using the formula below :

$$S = \sqrt{\frac{\Sigma fd^2}{N} - \left(\frac{\Sigma fd}{N}\right)^2} \times i$$

d in the formula above is calculated as $\frac{X-A}{i}$

where, f = Frequency of an observation.
A = Assumed mean
X = Mid-point of a class, and
i = Class interval.

Illustration 13 : Calculate the standard deviation for the following data on the age and number of persons in a village community.

Age (Y)	0-10	10-20	20-30	30-40	40-50	50-60	60-70	70-80	80-90
No. of persons (f)	80	120	140	145	110	95	89	30	5

The mean has been assumed as 50.

Solution :

Y	f	Mid point (X)	$d = \frac{X-A}{i}$	fd	fd²
0-10	80	5	− 4.5	− 360	1620
10-20	120	15	− 3.5	− 420	1470
20-30	140	25	− 2.5	− 350	875
30-40	145	35	− 1.5	− 217.5	326.25
40-50	110	45	− 0.5	− 55	27.5
50-60	95	55	0.5	47.5	23.75
60-70	89	65	1.5	133.5	200.25
70-80	30	75	2.5	75	187.5
80-90	5	85	3.5	17.5	61.25
	N = 814			Σfd = − 1129	Σfd² = 4791.5

$$S = \sqrt{\frac{\Sigma fd^2}{N} - \left(\frac{\Sigma fd}{N}\right)^2} \times i$$

$$= \sqrt{\frac{4791.5}{814} - \left(\frac{-1129}{814}\right)^2} \times 10$$

$$= \sqrt{5.89 - 1.93} \times 10$$

$$= 19.9$$

Merits of Standard Deviation

1. Standard deviation is based on all the values in the data set.
2. It is definite and rigidly defined.
3. It supports further algebraic treatment.
4. Squaring of deviations eliminates the problem of algebraic signs that arises in mean deviation.

Demerits of Standard Deviation

1. It gives more weight to the extreme items.
2. Calculation of standard deviation is cumbersome as compared to other measures of dispersion.

15.2.5. Coefficient of Variation

Coefficient of Variation (C.V.) is measured by the ratio of the standard deviation to the mean. While the standard deviation is an absolute measure, the coefficient of variation is a relative measure. It is useful in comparing the variability between two sets of data.

Computation of Coefficient of Variation

$$C.V. = \frac{\sigma}{\bar{X}} \times 100$$

Where, σ (sigma) stands for standard deviation, and
$\bar{X}$ stands for the mean of the data set.

Illustration 14 : The following data gives the monthly food expenditure of 25 households in a locality. Calculate the coefficient of variation.

Expenditure (X)	500-1000	1000-1500	1500-2000	2000-2500	2500-3000
No. of households (f)	5	8	6	4	2

Solution :
Assumed Mean (A) = 1000

X	f	Mid point (m)	d = (m – A)/500	fd	fd²
500-1000	5	750	– 0.5	– 2.5	1.25
1000-1500	8	1250	0.5	4	2
1500-2000	6	1750	1.5	9	13.50

2000-2500	4	2250	2.5	10	25
2500-3000	2	2750	3.5	7	24.50
	N = 25			Σfd = 27.5	Σfd² = 66.25

$$\text{Mean} = A + \frac{\Sigma fd}{N} \times i$$

$$= 1000 + \frac{27.5}{25} \times 500 = 1550$$

$$S = \sqrt{\frac{\Sigma fd^2}{N} - \left(\frac{\Sigma fd}{N}\right)^2} \times i$$

$$= \sqrt{\frac{66.25}{25} - \left(\frac{27.5}{25}\right)^2} \times 500$$

$$= \sqrt{2.65 - 1.21} \times 500$$

$$= \sqrt{1.44} \times 500$$

$$= 600$$

$$\text{C.V.} = \frac{\sigma}{\bar{X}} \times 100 = \frac{600}{1550} \times 100 = 38.7\%$$

Merits of Coefficient of Variation

1. Coefficient of variation is independent of unit of measurement as it is expressed as a percentage.
2. It facilitates comparison of data sets with different units of measurement and significantly different means.
3. It helps in measuring risk, especially in stock market investments.

Demerits of Coefficient of Variation

1. Coefficient of variation cannot be computed if the mean of a data set is zero.
2. It is misleading when there are positive and negative values in a data set.
3. It cannot be used to determine the confidence interval for mean as in case of standard deviation.

15.2.6. Lorenz Curve

Lorenz curve is a graphical method of studying the dispersion of data, named after Dr. Max O. Lorenz, who developed it in 1905. He studied the dispersion of wealth by graphical method. In order to construct a Lorenz curve, the items as well as the frequencies are cumulated and the total is considered as 100 percentage. Then percentages are calculated for the cumulated values. These percentages are plotted on a graph paper. If there is equal distribution of frequencies, the points would lie on a straight line. This line is known as the line of equal distribution or the line of equality. However, if the distribution is unequal, the curve would be away from the line of equality. The farther the curve from the line of equal distribution, the higher is the inequality or dispersion. Given below is the Lorenz curve depicting income distribution among households.

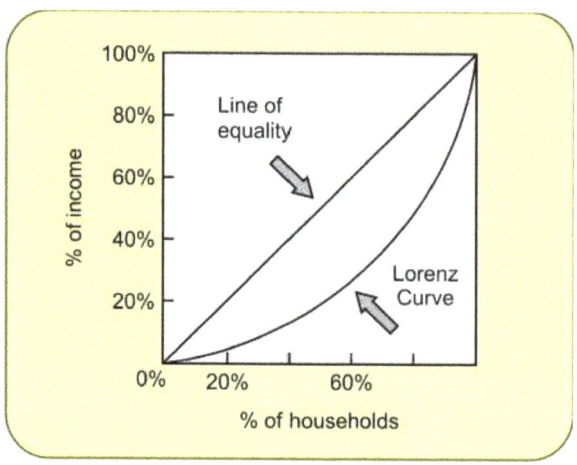

Fig. 15.2

1. **Dispersion**—In the words of A.L. Bowley, "Dispersion is the measure of the variation of the items".

2. The following are some of the most important measures of studying variation in the data :

    (i) **Range :** It is the difference between the largest and smallest value in the distribution.

    (ii) **Quartile Deviation :** It gives the average value by which the two quartiles differ from the median value.

    (iii) **Standard Deviation :** It is the square root of the average of the squared deviations from the mean. It measures the absolute deviation of the values from the mean.

    (iv) **Mean Deviation :** The mean deviation, also known as the average deviation, is the average difference between the values in the distribution and the mean or the median.

    (v) **Coefficient of Variation :** Coefficient of variation is measured by the ratio of the standard deviation to the mean.

    (vi) **Lorenz Curve :** Lorenz curve is a graphical method of studying the dispersion of data, named after Dr. Max O. Lorenz, who developed it in 1905. It is extremely useful in studying inequalities in distribution of income and wealth.

Exercise

◆ Short Answer Questions (2 marks)

1. Define measures of dispersion.
2. State any two measures of dispersion ?
3. What is a range ?
4. Calculate the range of 15, 8, 12, 22, 9, 2, 4, 12, 14, 7.
5. Differentiate between range and quartile deviation.
6. What is standard deviation ?
7. State the difference between a mean deviation and standard deviation.
8. What is a coefficient of variation ?
9. What is a Lorenz Curve ?

◆ Long Answer Questions (3-6 marks)

1. Discuss the various measures of dispersion of data.
2. Calculate the quartile deviation from the data given below :

Price	10	15	20	25	30	35	40
Quantity supplied	7	12	19	23	27	30	32

3. Calculate the standard deviation and coefficient of variation from the following data :

Advertisement exp.(in lakhs)	0-2	2-4	4-6	6-8	8-10
Units sold	9	25	52	54	55

4. The scores of 2 players in ten innings are given below. Calculate the coefficient of variation and state, out of the two, which player is more consistent.

Player 1	10	32	90	82	50	96	11	45	62	56
Player 2	12	25	40	80	90	95	50	42	96	90

5. Calculate the standard deviation and coefficient of variation for 2, 4, 6, 8, 12, 10.
6. Calculate the mean deviation from the following data on height of the students in a class.

Height (in cms.)	140	141	142	143	144	145
No. of students	15	22	13	20	18	12

7. The following data gives the height of 100 persons. Calculate the range.

Height (in inches)	62	63	64	65	66	67	68	69	70
No. of persons	2	6	10	23	22	19	9	8	1

8. The following are the marks obtained by 10 students in a class test. Calculate the standard deviation.

Roll No.	1	2	3	4	5	6	7	8	9	10
Marks	78	67	50	88	90	45	70	98	40	35

9. Calculate the quartile deviation of Tom's monthly income for a year.

Months	1	2	3	4	5	6	7	8	9	10
Income (in '000)	12	10	7	18	19	20	21	16	17	18

10. Find the mean yield of rice and the standard deviation for the distribution given below.

Year	1	2	3	4	5	6	7	8	9	10
Yield (per acre in lbs.)	236	481	604	576	419	333	217	402	384	432

11. Calculate the coefficient of variation of the following data.

Income	No. of workers
1000–2000	150
2000–3000	170
3000–4000	120
4000–5000	100
5000–6000	50
6000–7000	40
7000–8000	10

12. Calculate the standard deviation and the coefficient of variation from the following data on marks of students.

Marks	No. of students
10–30	40
30–50	30
50–70	20
70–90	10

16   Correlation

16.1. Introduction

We have already studied the concept of variables and the difference between dependent and independent variables. It is clear from these concepts that variables may be related to each other. For instance, demand and supply are related to the price of the commodity, agricultural output is dependent on the amount of rainfall, marks of students are dependent on time spent on learning, quantity demanded may depend on advertisement expenditure, consumption is dependent on income and so on. Correlation is a measure of the nature of relationship that exists between two or more variables. It ranges between –1 to +1. It helps in understanding the extent to which two variables are related and the direction of their relationship. In the words of Croxton and Cowden, *"When the relationship is of a quantitative nature, the appropriate statistical tool for discovering and measuring the relationship and expressing it in brief formula is known as correlation."*

16.1.1. Significance of the Study of Correlation

1. Correlation measures the strength of relationship between two or more variables. For example, the relationship between income and consumption expenditure, price and quantity demanded etc.

2. When the nature of relationship between variables is known, it is easy to predict the value of one variable when the other variable is known.

3. It helps in understanding the behaviour of various economic variables like, demand, supply, GDP, interest, money supply, inflation, income and expenditure and so on.

4. In business firms, it helps in making decisions on cost, price, sales, advertisement etc.

16.1.2. Types of Correlation

Depending upon the nature of relationship between variables and the number of variables under study, correlation can be classified into following types :

1. On the basis of direction of change—Positive and negative correlation
2. On the basis of number of variables—Simple, partial and multiple correlation.
3. On the basis of ratio of variation in the variables—Linear and non-linear correlation.

    1. **On the Basis of Direction of Change** :

    (i) **Positive Correlation** : Correlation between two variables is said to be positive when both the variables move in the same direction. This means, when one variable increases, the other also increases and when one decreases, the other also decreases. For instance, correlation between income and expenditure is said to be positive because as one's income increases, his expenditure also increases.

    (ii) **Negative Correlation** : Correlation between two variables is said to be negative when both the variables move in the opposite direction. This means, when one variable increases, the other decreases and when one decreases, the other increases. For example, the correlation between demand and price is said to be negative because as price increases, the quantity demanded decreases and as price decreases, the quantity demanded increases.

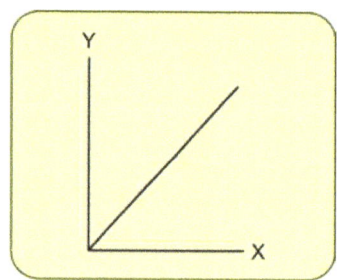
Positive Correlation

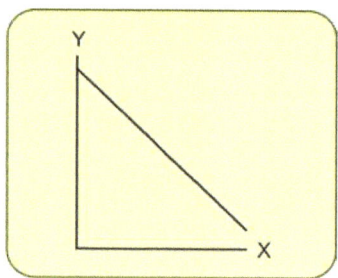
Negative Correlation

Fig. 16.1

2. On the Basis of Number of Variables :

Depending on the number of variables under study, correlation can be simple, partial or multiple.

(i) **Simple Correlation** : When the relationship between only two variables is studied, it is a simple correlation. In case of partial and multiple correlation, there are more than two variables that are related.

(ii) **Partial Correlation** : In a partial correlation, there are more than two variables that are related but the relationship between two variables alone is studied, assuming the other variables to be constant.

(iii) **Multiple Correlation** : In multiple correlation, the relationship between more than two variables is studied simultaneously.

For example, when quantity demanded is considered, it is affected by many variables like price, income, price of substitute products etc. In a partial correlation, we may study the relationship between quantity demanded and price of the commodity, assuming all other variables such as income, price of substitute products etc., to be constant. In multiple correlation, however, we study the relationship between quantity demanded and price, income and prices of substitutes, simultaneously.

3. On the Basis of Ratio of Variation in the Variables :

(i) **Linear Correlation** : When the ratio of change between two variables is constant, then the correlation is said to be linear. In linear correlation, the change in one variable is in a constant proportion to the other variable.

X	2	4	6	8	10
Y	5	10	15	20	25

In the above example, the variables X and Y change in the same ratio of 2 : 5. Hence, the correlation between the two variables would be linear.

(ii) **Non-linear Correlation** : When the ratio of change between two variables increases or decreases, then the correlation is said to be non-linear or curvi-linear.

In the example given below, the correlation between X and Y would be non-linear or curvi-linear because the ratio of change is not constant.

X	2	4	6	8	10
Y	5	10	16	23	32

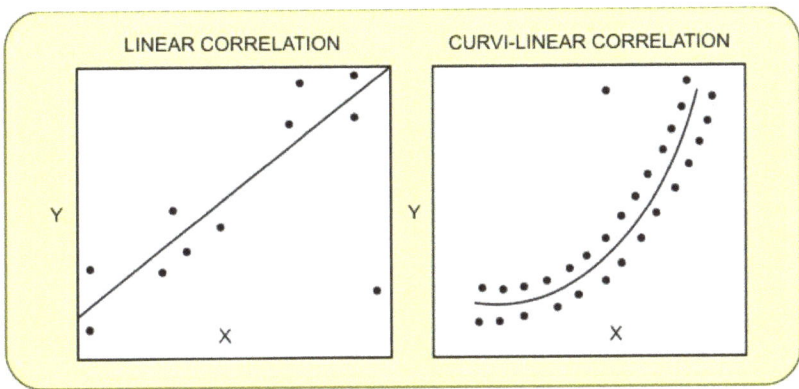

Fig. 16.2

16.2. Measures of Correlation

The most popular and commonly used methods of studying correlation between two variables are :

1. Scatter diagram method
2. Karl Pearson's coefficient of correlation
3. Spearman's rank correlation coefficient

16.2.1. Scatter Diagram Method

This is the simplest method of studying the relationship between two variables. In this method, the values of both the variables are plotted on a graph paper. If there are two variables, say X and Y, the variable X can be taken on the X-axis and Y on the Y-axis. For each pair of X and Y, a dot is plotted. Observing the way the points are scattered gives an idea as to how the two variables are related. Various degrees of correlation between two variables can be shown with the help of scatter diagrams as given below :

1. **Perfect Positive Correlation :** In a perfect positive correlation, all the dots lie in a straight line and are upward sloping. The correlation coefficient (r) would be equal to +1, when the correlation is perfectly positive.

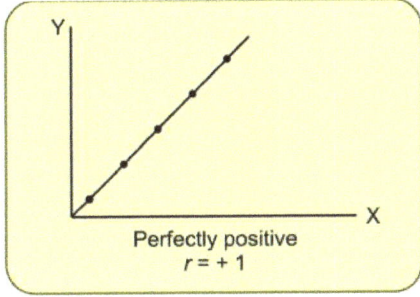

Fig. 16.3

2. Perfect Negative Correlation : In a perfect negative correlation, the dots lie on the same line and are downward sloping. The correlation coefficient (r) would be equal to –1, when the correlation is perfectly negative.

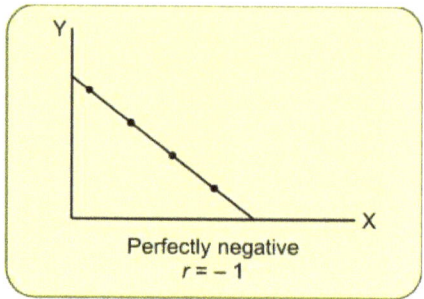

Fig. 16.4

3. High Degree of Positive Correlation : When the points come closer to a straight line and are moving from bottom left to top right, there is said to be a high degree of positive correlation. The value of the correlation coefficient (r) would lie between + 0.7 and + 1.

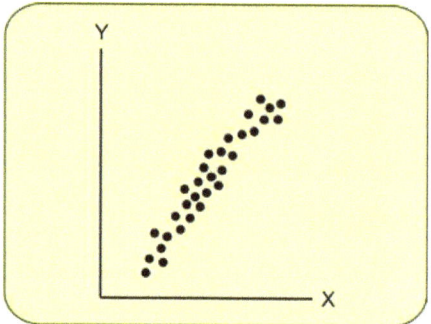

Fig. 16.5 : High degree of positive correlation

4. High Degree of Negative Correlation : When the points come closer to a straight line and are moving from top left to bottom right, there is said to be a high degree of negative correlation. The value of the correlation coefficient (r) would lie between – 0.7 and – 1.

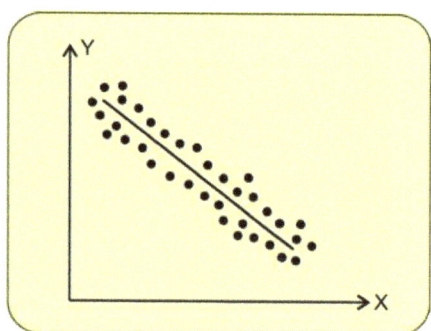

Fig. 16.6 : High degree of negative correlation

5. Low Degree of Positive Correlation : In this case, the points are widely scattered but are rising from lower left to upper right. The value of correlation coefficient (r) would be close to 0 but positive.

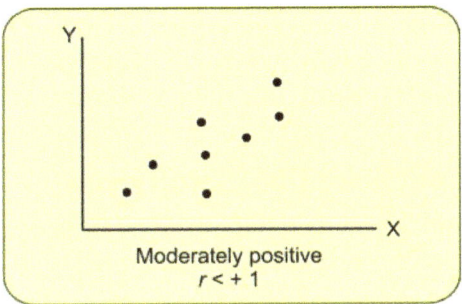

Fig. 16.7

6. Low Degree of Negative Correlation : In this case, the points are widely scattered but are falling from upper left to lower right. The value of correlation coefficient (r) would be close to 0 but negative.

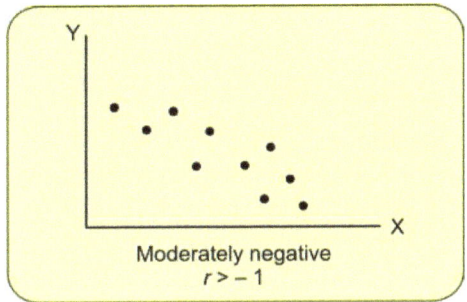

Fig. 16.8

7. No Correlation : When there is no relationship between variables, the points would be scattered all over and would not move in any direction. The value of correlation coefficient (r) would be equal to zero when there is no relationship between variables.

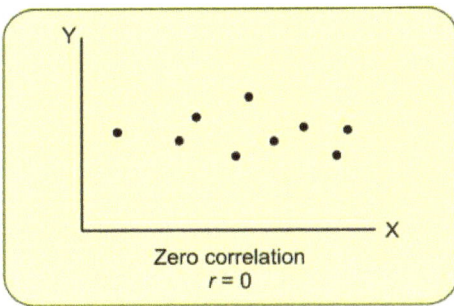

Fig. 16.9

Merits of Scatter Diagram Method

1. It is simple to understand as it is a non-mathematical method.
2. Relationship between variables can be understood by mere observation.
3. It is not affected by extreme items.
4. It is a preliminary step of investigating the relationship between two variables.

Demerits of Scatter Diagram Method

1. It is not an accurate measure of correlation. The scatter diagram only gives the direction of relationship and shows whether the correlation is high or low. However, it does not give the exact degree of correlation between two variables.
2. The method is useful only when number of observations is small. A scatter diagram does not give a precise measurement of correlation when there are large number of observations.

16.2.2. Karl Pearson's Coefficient of Correlation

The Karl Pearson's coefficient of correlation is denoted by r and can be used to measure correlation in case of both individual series as well as grouped data.

1. **Direct Method :** There are two ways to calculate coefficient of correlation under this method :

(i) First way to calculate coefficient of correlation under the direct method is by using the formula given below :

$$r = \frac{\Sigma(X-\bar{X})(Y-\bar{Y})}{\sqrt{\Sigma(X-\bar{X})^2}\sqrt{\Sigma(Y-\bar{Y})^2}}$$

Where, $\bar{X}$ = mean of variable X and
$\bar{Y}$ = mean of variable Y

Illustration 1: Calculate the Karl Pearson's coefficient of correlation for the following data on supply and price of a commodity and interpret the relationship between them.

Price (in ₹) (X)	5	6	7	8	9	10	11	12	13
Supply (Y)	25	32	35	40	42	50	58	60	63

Solution :

X	Y	$X - \bar{X}$	$(X - \bar{X})^2$	$Y - \bar{Y}$	$(Y - \bar{Y})^2$	$(X - \bar{X})(Y - \bar{Y})$
5	25	− 4	16	− 20	400	80
6	32	− 3	9	− 13	169	39
7	35	− 2	4	− 10	100	20
8	40	− 1	1	− 5	25	5
9	42	0	0	− 3	9	0
10	50	1	1	5	25	5
11	58	2	4	13	169	26
12	60	3	9	15	225	45
13	63	4	16	18	324	72
$\Sigma X = 81$	$\Sigma Y = 405$	$\Sigma(X - \bar{X}) = 0$	$\Sigma(X - \bar{X})^2 = 60$	$\Sigma(Y - \bar{Y}) = 0$	$\Sigma(Y - \bar{Y})^2 = 1446$	$\Sigma(X - \bar{X})(Y - \bar{Y}) = 292$

$$\bar{X} = \frac{\Sigma X}{n} = \frac{81}{9} = 9$$

and $\bar{Y} = \frac{\Sigma Y}{n} = \frac{405}{9} = 45$

Now, $r = \dfrac{\Sigma(X-\bar{X})(Y-\bar{Y})}{\sqrt{\Sigma(X-\bar{X})^2}\sqrt{\Sigma(Y-\bar{Y})^2}}$

$= \dfrac{292}{\sqrt{60}\sqrt{1446}} = 0.99$

Since the correlation coefficient is close to +1, it may be said that there is a high positive correlation between the price and the quantity supplied of a commodity.

(ii) When the mean is in decimals, then the calculation of deviations from the mean may become tedious. In such a situation, the following formula can be applied to compute the correlation directly without taking deviations.

$$r_{xy} = \frac{N\Sigma XY - \Sigma X \Sigma Y}{\sqrt{[N\Sigma X^2 - (\Sigma X)^2]}\sqrt{[N\Sigma Y^2 - (\Sigma Y)^2]}}$$

Where, N is the number of observations.

Illustration 2 : Calculate the coefficient of correlation from the following data :

Marks in Maths (X)	25	20	22	28	32	21	27	32	38	32
Marks in Science (Y)	32	25	28	32	42	21	20	35	25	30

Solution :

X	Y	X²	Y²	XY
25	32	625	1024	800
20	25	400	625	500
22	28	484	784	616
28	32	784	1024	896
32	42	1024	1764	1344
21	21	441	441	441
27	20	729	400	540
32	35	1024	1225	1120
38	25	1444	625	950
32	30	1024	900	960
ΣX = 277	ΣY = 290	ΣX² = 7979	ΣY² = 8812	ΣXY = 8167

$$r_{xy} = \frac{N\Sigma XY - \Sigma X \Sigma Y}{\sqrt{[N\Sigma X^2 - (\Sigma X)^2]}\sqrt{[N\Sigma Y^2 - (\Sigma Y)^2]}}$$

$$= \frac{10(8167)-(277)(290)}{\sqrt{10(7979)-(277)^2}\sqrt{(10(8812)-(290)^2}} = 0.38$$

Correlation coefficient of 0.38 indicates that there is a moderate positive correlation between marks in maths and marks in science.

2. Shortcut Method : When the actual mean is in fraction, deviations can also be taken from the assumed mean. When deviations are taken from the assumed mean, the following formula is applied to compute the correlation coefficient.

$$r = \frac{N\Sigma d_x d_y - (\Sigma d_x)(\Sigma d_y)}{\sqrt{[N\Sigma d_x^2 - (\Sigma d_x)^2]}\sqrt{[N\Sigma d_y^2 - (\Sigma d_y)^2]}}$$

Where, $d_x = X - A_x$ (A_x = Assumed mean of X)

$d_y = Y - A_y$ (A_y = Assumed mean of Y)

Illustration 3 : Calculate the coefficient of correlation for the following data on price and quantity demanded of a commodity.

Price (X) (in ₹)	78	90	100	61	79	60	68	62
Quantity Demanded (Y)	15	16	13	35	20	32	29	35

Solution :

Assumed mean of X (A_x) = 75

Assumed mean of Y (A_y) = 25

X	Y	$d_x = (X - 75)$	$d_y = Y - 25$	d_x^2	d_y^2	$d_x d_y$
78	15	3	− 10	9	100	− 30
90	16	15	− 9	225	81	− 135
100	13	25	− 12	625	144	− 300
61	35	− 14	10	196	100	− 140
79	20	4	− 5	16	25	− 20
60	32	− 15	7	225	49	− 105
68	29	− 7	4	49	16	− 28
62	35	− 13	10	169	100	− 130
ΣX = 598	ΣY = 195	Σd_x = −2	Σd_y = −5	Σd_x^2 = 1514	Σd_y^2 = 615	$\Sigma d_x d_y$ = −888

$$= \frac{N\Sigma d_x d_y - (\Sigma d_x)(\Sigma d_y)}{\sqrt{[N\Sigma d_x^2 - (\Sigma d_x)^2]}\sqrt{[N\Sigma d_y^2 - (\Sigma d_y)^2]}}$$

$$= \frac{8(-888)-(-2)(-5)}{\sqrt{8(1514)-(-2)^2}\sqrt{8(615)-(-5)^2}}$$

$$= -0.92$$

Correlation | **229**

The correlation coefficient of – 0.92 indicates a high negative correlation between price of the commodity and its quantity demanded.

Merits of Karl Pearson's Correlation Method
1. The Karl Pearson's coefficient of correlation gives the exact measure of correlation between variables.
2. It gives both the direction and the degree of relationship between variables.

Demerits of Karl Pearson's Correlation Method
1. It always assumes a linear relationship between variables.
2. The value of the coefficient is affected by the presence of extreme values.
3. It takes time to calculate the correlation coefficient using this method and it is a complicated method as compared to other measures of correlation.

16.2.3. Spearman's Rank Correlation Coefficient

The Karl Pearson's coefficient of correlation is computed based on the assumption that the observations are normally distributed. However, when the distribution of the observations is not known, then one can not use the previously mentioned methods of calculating correlation. Also, Karl Pearson's coefficient of correlation is unsuitable to study the correlation between two qualitative variables, such as honesty and beauty. In all such cases, Spearman's rank correlation coefficient can be applied to study the relationship between two variables. In this method, the variables need to be assigned ranks on the basis of their size from the smallest to the largest or from the largest to the smallest. This method is named after the British Psychologist Charles Edward Spearman, who developed it in 1904. Spearman's rank correlation coefficient is computed in the following manner :

1. **When Ranks are Given :** When the ranks have already been assigned to the items, following steps are to be used in calculating correlation :
    (i) Calculate the difference (D) between two ranks, i.e. Rx – Ry.
    (ii) The differences have to be squared (D^2) and their sum is to be taken as ΣD^2.
    (iii) Then the following formula is to be used to calculate the correlation coefficient :

$$R = 1 - \frac{6\Sigma D^2}{N(N^2 - 1)}$$

Where, R = Rank correlation coefficient
D = Difference in ranks of the paired items of the two variables
N = Number of items

Illustration 4 : The following are the ranks assigned to 10 competitors by 2 judges. Calculate the Spearman's rank correlation coefficient.

Competitors	1	2	3	4	5	6	7	8	9	10
Judge 1 (Rx)	9	8	10	6	5	7	4	3	2	1
Judge 2 (Ry)	3	8	4	5	6	10	2	9	7	1

Solution :

Competitors	Rx	Ry	D = Rx − Ry	D²
1	9	3	6	36
2	8	8	0	0
3	10	4	6	36
4	6	5	1	1
5	5	6	− 1	1
6	7	10	− 3	9
7	4	2	2	4
8	3	9	− 6	36
9	2	7	− 5	25
10	1	1	0	0
				ΣD² = 148

$$R = 1 - \frac{6\Sigma D^2}{N(N^2 - 1)}$$

$$R = 1 - \frac{6(148)}{10(10^2 - 1)} = 0.103$$

The Spearman's rank correlation coefficient of 0.103 represents a low positive correlation between the ranks given by the two judges.

2. **When Ranks are Not Given :** When the ranks are not already associated with the items and rather the marks or the values are assigned to each item, then the ranks have to be given to each item on the basis of the values or the marks attached to them. Following steps are to be followed when ranks are not given :

   (i)   First the rank is to be assigned to each item in the distribution. The variables can be assigned ranks on the basis of their size from smallest to largest or from largest to smallest.

  (ii)   Calculate the difference (D) of the two ranks, i.e. Rx − Ry.

 (iii)   The differences have to be squared (D²) and their sum is to be taken as ΣD².

 (iv)   Then the following formula is to be used :

$$R = 1 - \frac{6\Sigma D^2}{N(N^2 - 1)}$$

Where, R = Rank correlation coefficient
              D = Difference in ranks of the paired items of the two variables
              N = Number of items

Illustration 5 : Calculate the Spearman's rank correlation coefficient for the following data on the marks given by two examiners X and Y to the 10 students.

Roll No.	1	2	3	4	5	6	7	8	9	10
Marks given by X	75	70	65	62	80	85	43	40	90	45
Marks given by Y	91	43	64	62	50	90	40	45	92	60

Solution :

Firstly, the marks should be converted to ranks.

Roll No.	Marks given by X	Rx	Marks given by Y	Ry	D = Rx - Ry	D²
1	75	4	91	2	2	4
2	70	5	43	9	– 4	16
3	65	6	64	4	2	4
4	62	7	62	5	2	4
5	80	3	50	7	– 4	16
6	85	2	90	3	– 1	1
7	43	9	40	10	– 1	1
8	40	10	45	8	2	4
9	90	1	92	1	0	0
10	45	8	60	6	2	4
						ΣD² = 54

$$R = 1 - \frac{6\Sigma D^2}{N(N^2 - 1)}$$

$$= 1 - \frac{6(54)}{10(10^2 - 1)}$$

$$= 1 - \frac{324}{990}$$

$$= 1 - 0.33 = 0.67$$

The Spearman's rank correlation coefficient indicates a strong positive correlation between the marks given by the two examiners.

3. When Ranks are Equal : When there are equal ranks, for instance, when there are two 3rd ranks, then they are given the rank $\frac{3+4}{2} = 3.5$ and if there are three 3rd ranks, then it becomes $\frac{3+4+5}{3} = 4$. This adjustment is incorporated in the formula as follows :

$$R = 1 - \frac{6[\Sigma D^2 + \frac{1}{12}(m^3 - m) + \frac{1}{12}(m^3 - m) + ...]}{n^3 - n}$$

Where, D = Difference of rank in the two series
N = Total number of pairs
m = Number of times each rank repeats

Illustration 6 : Calculate the Spearman's rank correlation coefficient for the following data on the marks given by two examiners.

Roll No.	1	2	3	4	5	6	7	8	9	10
Examiner 1	75	70	65	62	80	85	40	40	90	45
Examiner 2	90	43	62	62	50	90	40	45	92	62

Solution :

Firstly, the marks should be converted to ranks.

Roll No.	Marks given by X	Rx	Marks given by Y	Ry	D = Rx - Ry	D²
1	75	4	90	2.5	1.5	2.25
2	70	5	43	9	– 4	16
3	65	6	62	5	1	1
4	62	7	62	5	2	4
5	80	3	50	7	– 4	16
6	85	2	90	2.5	– 0.5	0.25
7	40	9.5	40	10	– 0.5	0.25
8	40	9.5	45	8	1.5	2.25
9	90	1	92	1	0	0
10	45	8	62	5	3	9
						ΣD² = 51

It is to be noted here that the marks given by the examiner X contain marks which have been repeated i.e., 40 (2 times) and the marks given by the examiner Y contain 90 (2 times) and 62 (3 times). Hence, 40 would be given a rank of 9.5 (9+10/2)

90 would be given a rank of 2.5 (2+3/2)

And, 62 would be given a rank of 5 (4+5+6/3)

Since there are equal ranks, the formula to be applied is

$$R = 1 - \frac{6[\Sigma D^2 + \frac{1}{12}(m^3 - m) + \frac{1}{12}(m^3 - m) + ...]}{n^3 - n}$$

$$= 1 - \frac{6[51 + \frac{1}{12}(2^3 - 2) + \frac{1}{12}(2^3 - 2) + \frac{1}{12}(3^3 - 3)]}{10^3 - 10}$$

$$= 1 - 0.327$$

$$= 0.673$$

The Spearman's rank correlation coefficient indicates a strong positive correlation between the marks given by the two examiners.

Merits of Spearman's Rank Correlation Coefficient

1. It is simple to understand.
2. It is easy to calculate as compared to the Karl Pearson's correlation method.
3. It can be easily applied when the data is qualitative in nature. For example, the level of satisfaction derived by the two consumers from different products can easily be ranked and degree of correlation can be computed.
4. This method can also be applied when the data is not in the form of ranks. The actual data can be converted to ranks in such cases.

Demerits of Spearman's Rank Correlation Coefficient

1. This method cannot be applied when the data is in the form of grouped frequency distribution.
2. The calculation of Spearman's rank correlation coefficient becomes time consuming when the data is very large and when ranks are not given.

Summary

1. **Correlation**—Correlation is a measure of the nature of relationship that exists between two or more variables.
2. **Significance of the Study of Correlation**—
   (i) Correlation measures the strength of relationship between two or more variables.
   (ii) It helps in predicting the value of one variable when the other variable is known.
   (iii) It helps in understanding the behaviour of various economic variables.
   (iv) It helps in making business decisions.
3. **Types of Correlation**—
   (i) On the basis of direction of change—Positive and negative correlation
   (ii) On the basis of number of variables—Simple, partial and multiple correlation.
   (iii) On the basis of ratio of variation in the variables—Linear and non-linear correlation
4. **Positive Correlation**—Correlation between two variables is said to be positive when both the variables move in the same direction. When one variable increases, the other also increases and when one decreases, the other also decreases.
5. **Negative Correlation**—Correlation between two variables is said to be negative when both the variables move in opposite direction. When one variable increases, the other decreases and when one decreases, the other increases.

6. **Simple Correlation**—When the relationship between only two variables is studied, it is a simple correlation.
7. **Partial Correlation**—Studies the relationship between two variables, assuming all other variables to be constant.
8. **Multiple Correlation**—The relationship between more than two variables is studied simultaneously.
9. **Linear Correlation**—The ratio of change between two variables is constant.
10. **Non-linear Correlation**—The ratio of change between two variables increases or decreases.
11. **Methods of Correlation**—
    (i) Scatter diagram method
    (ii) Karl Pearson's coefficient of correlation
    (iii) Spearman's rank correlation coefficient
12. **Scatter Diagram Method**—This is the simplest method of studying the relationship between two variables. In this method, the values of both the variables are plotted on a graph paper. For each pair of X and Y, a dot is plotted. Observing the way the points are scattered gives an idea as to how the two variables are related.
13. **Degrees of Correlation**—
    (i) Perfect positive correlation
    (ii) Perfect negative correlation
    (iii) High degree of positive correlation
    (iv) High degree of negative correlation
    (v) Low degree of positive correlation
    (vi) Low degree of negative correlation
    (vii) No correlation
14. **Karl Pearson's Coefficient of Correlation**—It is a quantitative method of calculating correlation and can be used to measure correlation in case of both individual series as well as grouped data.
15. **Spearman's Rank Correlation Coefficient**—It is applied when the nature of distribution is not known and when the variables are in the form of ranks.

◆ Short Answer Questions (2 marks)

1. Define correlation.
2. State the significance of studying correlation between variables.
3. State the different types of correlation.

Correlation | 235

4. Differentiate between partial and multiple correlation.
5. Differentiate between linear and non-linear correlation.
6. What are the different methods of studying correlation ?
7. What is a scatter diagram ?
8. List out the merits and demerits of scatter diagram.
9. Differentiate between Pearson's and Spearman's correlation coefficients.
10. What is a rank correlation ?
11. What are the merits and demerits of Pearson's correlation coefficient ?
12. State the limitations of Spearman's rank correlation coefficient.

◆ **Long Answer Questions (3-6 marks)**

1. Explain the various types of correlation.
2. Discuss the different methods of studying correlation.
3. What are the various degrees of correlation?
4. Compute the Karl Pearson's coefficient of correlation for the following data on investments and number of people unemployed.

Investments (in millions)	500	575	600	620	700	750	800
No. of people unemployed (in '000)	75	65	60	62	60	45	48

5. Calculate the Spearman's coefficient of correlation between the marks in History and Geography for the following 10 students.

Roll No.	1	2	3	4	5	6	7	8	9	10
History	40	65	88	74	90	55	62	70	72	69
Geography	80	70	72	65	55	73	52	55	58	66

6. Calculate the Spearman's coefficient of correlation for the ranks given by two judges for the following students in a school competition.

Student	A	B	C	D	E	F
Judge 1	2	1	3	5	2	6
Judge 2	1	2	4	5	3	6

7. The scores of 8 students in two competitions are given below. Compute the Spearman's correlation coefficient.

Students	A	B	C	D	E	F	G	H
Competition 1	19	18	15	15	24	25	10	12
Competition 2	18	17	17	20	22	17	15	15

8. The following data provides information on the amount of advertisement expenditure and the sales revenue of a firm. Calculate the correlation coefficient.

Advertisement exp. (in '000)	25	45	40	60	65	70	80
Sales (in '000)	160	170	169	175	176	180	220

9. The grades of five students in Mathematics and Science are as follows :

Mathematics	55	40	68	72	90	85
Science	72	50	40	98	65	60

Calculate the Spearman's coefficient of correlation.

10. The heights and weights of 8 cricket players are as follows :

Height (in cms.)	180	185	178	190	193	198	201	202
Weight (in kgs.)	80	85	85	86	91	93	102	100

Calculate the Pearson's coefficient of correlation.

11. The following data provides the test scores of 10 students in Economics and Statistics. Calculate the Spearman's coefficient of correlation.

Economics	40	45	65	60	80	75	70	82	98	65
Statistics	55	50	72	80	72	65	90	85	85	72

Index Numbers

17.1. Meaning

Index numbers are measures that track the change in a variable or a set of related variables. According to Croxton and Cowden, "Index numbers are devices for measuring differences in the magnitude of a group of related variables." It is an average measure that denotes the change in a variable or related variables over a period of time. Price index, Index of Industrial Production (IIP), Sensex, Nifty, commodities index are common indices that we have heard of. Each of these indices tracks the change in a specific variable or a set of related variables. Following are some of the most important indices used in India :

1. **Wholesale Price Index (WPI)** : A price index captures the average prices for a given class of goods and services in a region for a certain period of time. The wholesale price index captures the prices of a basket of goods in the wholesale market. It compares the prices of goods in a specific year to the prices of the same goods in the base year. Some countries like Philippines follow the wholesale price index to measure their rate of inflation.

2. **Consumer Price Index (CPI)** : Consumer price index is based on the prices paid by the households for a basket of goods and services. Changes in CPI are followed by many countries as a measure of their rate of inflation. India, since 2014, has been following CPI as a measure of inflation.

3. **Index of Industrial Production (IIP)** : The index of industrial production, known as IIP, captures the growth of various sectors of the economy such as manufacturing, mining, power, infrastructure etc.

4. **Sensex and Nifty** : Sensex and Nifty capture the movement in prices of specific shares. While Sensex is made up of the stocks of 30 major companies, Nifty is made up of the stocks of 50 major companies.

17.2. Types of Index Numbers

Index numbers can broadly be classified into four categories. They are as follows :

1. **Price Index** : A price index compares the changes in prices from one period to another.

2. **Quantity Index** : A quantity index measures the changes in the quantity of a variable over a period of time.

3. **Value Index** : A value index measures the changes in the value of a currency.

4. **Special Purpose Index** : Special purpose index numbers combine a heterogeneous group of variables to obtain an index that tracks the changes in those variables.

17.3. Purpose of Index Numbers

Index numbers play a very important role in the economy as they serve as indicators for various purposes, which are listed below :

1. Index numbers are useful in tracking the changes in critical variables such as price, quantity etc.

2. They are useful in decision making. For instance, price index is useful in fixing the pay scale of the employees, market index is followed to make appropriate investment decisions etc.

3. They help in studying the trend and thereby, help in making predictions for the future.

4. While measuring the changes in the income, the absolute values are adjusted with the help of a price index in order to understand the real increase in the income.

17.4. Methods of Constructing Index Numbers

Numerous methods have been developed for constructing an index number. They are broadly classified as :

1. Simple or unweighted index numbers, and
2. Weighted index numbers

1. **Simple Index Numbers** : In simple index numbers, there are no weights assigned. The total of current year's price is divided by the base year prices and the quotient is multiplied by 100 to obtain the index value. Since weights are not assigned the relative importance of the items is not known in this method. Further, the units in which the variables are expressed can influence the value of the index.

Illustration 1. From the following data, construct an index for 2015 taking 2014 as the base year.

Commodity	Price in 2014 (in ₹)	Price in 2015 (in ₹)
Rice	45	50
Wheat	35	40
Maize	30	30
Pulse	70	80
Bajra	20	20

Index Numbers | 239

Solution:

Commodity	Price in 2014 (in ₹) P_0	Price in 2015 (in ₹) P_1
Rice	45	50
Wheat	35	40
Maize	30	30
Pulse	70	80
Bajra	20	20
	$\Sigma P_0 = 200$	$\Sigma P_1 = 220$

$$P_1 = \frac{\Sigma P_1}{\Sigma P_0} \times 100$$

$$= \frac{220}{200} \times 100 = 110$$

Illustration 2. Compute the index number for the following data taking 2008 as the base year.

Year	2008	2009	2010	2011	2012	2013	2014	2015	2016
Price of Milk (₹ per litre)	12	12	15	16	18	20	23	25	32

Solution:

Year	Price of Milk (in ₹)	Index Numbers (2008 = 100)
2008	12	100
2009	12	$\frac{12}{12} \times 100 = 100$
2010	15	$\frac{15}{12} \times 100 = 125$
2011	16	$\frac{16}{12} \times 100 = 133$
2012	18	$\frac{18}{12} \times 100 = 150$
2013	20	$\frac{20}{12} \times 100 = 167$

2014	23	$\frac{23}{12} \times 100 = 192$
2015	25	$\frac{25}{12} \times 100 = 208$
2016	32	$\frac{32}{12} \times 100 = 267$

2. Weighted Index Numbers: The weighted index assigns weights to the commodities in the index. While the simple index assigns equal importance to all the items, the weighted index assigns weights to the items according to their importance. A number of methods have been developed for computing weighted index. The most popular among them are :

(i) Laspeyres' method
(ii) Paasche's method
(iii) Fisher's Ideal method

(i) **Laspeyres' Method**: In Laspeyres' index method, the weights are determined according to the quantities in the base period. The formula used in this method is :

$$P_{01} = \frac{\Sigma p_1 q_0}{\Sigma p_0 q_0} \times 100$$

Where, p_1 = price of the current year
p_0 = price of the base year
q_0 = quantity of the base year

(ii) **Paasche's Method**: Paasche's method of computing the index is a slight variant of Laspeyres' method. Here, the weights are determined according to the quantities of the current year. While base period quantities are the weights in Lasperyres' method, the current period quantities are the weights in Paasche's method. Paasche's method is computed by the formula :

$$P_{01} = \frac{\Sigma p_1 q_1}{\Sigma p_0 q_1} \times 100$$

Where, q_1 indicates the quantity of the current year.

(iii) **Fisher's Ideal Index**: This is another method of constructing the index developed by Irving Fisher. Fisher's index is the geometric mean of Laspeyres' and Paasche's index. It is computed by the formula :

$$P_{01} = \sqrt{\frac{\Sigma p_1 q_0}{\Sigma p_0 q_0} \times \frac{\Sigma p_1 q_1}{\Sigma p_0 q_1}} \times 100$$

Fisher's index considers base year as well as current year's prices and quantities, hence, it is considered as an ideal index.

Illustration **3.** Given below is the data pertaining to the price and quantity of few commodities for two years.

Commodity	2010		2011	
	Price (₹)	Quantity (Kg.)	Price (₹)	Quantity (Kg.)
Sugar	30	9	50	8
Rice	60	13	80	15
Wheat	40	12	50	8
Milk	20	20	20	23

Compute :
(i) Laspeyres Index
(ii) Paasche's Index, and
(iii) Fisher's Index

Solution :

Commodity	p_0	q_0	p_1	q_1	$p_1 q_0$	$p_0 q_0$	$p_1 q_1$	$p_0 q_1$
Sugar	30	9	50	8	450	270	400	240
Rice	60	13	80	15	1040	780	1200	900
Wheat	40	12	50	8	600	480	400	320
Milk	20	20	20	23	400	400	460	460
					$\Sigma p_1 q_0$ = 2490	$\Sigma p_0 q_0$ = 1930	$\Sigma p_1 q_1$ = 2460	$\Sigma p_0 q_1$ = 1920

Laspeyres' Index—

$$P_{01} = \frac{\Sigma p_1 q_0}{\Sigma p_0 q_0} \times 100$$

$$P_{01} = \frac{2490}{1930} \times 100 = 129.02$$

Paasche's Index—

$$P_{01} = \frac{\Sigma p_1 q_1}{\Sigma p_0 q_1} \times 100$$

$$P_{01} = \frac{2460}{1920} \times 100 = 128.13$$

Fisher's Index—

$$P_{01} = \sqrt{\frac{\Sigma p_1 q_0}{\Sigma p_0 q_0} \times \frac{\Sigma p_1 q_1}{\Sigma p_0 q_1}} \times 100$$

$$P_{01} = \sqrt{\frac{2490}{1930} \times \frac{2460}{1920}} \times 100 = 128.57$$

17.5. Problems Involved in Constructing a Price Index Number

1. **Choice of the Base Period** : Index numbers are always computed with reference to a base period. Due care should be taken while choosing the base year to ensure that the base year is a normal one, free from events such as floods, earthquakes, depressions etc. It becomes difficult when a period without any abnormalities has to be chosen. In order to overcome this problem, sometimes the average of three or four years is taken as base year figures.

2. **Purpose of the Index** : Purpose of constructing the index must be clearly defined. Accordingly, the items to be included in the index should be decided. For instance, if an index is to be constructed to measure the cost of living of rural poor, adequate care should be taken to ensure that goods consumed by middle class or upper income group or by people in urban areas are not included in the goods chosen to be included in the index.

3. **Choice of Commodities** : Choice of items to be included in computing the index is another problem that arises. The items should be carefully chosen to fulfil the purpose of computing the index.

4. **Prices of Commodities** : Prices of the commodities should be accurate and unbiased. However, prices are subject to variation from one place to another. Hence, it becomes difficult to take a particular price for commodities in the index. Confusion also arises in deciding whether wholesale prices or retail prices of commodities should be considered.

5. **Choice of the Method** : Another problem that arises in computing the index is the choice of the method to be adopted, since there are different methods of computing an index. Generally, Fisher's index is chosen whenever greater accuracy is required.

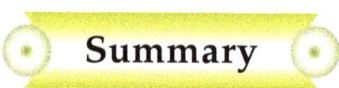

Summary

1. **Index Numbers**—Index numbers are measures that track the change in a variable or a set of related variables.
2. **Wholesale Price Index**—A wholesale price index captures the average wholesale prices for a given class of goods and services in a region, for a certain period of time.
3. **Consumer Price Index**—Consumer price index is based on the prices paid by the households for a basket of goods and services.
4. **Index of Industrial Production**—The index of industrial production, known as IIP, captures the growth of various sectors of the economy such as manufacturing, mining, power, infrastructure etc.
5. **Types of Index Numbers**—
    (i) Price index
    (ii) Quantity index
    (iii) Value index
    (iv) Special purpose index

Index Numbers | 243

6. **Methods of Constructing Index Numbers—**
   (i) Simple or unweighted index numbers
   (ii) Weighted index numbers
      (a) Laspeyres' method
      (b) Paasche's method
      (c) Fisher's ideal index
7. **Problems Involved in Constructing an Index—**
   (i) Choice of the base period
   (ii) Purpose of the index
   (iii) Choice of commodities
   (iv) Prices of commodities
   (v) Choice of the method

Exercise

◆ Short Answer Questions (2 marks)

1. What is an index ?
2. Differentiate between a wholesale price index and a consumer price index.
3. State the different types of index numbers.
4. State the methods of constructing index numbers.
5. What is the difference between a simple and weighted index number ?
6. State the formula for calculating the index number by Laspeyres' method.
7. Why is Fisher's index considered as an ideal index ?
8. State any two problems faced in computing an index.

◆ Long Answer Questions (3-6 marks)

1. Define an index number and state the purpose of constructing an index number.
2. Discuss the different methods of constructing index numbers.
3. From the following data construct an index for 2016 taking 2011 as the base year.

Commodity	Price in 2011 (in ₹)	Price in 2016 (in ₹)
Rice	50	80
Wheat	20	29
Maize	28	40
Pulse	60	80
Bajra	15	20

5. Compute the index number for the following data taking 2008 as the base year.

Year	2008	2009	2010	2011	2012	2013	2014	2015	2016
Price of Water (₹ per litre)	15	15	18	20	20	22	23	25	30

6. Compute the index number for the following data using Laspeyres', Paasche's and Fisher's methods.

Commodity	2001		2002	
	Price (in ₹)	Quantity	Price (in ₹)	Quantity
P	25	42	30	60
Q	20	15	18	25
R	40	30	45	50
S	15	28	10	30

4. Compute Laspeyres', Paasche's and Fisher's index from the following data.

Commodity	2010		2011	
	Price (in ₹)	Quantity	Price (in ₹)	Quantity
Gram	82	108	102	100
Flour	45	80	40	95
Maize	30	75	38	85
Sugar	35	115	55	12

❐❐

18 Mathematical Tools Used in Economics

18.1. Concept

Theories in economic analysis explain various economic problems by establishing relationships between economic variables. In other words, they model the relationships between two or more economic variables. In establishing such relationships, they apply numerous mathematical tools such as functions, equations, graphs, calculus, algebra, derivatives, etc., in order to quantify the facts.

In modelling the relationship between variables, some of the variables are explained within the theory and their values are dependent on the variables within the model itself. These variables are called endogenous variables. There are other variables outside the model that can have an influence on the variables in the model. These variables are called exogenous variables. The values of the exogenous variables are not dependent on the variables in the model. They are determined by factors outside the model.

For instance, while modelling the demand for a commodity, price is an endogenous variable that influences the demand for the product. Other variables such as income of the consumers, tastes and preferences, etc., are all exogenous variables since they are not influenced by the variables in the model.

18.2. Function

Economic models establish relationship between two or more economic variables. Such relationships may sometimes be expressed in the form of a function. A function is an expression of the relationship between two or more variables. A demand function is expressed as $Q_d = f(P)$, where Q_d represents the quantity demanded, P is the price of the commodity and f represents the functional relationship. It is read as "quantity demanded is a function of price".

18.3. Equation of a Straight Line

Equations are tools that are used to express the functional relationship between the variables. The demand function, for instance, is expressed in the form of an equation as

$$Q_d = a - bP$$

In the above equation 'a' is the intercept which is independent of the change in price. It shows the quantity of a commodity which will be demanded when the price is zero. Similarly 'b' is the rate of change which shows by how much the quantity demanded would change for a unit change in the price of the commodity. So 'b' is the coefficient of price.

The functional relationship between variables may be linear or non-linear. In a linear relationship, the ratio of change in the dependent variable to the change in the independent variable is constant. When the relationship is linear, the graph representing the relationship would be a straight line as shown below :

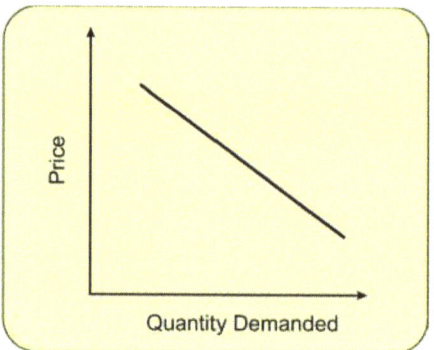

Fig. 18.1

When the relationship is non-linear, the graph showing the relationship between the variables would be a curve. When the ratio of change in the dependent variable to the change in the independent variable is not constant, then the line showing the relationship between the dependent and the independent variable would be a non-linear curve, as shown below :

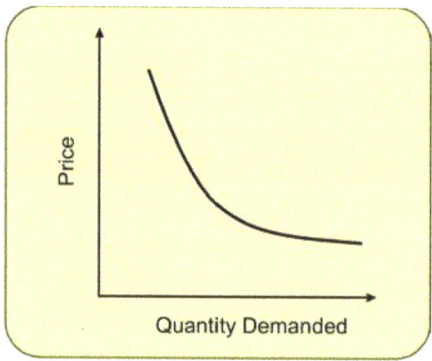

Fig. 18.2

18.4. Slope of a Line

The slope of a line is an important feature in studying the relationship between variables. It shows the rate of change in the dependent variable as the independent variable changes. The demand equation $Q_d = a - bP$ is a linear function, where b represents the slope of the demand curve. When b is negative, the line slopes down from left to right and when b is positive, the line slopes up from left to right.

The slope of a line is the ratio of change in the dependent variable to the change in the independent variable. It is mathematically expressed as :

$$\text{Slope} = \frac{\text{Change in Y}}{\text{Change in X}} = \frac{\Delta Y}{\Delta X}$$

Where, Y is the dependent variable and X is the independent variable.

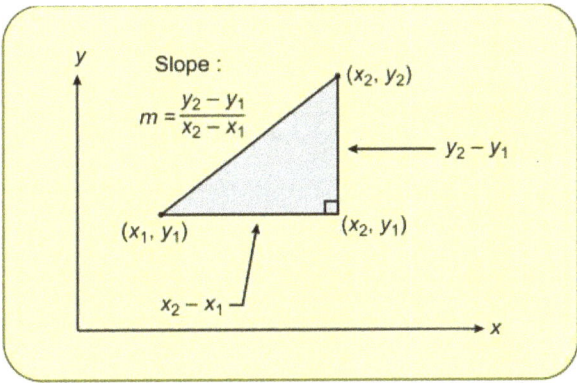

Fig. 18.3

Consider the demand equation, $Q_d = 25 - 2P$. Here, 25 is the Y intercept, which shows the demand that is independent of the price and -2 is the coefficient of price, which indicates that for a unit increase in the price, the quantity demanded would fall by 2 units.

Consider the supply equation, $Q_s = 25 + 2P$. Here, $+2$ is the coefficient of price and is positive. Thus, a unit increase in the price of the commodity would increase the quantity supplied by 2 units.

When the equation of a curve is known, it helps in predicting one variable when the other variable is given.

Illustration **1.** Given the equation of the demand curve $Q_d = 25 - 2P$, find the quantity demanded of the commodity when the price is ₹ 3.

Given, $Q_d = 25 - 2P$

Substituting P = 3 in the equation,

$Q_d = 25 - 2(3) = 19$.

Thus, the quantity demanded would be 19 units.

Illustration **2.** Given the supply equation, $Q_s = 10 + 4P$. Find the price of the commodity if the quantity supplied is 54 units.

Given, $Q_s = 10 + 4P$.

When, $Q_s = 54$

54 = 10 + 4P

P = 11.

Thus, the price of the commodity should be ₹ 11, if the quantity supplied is 54 units.

Summary

1. **Function**—A function is an expression of the relationship between two or more variables.
2. **Equation**—Equations are tools that are used to express the functional relationship between the variables.
3. **Slope of a Line**—Slope of a line shows the rate of change in the dependent variable as the independent variable changes.

Exercise

◆ Short Answer Questions (2 marks)

1. Differentiate between exogenous and endogenous variables.
2. What is a function ?
3. State the demand function.
4. Differentiate between a linear and a non-linear curve.
5. Give the equation of a straight line.

◆ Long Answer Questions (3-6 marks)

1. Discuss how mathematical tools are applied in economics.
2. How would you measure the slope of a straight line ?
3. Given the consumption function C = 1000 + 0.2Y, where C is the consumption (in units), and Y is the income. Find the amount of consumption when the income is ₹ 10000.
4. The equation of a demand curve is Q_d = 40 – 2P, find the quantity demanded of the commodity when the price is ₹ 5.
5. Given the supply equation, Q_s = 5 + 8P. Find the price of the commodity if the quantity supplied is 85 units.
6. The equation of the demand curve is Y = 4 – 2X. What is the slope of the curve ?
7. The equation of supply curve is given, Q_s = 20 + 5P. Find the quantity supplied when the price is ₹ 2, ₹ 4, ₹ 6, ₹ 8 and ₹ 10. Trace the supply curve.
8. When the price of a candy was ₹ 3, Jenny was willing to buy 10 of them. But when she reached the shop, she found that the price had increased to ₹ 4. She is now willing to buy only 7 of them. Find the slope of the demand curve.
9. A supplier was willing to supply 100 units of Good X when its price was ₹ 60. Now that the price has increased to ₹ 80, he is willing to supply 130 units. Find the slope of the supply curve.

PROJECT 1

Study consumer awareness among households through designing a questionnaire and collection of primary data.

All the researches related to the consumer involve collection of information directly from a sample of the consumers. Such kind of information is called as primary data. Primary data based researches provide the researcher first-hand information regarding various aspects of a consumer like preference, price expectations, desired aesthetics, attitude, knowledge, awareness etc. related to a product or service.

Process which is followed to conduct a research is given as under :

Step 1 : Identify the Problem

The very first step in the research process is to identify the problem which is required to be solved. The research problem may be to understand a consumer's requirements about a product, price he is ready to pay, type of communication required for reaching the right consumers, type of distribution channel appropriate for the target customers, changing preference of the consumer, behavioral aspects of consumer etc. This serves as the primary step of the study.

Step 2 : Determining the Specific Objectives of the Study

The next step involves the determination of the research objectives specifically. Specific objectives help in determining the right methodology of the research and the source of the data collection. For example, the objectives of a consumer awareness research may be the following :

1. To know whether a consumer pays attention to the information provided on a product box.
2. To assert whether a consumer takes the bill of the purchase.
3. To assert whether a consumer pays attention to the details of the bill.
4. To know whether a consumer knows about the grievance redressal bodies.

The sample questionnaire provided with this project has been developed by keeping these objectives in mind.

Step 3 : Determination of Research Methodology

After the determination of research objectives, the methodology to conduct the research is finalized. The research methodology includes the research design, sample size, method of sample selection, data collection tools etc. The methodology must be determined very cautiously because the success and effectiveness of research depends upon the methodology.

Step 4 : Collection of Data

After the research methodology is determined, the data is collected. There are two types of data which are collected in any research. The first is Primary data which is collected first hand for any research from the respondents from the field. Questionnaires are primarily used to collect primary data from the respondents. Some precautions must be taken to prepare a questionnaire. These are as follows :

1. There should be limited number of questions.
2. The questions must be logically sequenced.
3. The language of the questions must be simple.
4. Most of the questions must be close ended.
5. Questionnaire must be pre-tested.
6. Questions must be unbiased.
7. There should not be any effort to influence the responses of the respondents.

Second type of data is known as secondary data. It could be a data that has already been published or it may not have been published for various reasons and might have been kept only as a written record. Secondary data may be collected from various sources like newspapers, government reports, journals, magazines, internet etc.

Step 5 : Tabulation and Classification of Data

After collecting the data, the data is then classified on some predetermined basis and organized in various tables for further analysis.

Step 6 : Analysis of the Data

After tabulating the data, analysis of the data starts. The researcher analyze the data and makes inferences from the data by using various mathematical tools like correlation, regression, etc.

Step 7 : Presentation of the Report

Finally, report of the research is presented by organizing the whole process and data in the predetermined manner.

Sample Questionnaire

Name : _____

Address : _____

Gender : _____   Monthly Income : _____

1. Do you use toothpaste ?   Yes ☐   No ☐
2. Which brand do you use ?

   Pepsodent ☐   Colgate ☐   Close-Up ☐

Sensodyne ☐   Meswak ☐   Others ☐

3. How did you come to know about the brand ?

   Already used in family ☐   Relatives ☐

   Friends ☐   Newspaper ☐

   T.V. ☐   Others ☐

4. Do you check the information provided on the toothpaste box ?

   Yes ☐   No ☐

5. Put in sequence the information you check on the box :

   Price ☐   Date of Manufacturing ☐

   Date of Expiry ☐   Customer Care Details ☐

   Manufacturer's Details ☐   Others ☐

6. Do you take the bill of your purchase ?

   Yes ☐   No ☐

7. Do you check the information provided on the bill ?

   Yes ☐   No ☐

8. What information do you check on the bill ?

   Amount ☐   Date ☐   Particulars of Product ☐

   Amount of Tax ☐   Others ☐

9. Do you know the modes of complaints your brand provides to you ?

   Yes ☐   No ☐

10. Do you remember the Customer Care Email-Id or Telephone Number of the toothpaste you use ?

    Yes ☐   No ☐

11. Do you know the bodies which help you to resolve your complaint if the company possessing the brand fails to do so ?

    Yes ☐   No ☐

12. Which are they ?

   District Consumer Forum ☐   State Consumer Forum ☐

   National Consumer Forum ☐   Others ☐

The students are advised to make the following additions to the project :

1. The students must study the product/service of their choice.

2. The students must add or rewrite questions of their choice. But they must observe the principles of good questionnaire framing.

3. They must collect the data from at least 50 -100 households.

FINDINGS

Students are required to write their findings based on the analysis of the information collected in the form of a brief report.

SUGGESTED QUESTIONS FOR VIVA-VOCE

Q.1. What are the findings of the study ?
Q.2. What methodology have you adopted to make the research ?
Q.3. Why did you select this particular product for the study ?
Q.4. What difficulties did you face while collecting information from the respondents ?
Q.5. How did you deal with such difficulties ?

PROJECT 2

Prepare a report on productivity awareness among enterprises through use of statistical data from statistical tables published in Newspapers/RBI Bulletin/Budget/Census report/Economic survey etc.

India was industrially backward at the time of independence. In 1951-52, the share of industrial sector in national income was only 19 percent. But with the adoption of economic planning and economic reforms, India achieved industrialisation in the later years. This industrialisation resulted into relatively better growth rates in the earlier years but industrial growth became sluggish in the later period.

The industrial growth depends upon the availability of resources and the resources have always been scarce. So the productivity of resources is a matter of concern for the country. The productivity is measured in terms of labour productivity, capital productivity and total factor productivity.

The role of industrial sector has increased with every passing year. In 2016-17, the share of industrial sector in the GDP increased to about 31.2 percent which is a very positive sign. But, as far as factor productivity is concerned which is a ratio of output to inputs, many studies have found that the productivity has fallen in the post reform period. This means that for producing a given level of output, more and more units of inputs are required.

The students are required to develop this project on the basis of various government reports, RBI report, various studies etc. The students may develop the project by highlighting the following points :

1. Find out the rate of industrial growth in various years.

2. Find out the various challenges facing the industrial sector in this country.

3. Find out the employment opportunities provided by the industrial sector.

4. Find out the capital output ratio of the country.

5. Find out the rate of investment, GDP in real terms and the rate of employment generation by industrial sector.

The above questions may be designed by keeping in mind the selected sectors like automobiles, textiles or any other sector of your choice.

FINDINGS

Students are required to write their findings based on the analysis of the information collected and present it in a brief report.

SUGGESTED QUESTIONS FOR VIVA-VOCE

Q.1. What do you understand by productivity ?

Q.2. What are the factors which influence the productivity in manufacturing sector ?

Q.3. How can the productivity in the industrial sector be increased ?

Q.4. What efforts has the Indian government taken to increase the productivity in the industrial sector ?

PROJECT 3

Make a study of two co-operative institutions (example-milk co-operatives, etc.) with a view to compare the organizational and financial structure of the organisations, production capacity and output, marketing strategies, sales, market share, etc.

A co-operative society is an autonomous and voluntary association of persons who unite for the promotion of their common economic, social and cultural goals through a jointly-owned and democratically-controlled organisation.

Two such cooperatives are **Gujarat Cooperative Milk Marketing Federation Ltd.** (GCMMF), popularly known as **'AMUL',** which is the apex organisation of the Dairy Cooperatives of Gujarat and **Karnataka Cooperative Milk Producers' Federation Limited (KMF),** which is the apex body for the dairy co-operative movement in Karnataka.

AMUL

The formation of AMUL was a response by farmers to their exploitation by a cartel of local middleman in Anand, a small town in the state of Gujarat in Western India on the inspiration and suggestions of Sardar Vallabhbhai Patel.

In 1946, a co-operative organisation, the Kaira District Co-operative Milk Producers Union Ltd. began with just two village dairy co-operative societies and 247 litres of milk. Today, this Kaira District Co-operative Milk Producers Union Ltd. is popularly known as Amul Dairy.

The organisation which started with just 247 liters of milk from just two village dairy co-operative societies now has a milk procurement of approximately 18 million liters per day from 18,549 village milk cooperative societies, 18 member unions covering 33 districts, and 3.6 million milk producer members. Now AMUL has become India's largest food product marketing organisation with an annual turnover of US$ 4.1 billion in 2016-17.

AMUL operates through 56 Sales Offices and has a dealer network of 10000 dealers and 10 lakh retailers. Its product range comprises of milk, milk powder, paneer, ghee, butter, cheese, pizza cheese, ice-cream, health beverages, chocolates, traditional Indian sweets, etc.

AMUL follows the following organizational structure to move the milk from milk producers to the consumers :

Milk Producer ⟶ Village Dairy Cooperative Society ⟶ District Milk Cooperative Society ⟶ State Cooperative Milk Marketing Federation ⟶ The Consumer

KMF

The Karnataka Cooperative Milk Producers' Federation Limited (KMF) is the second largest dairy co-operative amongst the dairy cooperatives in the country.

The KMF was transformed from the Karnataka Dairy Development Cooperation (KDDC), which was the first ever World Bank/ International Development Agency funded Dairy Development Program in the country. It started in Karnataka on the AMUL pattern of dairy co-operatives with the organisation of Village Level Dairy Co-operatives in 1974.

KMF has 14 Milk Unions which cover all the districts of the State. They procure milk from Primary Dairy Cooperative Societies(DCS) and distribute milk to the consumers in various towns, cities and rural markets in Karnataka.

The sale of milk of KMF was only 95 thousand liters per day in 1976-77 which increased to 34.01 lakh liters per day in 2016-17.

The sales turnover of KMF which was merely ₹ 8.82 crores in 1976-77 increased to ₹ 12954 crores in 2016-17.

The KMF follows a three tiered organizational structure on co-operative principles and it has a democratically elected board from among the milk producers:

1. Dairy Co-operative Societies at grass root level.
2. District Co-operative Milk Unions at single / multi district level.
3. Milk Federation at State level.

The students are advised to develop the project further by adding and developing on the following points:

1. Find out the history of the development of cooperative institutions/societies in India.
2. Find the vision and mission of the organisations.
3. Present the organizational structures of both the organisations in detail.
4. Find out the various products offered by both the organisations.
5. Find out the pricing structure followed by both the organisations for their products.
6. Find out the promotional measures adopted by both the organisations for marketing their products.
7. Try to find out the respective market shares of both the organisations in their respective areas of operation.
8. Find out the local competitors of both the organisations.
9. Find out the various achievements made by both the organisations in their respective areas of operation.

FINDINGS

Students are required to write their findings based on the comparative analysis of the two cooperative institutions and present it in the form of a brief report.

SUGGESTED QUESTIONS FOR VIVA-VOCE

Q.1. What do you understand by a cooperative society ?

Q.2. How was the cooperative movement started in India ?

Q.3. Explain about the "White Revolution" in India.

Q.4. What kind of organizational structure is generally followed by both the cooperative organisations ?

Q.5. What differences have you found in the financial performance of both the organisations ?

Q.6. What is the difference between the marketing strategies of both the organisations ?

Project 4

Study in detail the South Asian Association for Regional Cooperation (SAARC) and its impact on Indian Economy

THE FORMATION

Since World War II, the countries of the world recognised and appreciated the importance of collectivism in the matters of diplomacy, development and trade. This resulted into the formation of International Monetary Fund (IMF), International Bank for Reconstruction and Development (IBRD) and General Agreement on Tariffs and Trade (GATT). The countries also started forming Regional Groupings to intensify the benefits of collectivism in various matters of a country's welfare. South Asian Association for Regional Cooperation (SAARC) is one such effort made by the countries of South Asia.

The South Asian Association for Regional Cooperation (SAARC) was established on 8th December, 1985 in Dhaka, Bangladesh by seven countries of South Asia, namely, Bangladesh, Bhutan, India, Maldives, Nepal, Pakistan, and Sri Lanka. Afghanistan became the eighth member of the organization in 2005. Its secretariat is in Kathmandu, Nepal.

SAARC consists of approximately 3 percent of the world's area while approximately 21 percent of the world's population resides in this area. In 2015, the combined GDP of the group was US$ 2.9 trillion which is about 3.8% of the global GDP.

The objective of SAARC is to bring about stability and development of South Asia by enhancing regional cooperation and economic integration.

OBJECTIVES OF SAARC

As per the Article One, the objectives of the Association are :

1. To promote the welfare of the people of South Asia and to improve their quality of life;

2. To accelerate economic growth, social progress and cultural development in the region and to provide all individuals the opportunity to live in dignity and to realise their full potentials;

3. To promote and strengthen collective self-reliance among the countries of South Asia;

4. To contribute to mutual trust, understanding and appreciation of one another's problems;

5. To promote active collaboration and mutual assistance in the economic, social, cultural, technical and scientific fields;

6. To strengthen cooperation with other developing countries;

7. To strengthen cooperation among themselves in international forums on matters of common interests; and

8. To cooperate with international and regional organisations with similar aims and purposes.

INITIATIVES

For strengthening economic relations between member countries, SAARC initiated various steps in the following manner :

1. An Inter-Governmental Group (IGG) was established in 1991 to formulate an agreement to establish a SAARC Preferential Trading Arrangement (SAPTA) by 1997. The Agreement was signed in 1993 which formally came into operation in December 1995.

2. The SAARC Chamber of Commerce and Industry (SCCI) was set up in 1992 to bring together the national chambers of commerce and industry of the member states under one umbrella so that the business communities of the member countries can coordinate their activities.

3. SAARC trade fairs and exhibitions are regularly organized since 1996 to provide a common platform to the industry and business houses of member countries for merchandising of their products.

4. South Asian Free Trade Area was formed on January 6th, 2004 in Islamabad, Pakistan. The agreement came into force on January 1st, 2006. The basic objective of the agreement was to remove all the barriers to free trade like tariffs, para-tariffs, and non-tariff barriers and to promote and facilitate smooth cross-border movement of goods.

5. SAARC members signed SAARC Agreement on Trade in Services (SATIS) on April 29th, 2010 in Thimphu, Bhutan to promote free trade in services.

All these initiatives by SAARC improved India's export performance, for example, in 1996-97, Indian exports to other SAARC Members were US$ 1.72 billion which increased to about US$ 15.11 billion in 2012-13. Similarly, the share of South Asian countries in India's total exports was 5.03 percent in 2012-13.

The students may expand the content of the report by paying attention to the following points :

1. The events that led to the formation of SAARC.
2. The structure of SAARC.
3. Benefits of SAARC to the member countries.
4. Investments flowing in India from the SAARC members.
5. Other areas of cooperation like banking, tourism, medicare, energy etc.

FINDINGS

Students are required to write their findings based on the analysis of the information provided in the form of a brief report.

SUGGESTED QUESTIONS FOR VIVA-VOCE

Q.1. Why did the formation of SAARC take place ?
Q.2. How did the SAARC affected trade between other members and India ?
Q.3. What steps have been taken by SAARC to improve business between its members ?
Q.4. What are the objectives of SAARC ?
Q.5. What are the benefits of SAARC to its members apart from trade ?

PROJECT 5

Prepare a Report on the various Poverty Alleviation and Employment Generation Programmes started in India, with special focus on MGNREGA

India has a population of approximately 1.27 billion and on the basis of purchasing power parity, it is the fourth largest economy of the world. In a recent government report, the per capita income of India was approximately ₹ 1.03 lakh. Though these figures look impressive in the beginning but as we dig deeper, we find that these figures are not sufficient. The income inequalities are very high in India. A small percentage of population control a very high percentage of national income while a very large percentage, i.e. approx. 22 percent of the population fall in the Below Poverty Line (BPL) category. On the basis of poverty estimates prepared by NSSO (National Sample Survey Organisation) in its 68th round survey, 25.7 percent of the rural population and 13.7 percent of the urban population was poor in 2011-12.

In India, poverty is estimated in terms of calorie consumption, i.e., when a person is not able to consume 2100 calories in urban areas and 2400 calories in rural areas, then such person is considered to be poor.

One of the major reasons which has been cited for poverty in India is the wide spread unemployment in the economy. In the 68th round of NSSO, the poverty was found to be 5.7 percent in rural areas and 5.5 percent in urban areas.

Various programmes have been devised by the government to deal with problems of poverty and unemployment in India. Following are the various programmes launched by the government at various points of time to deal with the dual curses of poverty and unemployment:

1. Integrated Rural Development Programme (IRDP)

IRDP was launched in India in 1978. It aims at providing self-employment opportunities to rural poor through acquisition of productive assets that could generate sufficient income. It is a centrally sponsored scheme and assistance is provided in the form of subsidies and bank credit. The programme provides 25 percent subsidy to small farmers, 33.3 percent subsidy to marginal farmers and 50 percent subsidies to families belonging to Scheduled Castes and Scheduled Tribes for acquiring capital assets. IRDP has been successful in providing additional income to a number of poor families. Yet, the major constraint is the lack of productive investment opportunities and adequate marketing infrastructure. The programme has also been criticised with respect to selection of families for assistance.

2. Training of Rural Youth for Self-Employment (TRYSEM)

This is another employment generation programme launched in 1979 that aims at providing technical and entrepreneurial skills to the rural poor in the age group of 18 to

35 years to enable them to take up income generating activities. The programme provides specialised training through recognised ITIs and polytechnics. An evaluation of the programme revealed that there was a mismatch in the job skills in 53.3 percent of the districts studied. It was also observed that many of them who underwent training under the programme remained unemployed. Only a small proportion of beneficiaries took up self-employment. Lack of funds for investment and inadequate credit facilities could also be cited as a reason for failure of the programme.

3. Development of Women and Children in Rural Areas (DWCRA)

This programme was introduced as a component of IRDP in 1982-83. It aims at the betterment of the living conditions of the poor women and children in rural areas. It provides access to employment opportunities, skill acquisition, training and credit facilities to the poor women. It also aims at making them self-reliant by promoting the habit of thrift among rural women. The programme also provides child care facilities to the beneficiary women. The programme, however, is said to suffer from several shortcomings such as lack of adequate funds, lack of productive investments, inadequate training and staffing etc.

4. Jawahar Rozgar Yojana (JRY)

JRY was launched in 1989 by merging the National Rural Employment Programme (NREP) and Rural Landless Employment Guarantee Programme (RLEGP). The main objective of this programme is to provide gainful employment to the unemployed rural poor. However, due to lack of adequate funds, the scheme could only generate very few jobs. JRY was re-launched in April 1999 as Jawahar Gram Samridhi Yojana (JGSY) with the objective of creating assets and infrastructure in the villages. It was again not successful due to inadequate funds and corruption.

5. Employment Assurance Scheme (EAS)

EAS was launched on October 02, 1993 and was meant for the drought prone, desert, hilly and tribal areas of the country. It aims at providing employment opportunities during the lean season. The Food for work programme which was started as part of the EAS programme, provided wages in the form of food grains to the poor and unemployed. All these programmes were merged to form Sampoorna Gramin Rozgar Yojana (SGRY) in 2001. The programme aimed at creating community assets and infrastructure and also aimed at providing food security for the rural poor.

6. Swaranjayanti Gram Swarozgar Yojna (SGSY)

Due to various shortcomings, the IRDP was replaced by SGSY in 1999. The million wells scheme and the DWCRA were merged into the SGSY scheme. The SGSY organised the poor into self-help groups and provided credit facilities to set up micro enterprises. The scheme also supported irrigation projects by way of subsidies.

7. Pradhan Mantri Gramodaya Yojana (PMGY)

PMGY, launched in 2000-01, is aimed at providing primary health care, education, drinking water and electricity in rural areas. Shelter being one of the basic requirements, the PMGY provides housing with sanitation facilities to the rural poor.

8. Rural Employment Generation Programme (REGP)

This programme was introduced in 1995 with the objective of creating self-employment in rural areas. The Khadi and Village Industries Commission (KVIC) is involved in the implementation of this programme. Assistance is provided under the scheme in the form of bank loans to set up village industries.

9. Prime Minister's Rozgar Yojana (PMRY)

This is another programme introduced in 1993 to provide self-employment opportunities to the educated unemployed youth whose family income is less than ₹ 40,000. Assistance is provided in the form of soft loans to educated youth to set up village industries.

10. National Food for Work Programme (FWP)

This programme was launched by the Central Government in 2004 in 150 most backward districts of India. It is a centrally sponsored scheme that provides work to the poor and unskilled labour. The wages are paid in the form of food grains. The States have a major responsibility in implementing this scheme.

11. Mahatma Gandhi National Rural Employment Guarantee Programme (MGNREGA)

In 2004, the UPA government under Prime Minister Dr. Manmohan Singh declared the National Rural Employment Guarantee Bill and National Rural Employment Guarantee Act (NREGA) was passed in September 2005. The programme was renamed as Mahatma Gandhi National Rural Employment Guarantee Act (MGNREGA) on October 02, 2009. The act aims at enhancing the lives of the rural poor by providing them 100 days of guaranteed employment during a financial year. The programme has made employment a right. The rural poor can, therefore, demand employment and the demand must be met within 15 days. In the event of failure to provide employment, an unemployment allowance should be given. The programme aims at providing employment opportunities by building rural infrastructure through watershed development, tanks, canals, land development, prevention of soil erosion, construction of roads etc. MGNREGA has also been subject to severe criticism for corrupt practices with respect to payment of wages and creation of assets. It also restricts the employment to just 100 days which is insufficient to meet the requirements of the rural poor.

Students may add more content to the report by adding

(i) The reasons for poverty and unemployment in India, and

(ii) The impact of various programmes launched by the government on the reduction of poverty and unemployment in India by exploring various government reports presented on the topic.

FINDINGS

Students are required to write their findings based on the analysis of the information and present it in the form of a brief report.

SUGGESTED QUESTIONS FOR VIVA-VOCE

Q.1. Who is considered as poor in India ?
Q.2. Who measures poverty and unemployment in India ?
Q.3. Explain any two programmes launched by the government for reducing poverty and unemployment in rural areas ?
Q.4. Give reasons for the prevalence of poverty and unemployment in India ?
Q.5. Explain about MGNREGA in detail.

PROJECT 6

Compare the status of women of your State with that at the National level for the last ten years, on the basis of educational level, employment etc.

Women represent half of the population on this earth. The nature has made both men and women equal to each other with their own unique characteristics which make them complementary to each other.

In the ancient India, this equal status of women given by nature was accepted and respected by society. This practice of equality resulted into the significant contribution of women in politics, religion, knowledge, literature, social development etc.

The position of women got undermined with the advent of foreign invaders in medieval India. The social position of women started changing and many biased practices like purdah pratha, dowry, sati pratha, talaq pratha etc. were started. This made women a secondary citizen of the society and these practices curtailed the freedom of women in India.

The situation of women which worsened in medieval India continued even after India got independence. The women used to be considered as the asset and grace of the family and were kept within the veil or curtain of the house. This deprived the women of their right to freedom which males enjoyed. Interestingly, most of the laws which were formulated in the British period also treated women as the second citizen of the country and did not give the rights to women which were at par with men. The British Government, however, abolished sati pratha on the behest of Raja Ram Mohan Roy.

The constitution of India provided the men and women equal status. Later, this helped the authorities to interpret the old laws and formulate the new laws which assigned women her righteous place in the society.

India is a country where development is taking place on all fronts including on women empowerment and women emancipation. Many schemes have been initiated for empowerment and upliftment of women. But the situation of women in India has not improved in most of the cases.

We have taken Uttar Pradesh as the state for this comparative study. The students from other states may gather the data regarding their own states.

Uttar Pradesh is situated in the north of India bordering Nepal. It is the most populous state of the country having 16 percent of India's population which is more than that of Brazil which is the 5th largest populous country in the world.

This project is an effort to find out whether the efforts which have taken place to empower women at the national level have also influenced the condition of women in Uttar Pradesh.

The decadal growth rate of female population at national level was 17.7 percent while it was 21.2 percent in Uttar Pradesh as per the census 2011. It indicates that the society's perception about women has changed positively in U.P.. This should be a positive sign towards woman empowerment in the state but the male-female ratio in the state (912) is well below the national sex ratio (943). It is a matter of concern. If we dig deeper and look at the child sex ratio (0-6 years), we find that this ratio is also very low in U.P. (902) which is again less than the national ratio (919) as per the census 2011.

Both these indicators reflect that despite the rise in the percentage of female population, the male-female ratio is not very encouraging in the state.

U.P. has also lagged behind other states with regard to the literacy rates among women. The national figure for literacy among women is 65.46 percent while it is only about 57.18 percent among the women in Uttar Pradesh. U.P. also has high material mortality and infant mortality rates. The cases of child marriage, missing children, crime against women, female foeticide etc. are also frequently reported from the state.

Students are advised to further develop this project on the following lines :

1. Find out the female health indicators for India and your state.
2. Find out the female enrolment ratio in different age groups for India and your state.
3. Find out the political achievements of the women in Union election, state election and local bodies elections.
4. Find out the percentage of employed females among the females of the state and compare it with the national average.
5. Find out the various Central and state government programmes which have been initiated for the improvement of status of women of your state.
6. You may also give suggestions to make improvements on all these indicators.

FINDINGS

Students are required to write their findings based on the analysis of the information provided and present it in the form of a report.

SUGGESTED QUESTIONS FOR VIVA-VOCE

Q.1. What is the status of education among the women of your state ?
Q.2. What is the status of health of women in your state ?
Q.3. What are the schemes launched by the government to make the women of your state self- dependent ?
Q.4. What steps would you suggest to improve health status of women of your state ?
Q.5. List down some of the areas where women in your state have been discriminated against ?

PROJECT 7

Prepare a report on the forest cover in India, highlighting the following aspects :
- **(a) Five states/Union territories having higher and lower forest cover and compare the extent of forest coverage.**
- **(b) Causes for decrease in forests in the country.**
- **(c) Measures adopted by the central/state governments to increase forest cover.**

India is a vast country having diversity in all its aspects. India is the seventh largest country of the world having the geographical area of 3287263 sq. kms. The geographical dimensions of the the country include the mountains, great plains, rivers, desert and the forests. India is one of the seventeen largest bio diverse regions of the world. Indian forest types include variety of tree families like swamps, tropical evergreens, mangroves, tropical deciduous, sub-tropical, scrub, sub-alpine and alpine forests etc.

As per the India State Forest Report 2015 presented by the Forest Survey of India, India's forest cover was 70.17 million hectare during October 2013 to February 2014. This is approximately 21.34 percent of the geographical area of the country. If the tree cover is also included in this data, then the total tree and forest cover reaches to 79.42 million hectare which is approximately 24.16 percent of the geographical area of the country.

This size of forest and tree cover acts as 7 billion tonnes of carbon sink - a natural reservoir that helps in absorbing carbon and countering the effects of global warming to some extent. This carbon sink is expected to increase by 2.5-3 billion tonnes by 2030. In an estimate, it has been observed that overall the India's forest cover improved in comparison to the world average. For example, average per capita forest cover the world over declined from 0.8 hectare to 0.6 hectare per person but in India, a net increase of 1.82% of forest cover has been registered in the past 30 years.

As per the data released by Forest Survey of India in 2015, top five states having the highest forest cover as a percentage of total geographical area are as follows :

1. Mizoram (88.93 percent of total geographical area)
2. Arunachal Pradesh (80.30 percent of total geographical area)
3. Nagaland (78.21 percent of total geographical area)
4. Meghalaya (76.76 percent of total geographical area)
5. Manipur (76.11 percent of total geographical area)

As far as the land area under forest cover is concerned, following are the top five states :

1. Madhya Pradesh (77,462 sq. Km.)
2. Arunachal Pradesh (67,248 sq. Km.)

3. Chhattisgarh (55,586 sq. Km.)
4. Maharashtra (50,628 sq. Km.)
5. Odisha (50,354 sq. Km.)

Similarly, bottom five states having the lowest forest cover as a percentage of total geographical area are as follows :

1. Punjab (3.52 percent of total geographical area)
2. Haryana (3.58 percent of total geographical area)
3. Rajasthan (4.73 percent of total geographical area)
4. Uttar Pradesh (6.00 percent of total geographical area)
5. Gujarat (7.48 percent of total geographical area)

Following are the bottom five states with least land area under forest cover :

1. Daman & Diu (19.61 sq. km.)
2. Chandigarh (22.03 sq. km.)
3. Lakshadweep (27.06 sq. km.)
4. Puducherry (55.38 sq. km.)
5. Dadra & Nagar Haveli (206 sq. km.)

As per the ecological principles, approximately one-third of the total land of a country must be under the forest cover while India's forest cover is only approximately one-fifth of the overall geographical area. There are various reasons which are responsible for the inadequate forest cover in India. They are as follows :

1. Expanding population and its impact on agriculture
2. Industrialisation
3. Urbanisation
4. Shifting cultivation
5. Infrastructure development

Government has made the following efforts to increase the forest cover in India :

1. The Forest Conservation Act of 1980
2. The National Forest Policy, 1988
3. National Forest Commission, 2002
4. The Indian National Forest Policy, 2009
5. The Green India Mission 2012

Students are advised to expand the report by adding the following points :

1. Explore the social, environmental and economic benefits of forests.
2. The causes of inadequate forest cover in India.
3. Gather information regarding various initiatives taken by the government to increase the forest cover in India.
4. Suggest steps to increase the forest cover in India.

FINDINGS

Students are required to write their findings based on the analysis of the information provided in the form of a report.

SUGGESTED QUESTIONS FOR VIVA-VOICE

- Q.1. What are the benefits of forests ?
- Q.2. Explain about the forest cover in India.
- Q.3. Is the forest cover in India adequate ? If no, what are the reasons ?
- Q.4. Which are the states/UTs with highest forest cover in absolute terms ?
- Q.5. What steps has the government taken to increase the forest cover in India ?

MODEL TEST PAPER-1

(Maximum Marks : 80)
(Time allowed : Three hours)

*(Candidates are allowed additional 15 minutes for **only** reading the paper. They must NOT start writing during this time.)*

*Answer **Question 1** (compulsory) from **Part I** and any **five** questions from **Part II**. The intended marks for questions or parts of questions are given in brackets [ ].*

PART I (20 Marks)
Answer all questions.

Question 1. [10 × 2]

Answer briefly each of the following questions (i) to (x).
- **(i)** Define economics as given by P.A. Samuelson.
- **(ii)** Differentiate between absolute poverty and relative poverty.
- **(iii)** Define statistics.
- **(iv)** What is meant by formal education ? How is it different from informal education ?
- **(v)** Differentiate between primary data and secondary data.
- **(vi)** What is meant by sustainable development ?
- **(vii)** Differentiate between total utility and marginal utility.
- **(viii)** Explain the meaning of disinvestment.
- **(ix)** State any two purposes of constructing index number.
- **(x)** Define cost push inflation.

PART-II (60 Marks)
Answer any five questions

Question 2.
- **(a)** State three differences between micro economics and macro economics. [3]
- **(b)** Discuss the features of production possibility curve, with the help of a diagram. [3]
- **(c)** Explain how price mechanism can be used to solve the basic problems in an economy. [6]

Question 3.
- **(a)** Explain three limitations of Per Capita Income Index. [3]
- **(b)** Discuss any three importances of human capital formation in economic development. [3]
- **(c)** Discuss any four causes of unemployment in India. [6]

Question 4.
- **(a)** Discuss any three measures undertaken by the government to improve agricultural marketing. [3]

(b) State one reason for each of the following types of loans being taken by farmers : [3]
  (i) Short-term loans (ii) Medium-term loans
  (iii) Long-term loans
(c) Explain four changes in the Indian economy after liberalisation. [6]

Question 5.
(a) Discuss three differences between growth and development. [3]
(b) Write short notes on the following Poverty Alleviation Programmes : [3]
  (i) MGNREGA (ii) Skill India Programme
(c) Define mixed economy. Explain four features of mixed economy. [6]

Question 6.
(a) Explain three benefits of organic farming. [3]
(b) Discuss two features of privatisation. [3]
(c) Discuss the various institutional sources of rural credit in India. [6]

Question 7.
(a) Explain any two effects of global warming. [3]
(b) Define Human Development Index. State its dimensions. [3]
(c) Explain any four effects of economic development on the environment. [6]

Question 8.
(a) Calculate Arithmetic mean from the data given below : [3]

Class Interval	0-10	10-20	20-30	30-40	40-50	50-60	60-70	70-80
Frequency	2	7	10	15	20	16	6	4

(b) Calculate median from the data given below : [3]

Class Interval	0-10	10-20	20-30	30-40	40-50	50-60
Frequency	5	10	18	9	5	3

(c) Using the data given below, calculate mode by grouping method : [6]

Marks	0-1	1-2	2-3	3-4	4-5	5-6	6-7	7-8
No. of Students	4	10	25	15	23	22	12	3

Question 9.
(a) From the data given below, calculate quartile deviation. [3]

Marks	0-10	10-20	20-30	30-40	40-50
Frequency	10	15	20	10	5

(b) Calculate Index Number by using Laspeyre's method : [3]

	Base year		Current Year	
	Price	Quantity	Price	Quantity
A	2	40	3	20
B	1.5	30	2.5	40
C	1	50	1.5	30
D	2.5	20	2	80

(c) With the data given below, calculate coefficient of correlation between the two variables X and Y, by using Karl Pearson's method : [6]

X	Y
10	7
12	9
11	12
13	9
12	13
14	8
9	10
12	12
14	7
13	13

❏❏

MODEL TEST PAPER-2

(Maximum Marks : 80)
(Time allowed : Three hours)

*(Candidates are allowed additional 15 minutes for **only** reading the paper.*
They must NOT start writing during this time.)

*Answer **Question 1 (compulsory)** from **Part I** and any **five** questions from **Part II**.*
The intended marks for questions or parts of questions are given in brackets [ ].

PART I (20 Marks)
*Answer **all** questions.*

Question 1. [10 × 2]

Answer briefly each of the following questions (i) to (x) :

(i) State and briefly explain Alfred Marshall's definition of Economics.
(ii) Explain the basic problem of 'How to produce' in an economy.
(iii) Briefly explain any one type of economy based on ownership of resources and one type of economy on the basis of nature.
(iv) State any two steps undertaken for promotion of foreign investment.
(v) State and briefly explain an important plan set during the Fifth five-year plan.
(vi) What is Absolute and Relative poverty ?
(vii) What is global warming ? Explain any one cause of global warming.
(viii) Explain with an example, what is qualitative classification of data ?
(ix) State any one merit and one demerit of calculating range.
(x) What is economic growth and development ? Give examples.

PART-II (60 Marks)
*Answer **any five** questions*

Question 2.
(a) State any three differences between Lionel Robbin's and Paul Samuleson's definitions of economics. [3]
(b) What is inflation ? Briefly explain the types of inflation. [3]
(c) What is the Production Possibility Curve ? Explain with a schedule and a diagram. [6]

Question 3.
(a) What do the following features of a capitalist economy mean ? [3]
  (i) Consumer is king
  (ii) Risk takers alone must control operations
  (iii) Individuals are driven by selfish motives and not altruism.
(b) Discuss three problems faced by the industrial sector in India post-globalisation. [3]
(c) State the objectives of economic planning in India. [6]

Question 4.
  (a) State the factors responsible for the Balance of Payments crisis in 1991 in India. [3]
  (b) What is organic farming ? [3]
  (c) What are the distinguishing socio-economic characteristics between Indian and Chinese economies? [6]

Question 5.
  (a) What is the meaning of privatisation ? Briefly state the drawbacks of privatisation. [3]
  (b) Distinguish between developed and developing economies. [3]
  (c) What is sustainable development ? Briefly explain the measures to achieve sustainable development. [6]

Question 6.
  (a) Globalisation acts as an engine of growth in India. Discuss. [3]
  (b) Rural poor get caught in a debt trap from which they cannot escape. Do you agree with this statement ? Give reasons. [3]
  (c) In the context of Law of Diminishing Marginal Utility, explain the relationship between Total Utility and Marginal Utility. Explain with a schedule and a diagram. [6]

Question 7.
  (a) Briefly explain how factors of production contributes to the national income. [3]
  (b) Briefly explain the basic problems of an economy. [3]
  (c) What is unemployment ? What are the various forms of unemployment ? [6]

Question 8.
  (a) Calculate the quartile deviation from the following data related to weight (in pounds) of students. [3]

Weight in pounds	No. of Students
120	1
122	3
124	5
126	7
130	10
140	3
150	1
160	1

  (b) Calculate the weighted arithmetic mean for following data : [3]

X	Weight (w)
4	4
2	2
3.5	2
3	4
2	3

(c) Compute the index number for the following data using Laspeyres', Paasche's and Fisher's methods. [6]

Items	2017		2018	
	Quantity	Price	Quantity	Price
A	24	20	30	24
B	30	14	40	10
C	48	10	40	18
D	10	32	10	28

Question 9.

(a) Calculate the coefficient of variation of marks in statistics between two students A and B. Which student's marks are more consistent [3]

Student	Mean	Standard Deviation
A	30	4
B	25	6

(b) Calculate the rank correlation coefficient from the ranks given by 2 judges. [3]

Rank 1	6	2	5	1	4	3	7
Rank 2	6	1	2	3	4	5	7

(c) Calculate the mode of the following series by grouping and analysis method. [6]

Class Interval	0-5	5-10	10-15	15-20	20-25	25-30	30-35
Frequency	1	2	10	4	10	9	2

❏❏